The Asian American

Clio Books/Pacific Historical Review Series

Norris Hundley, jr., Series Editor

#1. The American Indian

#2. The Chicano

#3. The Asian American

The Asian American:
The Historical Experience

Edited by Norris Hundley, jr.
Introduction by Akira Iriye

Essays by

Roger Daniels

Gary R. Hess

Lee and Chang-su Houchins

Harry H. L. Kitano

Stanford M. Lyman

H. Brett Melendy

John Modell

Shih-shan H. Ts'ai

CLIO BOOKS

AMERICAN BIBLIOGRAPHICAL CENTER—CLIO PRESS, INC.

SANTA BARBARA   OXFORD

The articles by Roger Daniels, Stanford M. Lyman, Harry H. L. Kitano, H. Brett Melendy, Lee and Chang-su Houchins, and Gary R. Hess are reprinted with permission and appeared previously in the *Pacific Historical Review*, Volume XLII, No. 4 (November 1974). The article by John Modell is reprinted with permission from the *Pacific Historical Review*, Volume XXXVIII, No. 2 (May 1969). The article by Shih-shan H. Ts'ai is reprinted with permission from the *Pacific Historical Review*, Volume XLII, No. 3 (August 1974).

Library of Congress Cataloging in Publication Data

Hundley, Norris, jr., comp.
  The Asian American.

   (Clio Books/*Pacific Historical Review* series)
   Chiefly essays from the *Pacific Historical Review*,
v. 38, No. 2, 1969; v. 42, No. 3–4, 1974.
   Includes index.
   1. The Asian Americans—History—Addresses, essays,
lectures. I. *The Pacific Historical Review.* II. Title.
E184.M5H86   973'.004'6872   75-2354
ISBN 0-87436-219-9
ISBN 0-87436-220-2 pbk.

American Bibliographical Center—Clio Press, Inc.
2040 Alameda Padre Serra
Santa Barbara, California

European Bibliographical Center—Clio Press
Woodside House, Hinksey Hill
Oxford OX1 5BE, England

Royalties earned from the sale of this book are used to further publication of the *Pacific Historical Review*.

Contents

Introduction   vii
   AKIRA IRIYE

American Historians and East Asian Immigrants   1
   ROGER DANIELS

Conflict and the Web of Group Affiliation in San Francisco's
   Chinatown ,1850–1910   26
   STANFORD M. LYMAN

Chinese Immigration through Communist Chinese Eyes: An
   Introduction to the Historiography   53
   SHIH-SHAN H. TS'AI

Class or Ethnic Solidarity: The Japanese American Company
   Union   67
   JOHN MODELL

Japanese Americans: The Development of a Middleman
   Minority   81
   HARRY H. L. KITANO

Filipinos in the United States   101
   H. BRETT MELENDY

The Korean Experience in America, 1903–1924   129
   LEE HOUCHINS and CHANG-SU HOUCHINS

The Forgotten Asian Americans: The East Indian Community in the United States   157
   GARY R. HESS

Index   179

Introduction

THE AWARENESS THAT the United States is a multiethnic society,
that it is a country of immigrants, is as old as American history.
Observers since the eighteenth century have stressed these facts
and sought to examine America's characteristics as well as its peculiar problems in terms of the relationship between ethnic diversity and national unity, between social segmentation and political
democracy, between pluralism and conformism, or between Old
World traditions and New World identity. All such problems have
made Americans one of the most self-conscious peoples in the
world, and American scholars among the most concerned with
national character and culture. In all of this discourse there has
been a feeling that America is a unique combination of particu-
larism and universalism. On one hand, the population largely consists of what Louis Hartz and others have called fragments of an-
tecedent units, whether they originate in Europe, Africa, or elsewhere. American society is particularistic in the persistence of these
fragments as a mode of maintaining social organization, and in the
sense that they all experience the shock of transplantation, as they
find themselves in a new physical setting, severed from the old
continents. On the other hand, there is the legacy of the Enlighten-
ment—traceable in fact to the Hellenistic tradition of Neopla-
tonism—which stresses the brotherhood of man and the unity of
mankind. The tradition posits the possibility that men of diverse
backgrounds may live in peace and harmony with one another,
since they are all potential equals and share common destinies.
America, in this view, is a Neoplatonic experiment.

The Asian American experience fits into such patterns of American history. Asian American communities have been fragmented
segments, each maintaining its unique cultural outlooks and systems of social control. They have had varying degrees of interac-
tions with other ethnic groupings. At the same time, Asian Americans have been part of the total picture, a test case for (or against)

the assertion that the United States tolerates and integrates all religious and nationality groups. Whether it does or not, the story
of Asian Americans tells a great deal about the country as a whole.

Thus, Asian Americans can be studied both in terms of the segments or of the whole. That scholars have tended to stress the latter
approach is well documented in Roger Daniels's essay in this book.
He gives an excellent summary of the literature dealing with East
Asian Americans, and shows that American historians and social
scientists have long been interested in immigrants from China and
Japan. Considering the fact they comprised only two percent of all
immigration during 1820–1971, and that today they constitute less
than one percent of the population, the amount of scholarly attention they have enjoyed would seem out of proportion to their numerical status. The basic reason for this is that histories of East
Asian Americans have tended to be written as part of white American history, as an episode in the history of American politics, immigration, or of racism, in which the main actors have remained white
Americans. The bulk of the literature on Asian immigrants deals,
in Daniels's words, with "the excluders rather than the excluded,"
with "the oppressors rather than the oppressed." The story of
anti-Oriental movements is an important part of American history, but to study Asian Americans in such a framework is like discussing European imperialism by focusing on the imperialists, leaving out of account those at the receiving end of imperialism.

Historians have nevertheless been inordinately interested in the
Asian immigration problem in the United States because it runs
so obviously counter to the credo of universal brotherhood. The
story of racial hostility and violence in a society espousing Neoplatonic doctrines must somehow be susceptible of scholarly explanation. Until recently, the basic interpretative strategy was to
employ a dichotomous scheme of civilization and say that the
United States was a Western country. Its civilization was Western
and, apart from the indigenous Indians and the imported Africans,
its people were European. All the talk about cultural diversity and
ethnic heterogeneity was sensible only within the framework of
Western tradition. Asia was qualitatively different from the West,
and Asians were a threat to Western ways of life. This was not only
the way the exclusionists justified their assault on Asian immigrants, but also how scholars interpreted the phenomenon. William

Graham Sumner wrote in *Folkways* (1906), "The two great cultural divisions of the human race are the oriental and the occidental. Each is consistent throughout; each has its own philosophy and spirit; they are separated from top to bottom by different mores, different standpoints, different ways, and different notions of what societal arrangements are advantageous." Such an interpretation helped explain, so it was felt, the extraordinary sense of antagonism expressed by white Americans toward Asian Americans. On the other hand, to the extent that the latter made good in the United States, this was often analyzed in terms of their successful Westernization. They became "Westerners from Asia" or, in sociologist Robert Park's words, cultural Occidentals though remaining racially Oriental.

The recent rise and development of Asian American studies, some of the fruits of which are printed in this volume, reflect the erosion of the once prevalent frameworks in which the subject matter was discussed. The thematic stress on white American attitudes toward Asians, and the conceptual framework of East-West differences, have been superseded by attempts at looking at Asian Americans, their ideas and ways of life, on their own terms, and to relate them as much to Asian history as to United States history. Such a trend has been facilitated and promoted by many factors, but two in particular stand out. First, the spectacular growth of the social sciences after the Second World War has been based upon, and further fortified, the assumption that methodological tools for examining social and personal behavior are as applicable to primitive tribes as to advanced societies. No people is peculiar: all communities are susceptible of analysis in terms of certain methodologies and conceptual tools. It follows that Asian Americans are just as serious objects of study as other groups in the United States. Conversely, to study America it becomes imperative to devise schemes and frameworks that will work with regard to all groups. A theory is seriously deficient if it cannot explain a particular minority except by saying the theory excludes the latter. The development of social science research has thus had a leveling tendency and a universalizing effect.

Second, international affairs since the 1930s have undermined the once dominant notion of Western unity and superiority. As Pitrim Sorokin wrote in *The Crisis of Our Age* (1941), "the present

crisis is not ordinary but extraordinary. It is not merely an economic or political maladjustment, but involves simultaneously almost the whole of Western culture and society, in all their main
sectors . . . a crisis involving almost the whole way of life, thought,
and conduct of Western society." The crisis of Western civilization
—more seriously, as Sorokin's words reflected, the crisis of Western
consciousness—created an atmosphere conducive to studying other
cultures, not merely as objects of curiosity or anthropological inquiry, but also as genuinely revealing entities. Efforts began to try
to understand non-Western peoples as they themselves perceived
their cultures and societies. Their traditions came to be studied as
fascinating phenomena in their own terms, not in terms of the
Western impact upon or prejudice against them.

Nowhere have these trends been more manifest than in the field
of American-Asian relations. Political scientists, sociologists, an-
thropologists, economists, and others have sought to analyze Asian
societies in social-scientific frameworks, ranging from theories of
economic modernization to those of social integration. They have
proposed various conceptual tools for examining social systems and
personality types, and the result has been an impressive accumula-
tion of data and hypotheses about the structure and functioning of
these societies. At the same time, students of history and literature
have combed documentary evidence in the original languages
to see how Asians view the outside world as they interact with
other peoples. All these efforts have served to raise the level of
scholarship on American-Asian relations to a degree of sophisti-
cation lacking in traditional studies of diplomatic history and international affairs. Today it is no longer sufficient to treat the subject merely in the context of United States policy, American missionary activities, and the like. More and more writers are dealing
with the Asian side of the picture as extensively as the American.
The fundamental assumption is that international relations must
be studied as intercultural relations; what an Asian does and thinks
is as important as an American's behavior and thought, and the
latter's activities, perceptions, and prejudices become meaningful
only when they are related to those of the former.

It is obvious, then, that a study of Asian Americans today is valuable only when it proposes a new methodology or workable conceptual framework, when it is based upon a substantial body of

primary evidence, or when it is integrated into the histories and cultures of the societies from which they or their ancestors have come. The articles in this volume dealing with Chinese, Japanese, Korean, Filipino, and East Indian immigrants are all substantial contributions in this regard, although the specific nature of the contributions varies from essay to essay. For instance, Stanford M. Lyman's analysis of San Francisco's Chinatown before 1910, while based entirely on English-language material, offers an interpretation in terms of the sociology of conflict. As he writes, the Chinese were "bound to one another not only because of external hostility but also because of deadly internal factionalism." They were constantly engaged in feuds and conflicts, but their very existence ensured the growth of a sense of community. Actors in the power struggles were always exclusively Chinese, many of whom were members in a number of associations, both legitimate and clandestine. Subgroup loyalties and conflicts fostered an awareness of affiliation with the total community which developed its own rituals, conventions, and systems of arbitration and jurisdiction. In this way Chinatown defined a specific boundary within American society, a boundary which was not only forced on it by white Americans, but beyond which the Chinese found it neither necessary nor comfortable to move.

Harry H. L. Kitano's essay seeks to define precisely how Japanese Americans fit into the total system, and he employs the theory of "middleman minority." The basic assumption is that America is a society that tolerates middleman minorities, those groups that are neither at the bottom nor likely to make it to the top. Stressing the social structure and value system of Meiji Japan from which first-generation Japanese Americans came, Kitano suggests that they were ideally fitted to play such a role. As he says, their "quest to be accepted by the group in power led to a strategy of high achievement, conformity, productivity, and a rise above the basement, but in such a way as not to threaten the status of the dominant group." A key question, of course, is whether Japanese Americans would long be content to remain in this middle position, and whether American society would be systemically flexible enough to accommodate their upward moves. An excellent case study that gives some clues to these problems is provided by John Modell's essay on the unionization episode in Los Angeles during the

1930s. Japanese American fruitstand employees and retail clerks
—now increasingly Nisei—were in effect compelled to choose between ethnic and class interests. Unionization and a class struggle
in cooperation with white American laborers might weaken community solidarity, but they might provide an opportunity for
Japanese Americans to gain a foothold in the labor movement
which had traditionally been fiercely anti-Oriental. The solution
at that time was an all-Japanese union. Such an episode is an excellent example of how a segmented community in the United States
sought to maintain, or to put an end to, its isolated existence. It
also shows resistance, both inside and outside the Japanese American community, to vertical moves in the social hierarchy.

Lee and Chang-su Houchins's essay on the Korean experience
in the United States is the only study in this collection based on
non-English sources. In the absence of a comprehensive history
of Korean Americans, this article should serve as the basic starting
point for future research. The authors emphasize the political
ideologies and activities of this immigrant group, demonstrating
that, in contrast to Chinese and Japanese who had a choice of returning to the homeland if they wished, a minority whose country
no longer existed as a sovereign entity had to spend much of its resources on purely political matters.

Chinese, Japanese, and Korean immigrants can be grouped together as East Asian Americans. The articles cited above show that
much progress has been made in studying them. The Philippines
and India, on the other hand, are not part of the East Asian tradition, and there may even be some argument as to whether Filipinos
and East Indians are in fact Asians—if indeed there are such peoples
as "Asians." Today "Asia" seems no more valuable a concept than
"Orient." It is nevertheless useful to have scholarly accounts of
Filipino and East Indian Americans to contrast their experiences
in the United States to those of East Asians. This is made possible
thanks to the pioneering essays by H. Brett Melendy and Gary R.
Hess. Filipinos were subjects of the American colonial empire, and
East Indians of the British empire. Ethnically they were distinguishable from Chinese, Japanese, and Koreans. And yet, as Me-
lendy and Hess demonstrate, all these groups came to the United
States under similar circumstances and encountered white preju-

dice which was often expressed in identical vocabulary. They were alike victimized by economic forces in America and by uncertainties of political status. Not the least important was the tendency of each nationality group to assert its superiority to the others, rather than to foster a pan-Asianist sentiment.

Finally, Shih-shan H. Ts'ai's article stands by itself. It summarizes Chinese historiography on the immigration dispute. It is amazing, as the author notes, how much has been accomplished by writers in China, in compiling data and collecting documents dealing with the anti-Chinese outbursts in the United States. Chinese historians tend to interpret the phenomenon in orthodox Marxist frameworks, most of which are inadequate to account for the symbolism of the exclusionist movement. But, as Ts'ai says, "we must recognize that the Communist Chinese researchers have added a considerable array of new data to the study of Chinese immigration." One should probably go a step further and argue that no significant progress is possible in the study of Chinese and other Asian Americans without intensive collaboration between American and Asian scholars. This seems important for at least three reasons. One, it is obviously desirable to gain access to archival and other kinds of evidence that remains in the countries from which Asian immigrants originated. Second, to the extent that the study of Asian Americans entails a study of Asian societies themselves, it is essential to make use of the findings by Chinese historians, Japanese sociologists, and the like in developing the field of Asian American studies. Third, insofar as the history of Asian Americans is an integral part of United States history, such international collaboration should serve to raise fresh questions about American history. In tracing the tension between Asian American communities and American society, between fragments and the whole, both symbolically and materially, it will be extremely useful and valuable to obtain insights developed by historians and social scientists in Asia. Asian American studies will then become of far more than sectarian or antiquarian interest; they will bridge the academic communities across the Pacific and emerge as a vital force in promoting international scholarly exchanges.

Akira Iriye
University of Chicago

American Historians and East Asian Immigrants

Roger Daniels

The author is professor of history in the State University of New York, Fredonia.

IN JULY 1973, during the televised Watergate hearings, an attorney representing elements of the Nixon administration attacked one of the Senate panel's more persistent interrogators as that "little Jap." This racist slur directed at Senator Daniel Inouye (D-Hi.) produced a national reaction, all of it favorable to the senator and against the lawyer; a later Gallup Poll gave Inouye the highest positive rating of any committee member, eighty-three percent. No other single incident so symbolizes the rapid reversal in the public image of the Asian American: just three decades previously most mainland Japanese Americans were imprisoned in desolate barbed wire enclosures, euphemistically called "relocation centers." Historians, too, have recorded a 180° turn in their treatment of Asian Americans.[1] Beginning in the late nineteenth century, writers like Hubert Howe Bancroft were ideological abettors of the anti-Oriental movements. Shortly thereafter, other writers, for whom Mary Roberts Coolidge can stand as surrogate, defended immigrants from Asia, not as equals but rather as needed hewers of wood and drawers of water. With the rise of professional historianship in the early twentieth century, other attitudes were brought into play: diplomatic historians,[2] for example, saw mistreatment of

---

[1] For a masterful analysis of the views of historians toward European immigrants, see Edward N. Saveth, *American Historians and European Immigrants, 1875–1925* (New York, 1948).

[2] Works that are essentially diplomatic history, with one or two exceptions, will not be treated here. An excellent historiographical survey of the diplomatic oriented history is Ernest R. May and James C. Thompson, eds., *American-East Asian Relations: A Survey* (Cambridge, Mass., 1972).

Asian immigrants as a disturbing and essentially irrational element in our relations with the Far East, while historians of labor saw hostility toward Asian competitors as the necessary cement which held western workingmen's organizations together. In more recent years, as perceptions about race have changed, historians have come to see mistreatment of Asian immigrants and their descendants not so much as a discrete phenomenon, but rather as an integral if minor part of a larger whole, American racism. Yet there remain striking continuities in the treatments from Bancroft to the present: Asian Americans are still seen largely as the objects rather than the subjects of history. A recent California history text by the liberal dean of western historians, while deploring the major manifestations of anti-Asian racism, still fails to mention one Asian American by name.[3]

Before commencing the analysis of individual works which will comprise the bulk of this essay, it might be well to put the essential historical and demographic facts into perspective. The migration of Asians to the United States can be divided conveniently into five periods:[4]

1. 1849–1882: A period of heavy Chinese immigration, punctuated by the anti-Chinese movement and ended by the Chinese Exclusion Act of 1882. A very small number of other Asians come during this period.

---

[3] John W. Caughey, *California: A Remarkable State's Life History* (3rd ed., Englewood Cliffs, N.J., 1970). Similarly, although now aware that "today's authors are obligated to let Negroes or Mexican-Americans or Indians speak loudly from their pages," the leading interpreter of western history cannot find space, in a work of 662 pages, to mention anti-orientalism. His only mention of Chinese—as laborers on the Central Pacific—significantly understates their number. Ray Allen Billington, *Westward Expansion: A History of the American Frontier* (4th ed., New York, 1974), vii, 555–556. Roger Zuercher, "The Treatment of Asian Minorities in American History Textbooks," *Indiana Social Studies Quarterly*, XXII (1969), 19–27, is an analysis of twelve secondary level texts. See also Dennis Ogawa, *From Japs to Japanese: The Evolution of the Japanese American Stereotype* (Berkeley, 1971).

[4] A brief narrative account of immigration law before 1924 is found in Roger Daniels, *The Politics of Prejudice: The Anti-Japanese Movement in California and the Struggle for Japanese Exclusion* (Berkeley and Los Angeles, 1962), 93–94; Milton R. Konvitz, *The Alien and the Asiatic in American Law* (Ithaca, N.Y., 1946), is a superb legal analysis. Robert A. Divine, *American Immigration Policy, 1924–1952* (New Haven, 1957), contains good treatments of legislation aimed at Filipinos and of the passage of the McCarran Act. Fred Riggs, *Pressures on Congress* (New York, 1950), is an account of the 1943 repeal of the Chinese Exclusion Act. On the 1965 immigration act I have been guided by an excellent seminar paper, Richard L. Boylan, "The Immigration Act of 1965" (Fredonia, N.Y., 1972), which is in my possession. The 1965 law may be found in *U.S. Statutes at Large*, LXXIX, 911.

2. 1890–1924: Initial period of Japanese immigration, punctuated by an anti-Japanese movement, alien land acts, the Gentlemen's Agreement, and other executive compacts to limit immigration and ended by the exclusion of all Asians (except Filipinos) by the immigration act of 1924.
3. 1924–1952: Generally, the period of Asian exclusion, but also the initial period of heavy Filipino immigration, 1920–1934, since Filipinos, as nationals, were not affected by the immigration laws. One of the side effects of the Philippine Independence Act of 1934 was to cut Filipino immigration to a token 50 newcomers per year. The Chinese received a similar token quota of 100 as a wartime gesture in 1943. Chinese, Japanese, Filipinos, and other Asians remain ineligible for naturalization.
4. 1952–1965: The era of the McCarran Act, which, while continuing, in essence, the quotas of the 1924 act, ends all racial bars to naturalization and gives token quotas, usually 105 per year, to most Asian nations. Relatively large numbers of Asians, chiefly Japanese and Chinese, come in as "non quota" immigrants, relatives of citizens, war brides, and so forth.
5. 1965 to present: Under the totally revamped immigration act of the Lyndon Johnson administration all racial and ethnic quotas are removed. Asians begin to comprise a much larger percentage of total annual immigration than ever before.

The total number of enumerated legal immigrants from Asia, 1820–1971, was 1,173,130, about 2.5 percent of all immigration in that period. By country, the count breaks down as follows:[5]

	Total immigrants, by country of origin 1820–1971
China	450,900
Japan	370,033
Philippines	145,371
Hong Kong	98,511
Korea	54,463
India	53,852

In the years 1969, 1970, 1971—the first years in which the nondiscriminatory 1965 act was fully in effect—immigrants from Asia comprised between 15 and 20 percent of all immigrants, the high-

---

[5] U.S. Dept. of Commerce, *Statistical Abstract of the United States, 1972* (Washington, D.C., 1972), 92.

est percentages in U.S. history. Whether this will, in turn, produce a nativist reaction, remains to be seen, but at this writing, mid-1974, no such reaction is apparent. After all, according to the 1970 census, East Asians comprised less than one percent of the population, and more than half of them lived in just two states, California and Hawaii.[6]

* * *

Hubert Howe Bancroft, the premier historian of California, saw the Chinese as aliens "in every sense."

The color of their skins, the repulsiveness of their features, their undersize of figure, their incomprehensible language, strange customs and heathen religion . . . conspired to set them apart had they not themselves exhibited a disposition to hold aloof from the white race. Their camps

---

[6] U.S. Dept. of Commerce, Bureau of the Census, *Japanese, Chinese, and Filipinos in the United States*, Subject Report PC (2)–1G, 1970 Census of Population (Washington, D.C., 1973), contains the most detailed compilation of statistics on Asian Americans ever assembled for a single census. The data in this report are based on samples rather than the complete count. As the table below shows, there are differences, although most of them are slight. My own practice will be to use the 20 percent sample figure (column 2 below).

Comparison of Complete-Count and 20- and 15-Percent Sample Data on the Population
by Race, for the United States: 1970
[Minus sign (—) denotes decrease]

		20-percent sample			15-percent sample		
			Difference from complete count			Difference from complete count	
Race	Complete count	Total	Number	Per-cent	Total	Number	Per-cent
Total	203,211,926	203,212,877	951	0.0	203,210,158	—1,768	0.0
White	177,748,975	178,107,190	358,215	0.2	178,119,221	370,246	0.2
Negro	22,580,289	22,549,815	—30,474	—0.1	22,539,362	—40,927	—0.2
American Indian	792,730	763,594	—29,136	—3.7	760,572	—32,158	—4.1
Japanese	591,290	588,324	—2,966	—0.5	586,675	—4,615	—0.8
Chinese	435,062	431,583	—3,479	—0.8	433,469	—1,593	—0.4
Filipino	343,060	336,731	—6,329	—1.9	336,823	—6,237	—1.8
All other	720,520	435,640	—284,880	—39.5	434,036	—286,484	—39.8
Korean (excludes Alaska)	(NA)	65,510	..	..	70,598	..	..
Hawaiian (excludes Alaska)	(NA)	99,958	..	..	98,836	..	..
Aleut (in Alaska)...	(NA)	6,292	..	..	6,352	..	..
Eskimo (in Alaska).	(NA)	28,233	..	..	28,186	..	..

In geographical terms, a very high concentration of Asian Americans exists in two states, California and Hawaii.

	Total U.S.	California	Hawaii
Japanese Americans	588,324	213,277	217,175
Chinese Americans	431,583	170,419	52,583
Filipino Americans	336,731	135,284	95,680
Korean Americans	69,510	15,909	na*
	1,426,148	534,889	365,438

*The report does indicate that 8,914 Korean Americans lived in the Honolulu standard metropolitan statistical area, but it gives no figure for the entire state.

were always removed to a comfortable distance from the camps of the white miners, as much from choice as from recognition of the unfriendliness visible in the looks and acts of their American and European neighbors.[7]

In a final volume published at the height of the Progressive era, Bancroft's views, while still racist, had changed. He devoted a chapter, "Asia and Africa in America," to arguing that Asian labor was necessary: "we want the Asiatic for our low-grade work, and when it is finished we want him to go home and stay there until we want him again." As for Japanese, not the "Japanese working man," but the "educated and ambitious class," which "delights in stirring up strife and making trouble," should be excluded. The hard-working Asian laborers were contrasted favorably not only with the "lazy and licentious" Negro, in whom "the animal overbalances the mental," but also with those whom Bancroft regarded as elements from "the cesspools of Europe." The Chinese were not "anarchistic dirty and revengeful like the Italian, thieving and vermiparous like the Slav, or impudent and intermeddling like the Celt and Teuton," nor would they make love to our women or "breed a few million yellow piccaninnies for American citizenship." He even took up the yellow peril theme, although unlike most of his contemporaries, he found China rather than Japan the real threat, foreseeing the day when she would send "five thousand airships sailing over America and Europe, dropping bombs into the large cities."[8]

The yellow peril theme, the notion that immigrants from Asia were only the first and peaceful wave of what would become an armed invasion, had not been a major theme of nativist literature in the nineteenth century, although there are a few obscure examples.[9] The general nativist view, denigrating Indians and Mexican Americans, predominated, but a few antinativist voices were raised. The most important of these spokesmen, Josiah Royce and

---

[7] Hubert Howe Bancroft, *History of California, Vol. VII, 1860–1890* (San Francisco, 1890), 336 (*Works*, Vol. XXIV).

[8] Bancroft, *Retrospection, Political and Personal* (New York, 1912), 345–374.

[9] See, for example, H. J. West, *The Chinese Invasion* (San Francisco, 1873), and Robert Woltor, *A Short and Truthful History of the Taking of California and Oregon by the Chinese in the Year A.D. 1899* (San Francisco, 1882). The fullest treatment is Richard Austin Thompson, "The Yellow Peril, 1890–1924" (Ph.D. dissertation, University of Wisconsin, 1957); see also Daniels, *Politics of Prejudice*, 65–78, and Fred H. Matthews, "White Community and 'Yellow Peril'," *Mississippi Valley Historical Review*, L (1964), 612–633.

Helen Hunt Jackson, were not particularly concerned with defend-
ing Asians. Most of the several dozen "pro-Chinese" voices belonged
to obscure polemicists. Most of them had a special interest in the
Chinese question; they were merchants interested in trade with the
Far East, manufacturers and agriculturists who wished to keep the
wage level as low as possible, middle-class spokesmen interested in
a cheap and docile solution to the servant problem which seemed
quite important in a Gilded Age America, and, perhaps most important, a number of Protestant clergymen, especially those engaged
in missionary activity on both sides of the Pacific or connected with
denominations that were so engaged. That these "defenders" of the
Chinese were not, in a modern sense, egalitarians, almost goes without saying. The most notable of the clerical champions of the Chinese was the Reverend Otis Gibson, who insisted that "it is the
God-taught principle that *all men are born free and equal.*" Gibson,
who ran a San Francisco mission for reformed Chinese prostitutes,
was not without prejudice: he reports that one of his charges was
married to a "white man," but quickly adds "of course, not to an
American citizen."[10] Gibson's writings, and other books and pamphlets on the Chinese question from all points of view, were the
literary aspect of the political struggle over Chinese exclusion
which was settled for all practical purposes by the Exclusion Act of
1882.[11] The western view of the Chinese question also came to prevail among most eastern historians. Woodrow Wilson, for example,
wrote in his popular five-volume *History of the American People*:

Chinese laborers had poured in [to the Pacific Coast], first by hundreds,
then by thousands, finally by hundreds of thousands, until the labor
situation of the whole coast had become one almost of revolution.
Caucasian laborers could not compete with the Chinese, could not live
upon a handful of rice and work for a pittance, and found themselves
being steadily crowded out from occupation after occupation by the

---

[10] Otis Gibson, *The Chinese in America* (Cincinnati, 1877), 275. Robert Seager,
"Some Denominational Reactions to Chinese Immigration to California, 1856–1892,"
Pacific Historical Review, XXVIII (1959), 49–66, is a survey of Protestant reactions.
For a biography of an anti-Chinese Catholic priest, see John B. McGloin, *Eloquent
Indian: the Life of James Bouchard, California Jesuit* (Stanford, 1949). Lionel U.
Ridout, "The Church, the Chinese and the Negroes in California," *Historical Maga-
zine of the Protestant Episcopal Church*, XXVII (1959), 115–138, examines reactions
within one denomination.

[11] The most complete listing of these materials is Robert E. Cowan and Boutwell
Dunlap, *Bibliography of the Chinese Question* (San Francisco, 1909). A. P. C. Griffin,
Select List of References on Chinese Immigration (Washington, D.C., 1904) is a good
guide to governmental sources, including the *Congressional Record*.

thrifty, skillful Orientals, who, with their yellow skin and debasing habits of life, seemed to them hardly fellow men at all, but evil spirits, rather.[12]

The first full-scale treatment of the Chinese in the United States that can be called history was Mary Roberts Coolidge's *Chinese Immigration,* published in 1909 in the Holt "American Public Problems" series. Coolidge (1860–1945) was an almost hypertypical WASP reform intellectual. The daughter of a college professor (her second husband was a distant kinsman of the thirtieth President), she earned two degrees from Cornell and a Ph.D. in sociology from Stanford in 1896. She had taught history at private schools and at Wellesley College, taught sociology at Stanford (1896–1903) and at Mills College (1918–1927), and worked in a settlement house (1905–1906). She was a Unitarian, a Republican, and a member of the American Indian Defense Association; her public service included a term on the California State Board of Education (1928–1932) and serving as a trustee of the Pacific Colony for the Feeble-minded. Her 1909 volume was her only publication on Asian Americans, although she also published books on Indians, the woman question, and social work.[13]

Coolidge's book is a partial defense of the Chinese and a vehement attack on the anti-Chinese forces. Denying the unassimilability of the Chinese, she insisted that a comparison of them to "the Italians, Mexicans and Greeks in San Francisco discloses that they are being Americanized quite as rapidly, and, in some respects, make better citizens because of their superior intellectual capacity." She had no understanding of the social forces which created anti-Orientalism, and wrote off the anti-Japanese agitation then coming to a head as "a superficial demonstration confined to a class of workingmen, and reflected by political aspirants of a lower grade but ignored by the majority."[14] Despite its polemic nature, *Chinese Immigration* was a clear historiographical advance, although its patrician view of the California labor movement and of popular movements generally resulted in a serious underestimation of the

---

[12] Woodrow Wilson, *A History of the American People* (6 vols., New York, 1901), V, 185; see also James Ford Rhodes, *History of the United States from Hayes to McKinley, 1877–1896* (New York, 1919), 180–196.

[13] Mary Roberts Coolidge, *Chinese Immigration* (New York, 1909; reprinted, 1969). Biographical data from *Who Was Who in America, 1943–1950* (Chicago, 1950), 138, and *New York Times,* April 14, 1945.

[14] Coolidge, *Chinese Immigration,* 441, 253.

strength of anti-Orientalism. Some of this bias was dispelled in the following year with the publication of Lucille Eaves, *A History of Labor Legislation in California,* a work of much broader significance than its title implies. In the process of evaluating the growth of the California labor movement, Eaves argued convincingly that the struggle against the Chinese "contributed more than any other one factor" to the cohesiveness of the state's labor movement.[15]

For three decades after Coolidge's work, little of primary importance was published.[16] Then in 1939 Elmer C. Sandmeyer published his 1932 Illinois dissertation, *The Anti-Chinese Movement in California,* which can be considered the first account to meet the demands of contemporary scholarship. What sets his work off from what had gone before was that it was an attempt to understand rather than to denigrate. Without in any way "approving" the anti-Chinese movement, he demonstrated that its roots were in deeply felt social and economic grievances. Sandmeyer understood that while "diverse motives" were responsible for its growth and success, the fundamental element was racial "antagonism, reinforced by economic competition."[17] His research, largely in newspapers, pamphlets, government documents, and the periodical press, established clearly and precisely the successive manifestations of anti-Chinese sentiment, which coalesced into a movement that triumphed successively on the local, state, regional, and, finally, national level. If the writing and level of analysis are somewhat pedestrian, the work is accurate, and, in the three and a half decades since its publication, no scholar has thought it necessary to redo Sandmeyer's effort. Nor is any such reexamination likely.

In the last few years, however, two important books have appeared which reevaluate, in a most fundamental way, the signifi-

---

15 Lucille Eaves, *A History of Labor Legislation in California* (Berkeley, 1910), 6; for a specific example of trade union discrimination, see Paul S. Taylor, *The Sailor's Union of the Pacific* (New York, 1923), 156; for a theoretical discussion of the meaning of labor discrimination against Asians, see Isabella Black, "American Labour and Chinese Immigration," *Past and Present,* XXV (1963), 59–76, and Roger Daniels, "American Labour and Chinese Immigration," *Past and Present,* XXVII (1964), 113–114.

16 Of chief significance were two competent monographic studies by scholars born in China and working at American institutions: Tien-Lu Li, *Congressional Policy of Chinese Immigration; or Legislation Relating to Chinese Immigration to the United States* (Nashville, 1916), and Ta Chen, "Chinese Migrations," *Bulletin of the Bureau of Labor Statistics No. 340* (Washington, D.C., 1923).

17 (Urbana, 1939), 109. A 1973 reprinting contains a supplementary bibliography by Roger Daniels covering publications between 1939 and 1973.

cance of the anti-Chinese movement. Appearing after the post-1954 civil rights movement had placed race and racism high on the domestic agenda, Stuart Creighton Miller and Alexander Saxton each related what had previously been treated as a discrete regional phenomenon to the national dilemma.

Miller's *The Unwelcome Immigrant: The American Image of the Chinese, 1785–1882* was the first major work directly to relate discrimination against Chinese to the mainstream of American racism.[18] Essentially a work of intellectual history, Miller demonstrated, quite conclusively, that the American image of China and the Chinese was, even before the American Civil War, not only largely negative, but also distinctly racist. This was in direct opposition to the then established view, crystallized by Harold Isaacs but held by most scholars who had dealt with the genesis of Sino-American relations, that there had existed an "Age of Respect" before 1840 in the American image of China.[19]

Saxton's *The Indispensable Enemy: Labor and the Anti-Chinese Movement in California* also dealt with ideology.[20] Focusing on the California labor movement, which all authorities agree was the *fons et origo* of organizational opposition to Chinese in the United States, he showed that there were eastern roots for what had been assumed to be an indigenous far western movement. Where Miller examined the thoughts of men like Ralph Waldo Emerson and John Quincy Adams, Saxton discovered some of the genesis of anti-Chinese sentiment in the murky ideology of Jacksonian America. His thesis, that the presence of large numbers of Chinese provided the indispensable cement to hold together the relatively very strong California labor movement, was not new, having been put forth by Ira Cross, but it had never before been so convincingly demonstrated.[21]

---

18 (Berkeley and Los Angeles, 1969). See also his "An East Coast Perspective to Chinese Exclusion, 1852-1882," *Historian*, XXXIII (1971), 183–201.

19 Harold Isaacs, *Scratches on Our Mind: American Images of China and India* (New York, 1958). For a most important recent article on Chinese immigration, see Shih-shan H. Ts'ai, "Chinese Immigration through Communist Chinese Eyes: An Introduction to the Historiography," *Pacific Historical Review*, XLIII (1974), 395–408. By using Chinese language sources, some of them going back to the mid-nineteenth century, it makes a breakthrough that future scholarship ought to exploit.

20 (Berkeley and Los Angeles, 1971).

21 Ira B. Cross, *A History of the Labor Movement in California* (Berkeley, 1935). A number of articles and theses throw light on the interconnections between organized labor and anti-Chinese activity. Among the more significant are Donald Rowland, "The United States and the Contract Labor Question in Hawaii, 1862-1900,"

Most of the scholarship about Chinese in America, and in fact about Asian Americans generally, has focused on the opposition which they aroused, on the excluders rather than the excluded. There are many reasons for this: the lack of manuscript materials, the inability of most scholars interested in United States history to utilize Asian languages, and, perhaps most important of all, a first overt and then covert kind of racism which tended to ignore the victims even while dissecting the oppressors. Given the current interest in and urgency about ethnic studies in the United States, one can expect a burgeoning of Asian American studies in general and Chinese American studies in particular.

There are two broad histories of Chinese in the United States. The earlier work, Rose Hum Lee's *The Chinese in the United States of America,* is a treatment by a sociologist and badly flawed by a lack of historical understanding and factual errors.[22] Much more useful is the recent treatment by Betty Lee Sung.[23] While written for the general reader rather than the scholar, it is an accurate and often perceptive synthesis which should become a point of departure for more detailed and sophisticated studies. One recent ambitious work by a professional historian did break new ground

Pacific Historical Review, II (1933), 249–269; Rodman W. Paul, "The Origin of the Chinese Issue in California," *Mississippi Valley Historical Review,* XXV (1938), 181–196; Paul Crane and Alfred Larson, "The Chinese Massacre," *Annals of Wyoming,* XII (1940), 47–55, 153–160; Ralph Kauer, "The Workingmen's Party of California," *Pacific Historical Review,* XIII (1944), 278–291; Frederick Rudolph, "Chinamen in Yankeedom: Anti-Unionism in Massachusetts in 1870," *American Historical Review,* LIII (1947), 1–29; Jules A. Karlin, "The Anti-Chinese Outbreaks in Seattle," *Pacific Northwest Quarterly,* XXXIX (1948), 103–130; Nicholas A. Somma, "The Knights of Labor and Chinese Immigration" (M.A. thesis, Catholic University, 1952); Arthur Mann, "Gompers and the Irony of Racism," *Antioch Review,* XIII (1953), 203–214; Leonard Pitt, "The Beginnings of Nativism in California," *Pacific Historical Review,* XXX (1961), 23–38; Lynwood Carranco, "Chinese Expulsion from Humboldt County," *Pacific Historical Review,* XXX (1961), 329–340; R. E. Wynne, "Reaction to the Chinese in the Pacific Northwest and British Columbia" (Ph.D. dissertation, University of Washington, 1964); Roy T. Wortman, "Denver's Anti-Chinese Riot," *Colorado Magazine of History,* XLII (1965), 275–291; Robert E. Wynne, "American Labor Leaders and the Vancouver Anti-Oriental Riot," *Pacific Northwest Quarterly,* LVII (1966), 172–179; Alexander Saxton, "The Army of Canton in the High Sierra," *Pacific Historical Review,* XXXV (1966), 141–152; Arlen Ray Wilson, "The Rock Springs, Wyoming, Chinese Massacre, 1885" (M.A. thesis, University of Wyoming, 1967); Alexander Saxton, "Race in the House of Labor," in Gary Nash and Richard Weiss, eds., *Race in the Mind of America* (New York, 1970), 98–120; Herbert Hill, "Anti-Oriental Agitation and the Rise of Working-Class Racism," *Society,* X (1973), 43–53.

22 (Hong Kong, 1960).

23 *Mountain of Gold* (New York, 1967); the paperback edition is entitled *The Story of the Chinese in the United States* (New York, 1970).

in a crucial area of Chinese American history. Gunther Barth's *Bitter Strength* is a history of the Chinese in the United States during the first two decades of their experience.[24] Seriously hampered by an almost total absence of documentary evidence telling the story from a Chinese point of view, Barth resorted heavily to the argument from analogy, comparing Chinese immigration to the United States with that of Chinese to various parts of Southeast Asia. Using a broad-based social science approach typical of the students of Oscar Handlin, he characterized the Chinese as essentially "sojourners" who eventually became immigrants. There are, as yet, no sophisticated monographic studies of the major Chinese American communities like San Francisco and New York. The best regional study of a Chinese American community is James W. Loewen's *The Mississippi Chinese,* but it treats a microgroup whose experiences are significantly different from those of the overwhelming majority of their compatriots.[25]

The historiography of Japanese Americans is, for a variety of reasons, more fully developed. Japanese came to the United States later and received a good deal of attention from contemporary

---

24 *Bitter Strength: A History of the Chinese in the United States, 1850–1870* (Cambridge, Mass., 1964). See also his "Chinese Sojourners in the West: The Coming," *Southern California Quarterly,* XLVI (1964), 55–67.

25 *The Mississippi Chinese: Between Black and White* (Cambridge, Mass., 1971). Other studies of the Chinese American community include William Hoy, *The Chinese Six Companies* (San Francisco, 1942), a filiopietistic treatment of a subject that needs serious attention; Francis L. K. Hsu, *Americans and Chinese: Two Ways of Life* (New York, 1953); Stanford M. Lyman, "The Structure of Chinese Society in Nineteenth Century America" (Ph.D. dissertation, University of California, Berkeley, 1961); S. W. Kung, *The Chinese in American Life: Some Aspects of Their History, Status, Problems and Contributions* (Seattle, 1962); Kwang Ching Liu, *Americans and Chinese* (Cambridge, Mass., 1963); Ping Chiu, *Chinese Labor in California, 1850–1880* (Madison, Wis., 1963); David T. Yuan, "Voluntary Segregation; A Study of New York Chinatown," *Phylon,* XXIV (1963), 255–265, and "Chinatown and Beyond: The Chinese Population in Metropolitan New York," *ibid.,* XVII (1966), 321–332; Calvin Lee, *Chinatown, U.S.A.* (New York, 1965); Roger Daniels, "Westerners from the East: Oriental Immigrants Reappraised," *Pacific Historical Review,* XXXV (1966), 373–383; Larry D. Quinn, "Chink, Chink Chinaman: The Beginnings of Nativism in Montana," *Pacific Northwest Quarterly,* LVIII (1967), 82–89; Philip P. Choy, "Golden Mountain of Lead: The Chinese Experience in California," *California Historical Quarterly,* L (1970), 267–276; George Chu, "Chinatowns in the Delta: The Chinese in the Sacramento-San Joaquin Delta, 1876–1960," *ibid.,* 277–286; Stanford M. Lyman, *The Asian in the West* (Reno and Las Vegas, Nev., Desert Research Institute, 1970); Francis L. K. Hsu, *The Challenge of the American Dream: The Chinese in the United States* (Belmont, Calif., 1971); and Sally Ken, "The Chinese Community of Augusta, Georgia, from 1873 to 1971," *Richmond County History,* IV (1972), 51–60; Ivan Light, "From Vice District to Tourist Attraction: The Moral Career of American Chinatowns, 1880–1940," *Pacific Historical Review,* XLIII (1974), 367–394.

scholars, some of it inspired by the Japanese government. During much of the twentieth century, Japanese American relations were central rather than peripheral. And finally, of course, the atrocious treatment meted out to the West Coast Japanese Americans during World War II facilitated a comprehensive collection of data unsurpassed in the history of American ethnic groups and at the same time stirred the conscience and the interest of many Americans.

As was the case with Chinese, Japanese American historiography started with pamphlet controversies but very quickly took on a scholarly dimension. Anti-Japanese pamphlets began to appear as early as 1907, and two years later the whole Japanese immigration controversy was of enough moment that several articles in the prestigious *Annals of the American Academy of Political and Social Sciences* were devoted to it.[26] In 1911 a volume of the *Reports of the United States Immigration Commission* was devoted to "Japanese and Other Immigrant Races in the Pacific Coast and Rocky Mountain States." Although most of the surviving members of the commission, including Henry Cabot Lodge, would eventually support exclusion in 1924, the report itself, prepared by a social scientist, H. A. Millis, is an accurate and not unfavorable account.[27] One of his investigators, Yamato Ichihashi, a Japanese-born scholar who had earned a Ph.D., published in 1913 a brief account of *Japanese Immigration: Its Status in California,* which, although something of an apology, is also a work of useful scholarship, and the forerunner of his much fuller *Japanese in the United States.*[28]

In addition to these scholarly works, there was an extensive polemical literature. The two most significant champions of the Japanese immigrants were an American clergyman, Sidney Lewis Gulick, and a Japanese-born publicist, K. K. Kawakami. Gulick seemed to be a mass movement all by himself: he was executive secretary and organizer of the National Committee for Constructive

---

26 *Annals of the American Academy of Political and Social Sciences,* XXXIV (Sept., 1909).

27 U.S. Immigration Commission, *Reports of the Immigration Commission: Japanese and Other Immigrant Groups in the Pacific Coast and Rocky Mountain States* (Washington, D.C., 1911), Vol. 23. Millis published much of the same material in *The Japanese Problem in the United States: An Investigation for the Commission on Relations with Japan Appointed by the Federal Council of Churches of Christ in America* (New York, 1911).

28 *Japanese Immigration: Its Status in California* (San Francisco, 1913); *Japanese in the United States* (Stanford, Calif., 1932).

Immigration Legislation, secretary of the Committee on American-Japanese Relations, and a member of the Commission on Relations with Japan of the Federal Council of Churches of Christ in America. Between 1914 and 1924 he wrote at least twenty-four books and pamphlets on the Japanese question, published dozens of magazine articles, and gave hundreds of lectures and sermons. His basic position was set forth in 1914 in his first major work on the subject, *The American Japanese Problem,* and his line of argument is quite similar to Coolidge's. He excoriated the anti-Japanese movement as "needless," "hysterical," "unscientific," and "unChristian." He was sure that Japanese were superior to immigrants from southern Europe and to Negroes. "The Japanese race," he asserted, "already contains considerable white blood." He was opposed to the "free intermarriage of the races" and to "unlimited immigration" and became one of the earliest proponents of a quota system.[29] Kawakami, sometime Washington correspondent for the Tokyo *Hochi Shimbun,* defended not only the Japanese immigrants, but also became an apologist for Japanese expansion in East Asia.[30]

But the anti-Japanese polemicists were much more numerous and influential. They ranged from the crude pamphleteers of the California labor movement to slick novelists like Wallace Irwin and Peter B. Kyne and even included a minor military prophet, Homer Lea.[31] Each of the several Japanese American crises—the San Francisco School Board affair of 1907, the war scares of the pre-World War I era, the controversies over alien land acts in 1913 and 1920, and the enactment of Japanese exclusion in 1924—produced a spate of printed materials.[32] The first significant scholarly attempt to analyze this diverse movement came in a two-part article published in 1922–1923 by a political scientist, Raymond Leslie Buell, while five years later the sociologist R. D. McKenzie made the

---

29 *The American Japanese Problem* (New York, 1914), 184–196, 72, 152–153, 157–160.

30 *The Real Japanese Question* (New York, 1921) and *Japan Speaks* (New York, 1932) are representative.

31 See, for example, Asiatic Exclusion League, *Proceedings* (San Francisco, 1907–1912); Wallace Irwin, *Seed of the Sun* (New York, 1921); Peter B. Kyne, *The Pride of Palomar* (New York, 1921); and Homer Lea, *The Valor of Ignorance* (New York, 1909).

32 Among the more interesting are Herbert B. Johnson, *Discrimination Against Japanese in California* (Berkeley, 1907); William G. Burke, *The Japanese School Segregation Case: Respondents' Brief* (San Francisco [?], 1907 [?]); Montaville Flowers, *The Japanese Conquest of American Public Opinion* (New York, 1917); George Shima, *An Appeal to Justice* (Stockton, Calif., 1920); and Cornelius Vanderbilt, Jr., *The Verdict of Public Opinion on the Japanese-American Question* (New York, 1920).

first noteworthy attempt to generalize about anti-Oriental move-ments.[33]

Like the owl of Minerva, historians arrive on the scene much later. In 1934 Thomas A. Bailey published *Theodore Roosevelt and the Japanese-American Crisis.* Although primarily a work of diplomatic history, it represents the first enduring historical analysis of the forces involved in the anti-Japanese movement. Without in any way "approving" its excesses, Bailey understood, as his prede-cessors had not, that the movement represented the real aspirations of the "man in the street."[34] Other mature evaluations were much longer in coming. In 1946 a legal historian, Milton R. Konvitz, published *The Alien and the Asiatic in American Law,* a detailed analysis of continuing discriminatory treatment.[35] And, in the next decade, two works appeared which, although not chiefly directed at the Asian American experience, cast much light upon it. In *The Japanese Frontier in Hawaii, 1868–1898,* Hilary Conroy explained, for the first time, the complex process by which Japanese immi-grated to Hawaii, which served as a staging area for migration to the mainland.[36] John Higham, *Strangers in the Land,* while only marginally concerned with Asian Americans, painted, in broad

---

[33] Raymond Leslie Buell, "The Development of the Anti-Japanese Agitation in the United States," *Political Science Quarterly,* XXXVII (1922), 605–638, and XXXVIII (1923), 57–81; and R. D. McKenzie, *Oriental Exclusion* (Chicago, 1928). Other social-science treatments of these years include M. Fujita, "The Japanese Associations in America," *Sociology and Social Research,* XIV (1929), 211–217; Edward K. Strong, *The Second Generation Japanese Problem* (Stanford, Calif., 1934); John A. Rade-maker, "The Japanese in the Social Organization of the Puget Sound Region," *Ameri-can Journal of Sociology,* XL (1934), 338–343; Eleanor Tupper and George E. Mc-Reynolds, *Japan in American Public Opinion* (New York, 1937); and S. Frank Miya-moto, *Social Solidarity Among the Japanese in Seattle* (Seattle, 1939).

[34] (Stanford, Calif., 1934). Bailey also published "California, Japan and the Alien Land Act Legislation of 1913," *Pacific Historical Review,* I (1932), 36–59. Both suf-fered from the unavailability at that time of the papers of California politicians, especially those of Hiram W. Johnson. Two contrasting brief historical treatments of the enactment of Japanese exclusion are Earl H. Pritchard, "The Japanese Ex-clusion Bill of 1924," *Research Studies of the State College of Washington,* II (1930), 65–76; and Rodman W. Paul, *The Abrogation of the Gentlemen's Agreement* (Cam-bridge, Mass., 1936). See also Dudley O. McGovney, "The Anti-Japanese Laws of California and Ten Other States," *California Law Review,* XXV (1935), 7–60.

[35] (Ithaca, N.Y., 1946).

[36] (Berkeley and Los Angeles, 1953). See also his (with Yukiko Irwin) "R. W. Irwin and Systematic Immigration to Hawaii," and Masajii Marumoto's "'First Year' Immi-grants to Hawaii and Eugene Van Reed," both in Conroy and T. Scott Miyakawa, eds., *East Across the Pacific: Historical and Sociological Studies of Japanese Immigra-tion and Assimilation* (Santa Barbara, Calif., 1972).

strokes, the patterns of post-Civil War American nativism.[37] In 1962, using the newly available papers of Hiram W. Johnson, James D. Phelan, and other California politicians, Roger Daniels published *The Politics of Prejudice*, a detailed analysis showing that both labor unions and those forces usually labeled "progressive" had been the prime movers of anti-Japanese legislation at the state and national levels.[38]

In the meantime, the great Pacific War of which the yellow perilists had written finally took place. The battles on American soil that Homer Lea and others[39] had predicted never happened; instead, American concentration camps were set up for all persons of Japanese ancestry in the far western United States. This tragedy, sometimes called "our worst wartime mistake," has produced the fullest and most varied literature on any aspect of Asian American studies. Even before the West Coast Japanese had been rounded up, an ambitious, well-financed social-science research project was established at the University of California, Berkeley, to study the whole process. The University of California Japanese American Evacuation and Resettlement Study was directed by Dorothy S. Thomas, then a professor of rural sociology at Berkeley, and never included either a professional historian or an archivist on its staff.[40] It received much cooperation from the federal government, and, in return, those involved in the study pledged not to publish or discuss publicly the evacuation during the war. Since the scholars in the best position to discuss the evacuation were silent, the earliest accounts were either journalistic or government propaganda.

The latter falls into two main categories: material published by the United States Army, which was mendacious, and that published by the War Relocation Authority, which was self-serving. The Army's major contribution, entitled *Final Report: Japanese Evacuation from the West Coast, 1942*, was largely written by Colonel

---

37 *Strangers in the Land: Patterns of American Nativism, 1860–1925* (New Brunswick, N.J., 1955).

38 *The Politics of Prejudice: The Anti-Japanese Movement in California and the Struggle for Japanese Exclusion* (Berkeley and Los Angeles, 1962).

39 For perhaps the last such prediction, see Whitman Chambers, *Invasion!* (New York, 1943).

40 The lack of an archivist was particularly unfortunate and resulted in the mutilation of some of the project's files which are now located in the Bancroft Library, Berkeley. For an analytical memoir account by one of the project's researchers, see Rosalie H. Wax, *Doing Fieldwork: Warnings and Advice* (Chicago, 1971), 59–176.

Karl R. Bendetsen, a major architect of the evacuation. It pictured the evacuation as dictated by "stern, military necessity."[41] The publications of the War Relocation Authority, one of which, *Wartime Exile,* criticizes the evacuation, contain much information, but often suppress those aspects of life in American concentration camps likely to reflect badly on the keepers. The general tone of these publications may be inferred from the title of the agency's self-history, *WRA: A Story of Human Conservation.*[42]

One of the great wartime weaknesses of the American press was its failure to cover, in any adequate way, the evacuation story. A few journalists, of whom Carey McWilliams is the most notable, did write accurate and indignant stories, but they received little attention.[43] Only as the war was ending did an eloquent condemnation of the evacuation attract national attention when Eugene V. Rostow published a vigorous denunciation entitled "Our Worst Wartime Mistake."[44]

---

[41] U.S. Dept. of War, *Final Report: Japanese Evacuation From the West Coast* (Washington, D.C., 1943). Lt. Gen. John L. De Witt was officially responsible for the document.

[42] The major publications are U.S. Dept. of the Interior, War Relocation Authority, *The Relocation Program: A Guidebook for the Residents of Relocation Centers* (Washington, D.C., 1943); *Administrative Highlights of the WRA Program* (Washington, D.C., 1946); *Community Government in War Relocation Centers* (Washington, D.C., 1946); *The Evacuated People: A Quantitative Description* (Washington, D.C., 1946); *Legal and Constitutional Phases of the WRA Program* (Washington, D.C., 1946); *People in Motion: The Postwar Readjustment of the Evacuated Japanese Americans* (Washington, D.C., 1946); *The Relocation Program* (Washington, D.C., 1946); *WRA: A Story of Human Conservation* (Washington, D.C., 1946); *Wartime Exile: The Exclusion of the Japanese Americans from the West Coast* (Washington, D.C., 1946); *The Wartime Handling of Evacuee Property* (Washington, D.C., 1946), all of which are being reprinted by the AMS Press. Another 1946 volume has been reprinted as Edward H. Spicer, Asael T. Hansen, Katherine Luomala, and Marvin K. Opler, *Impounded People: Japanese Americans in the Relocation Centers* (Tucson, Ariz., 1969); the 1969 edition contains a valuable "Bibliography of Life in the War Relocation Centers," prepared by Edward H. Spicer and Janet R. Monroe. The WRA director, Dillon S. Myer, has published his memoirs under the title, *Uprooted Americans* (Tucson, Ariz., 1971). Alexander Leighton's *The Governing of Men: General Principles and Recommendations Based on Experience at a Japanese Relocation Camp* (Princeton, N.J., 1945) is the only book by an insider that is significantly critical. A thorough study of this agency of benign incarceration is badly needed.

[43] Most significant was Carey McWilliams, *Prejudice: Japanese Americans: Symbol of Racial Intolerance* (Boston, 1945); his earlier publications include a pamphlet, *What About Our Japanese Americans?* (New York, 1944). For an insightful critique of McWilliams and others on the Left, see William Petersen, *Japanese Americans: Oppression and Success* (New York, 1971), 73–81.

[44] "Our Worst Wartime Mistake," *Harper's Magazine,* CXCI (Sept. 1945), 193–201; a more scholarly version is Rostow's "The Japanese American Cases—A Disaster,"

The war over, the works of the Berkeley study began to appear. Four books have emanated from the project, three of which appeared under its aegis. The director, Dorothy S. Thomas, was the senior author of two works, *The Spoilage* (1946) and *The Salvage* (1952).[45] The first concerned itself solely with the large minority of Japanese Americans, who sought, at one time or another, repatriation to Japan, while the second is a collection of case histories of evacuees gathered by participant observers in assembly centers and relocation camps. In 1949 Morton Grodzins published *Americans Betrayed*. Although, as a doctoral candidate in political science, he had worked on the Berkeley project as a principal investigator of its political aspects, his work was neither published nor approved by the project; in fact there was some legal effort to inhibit the publication of his study. Grodzins, who was able to use only those documents which government officials at the time were willing to show him, felt that the chief responsibility for the evacuation lay with economic pressure groups and, to a lesser degree, politicians. His work, along with that of McWilliams and Bradford Smith,[46] may be called a kind of simplistic Beardianism, which delighted in discovering an apparent direct relationship between economics and politics.[47] The fourth book and the third volume of the project, Jacobus tenBroek, Edward N. Barnhart, and Floyd W. Matson, *Prejudice, War and the Constitution*, appeared only in 1958.[48]

Yale Law Review, LIV (1945), 489–553, which is reprinted in his *The Sovereign Prerogative: The Supreme Court and the Quest for Law* (New Haven, Conn., 1962). It should be noted that Rostow challenged the legality of the evacuation even while accepting—for want of evidence to the contrary—some of the misstatements in the U.S. War Department's *Final Report*. Another important early legal article is Nanette Dembitz, "Racial Discrimination and the Military Judgment: The Supreme Court's Korematsu and Endo Decisions," *Columbia Law Review*, XLV (1945), 175–239.

45 Dorothy S. Thomas and Richard S. Nishimoto, *The Spoilage* (Berkeley and Los Angeles, 1946), and Dorothy S. Thomas, *The Salvage* (Berkeley and Los Angeles, 1952). See also her "Some Social Aspects of Japanese-American Demography," *Proceedings of the American Philosophical Society*, XCIV (1950), 459–480.

46 Bradford Smith, *Americans From Japan* (New York, 1948).

47 Morton Grodzins, *Americans Betrayed: Politics and the Japanese Evacuation* (Chicago, 1949). Despite my criticism of both his method and assumptions, Grodzins's conclusion—the most significant and ominous aspect of the evacuation was that it gave "precedent and constitutional sanctity for a policy of mass incarceration under military auspices . . . that . . . betrayed all Americans"—still seems to me most perceptive.

48 *Prejudice, War and the Constitution* (Berkeley and Los Angeles, 1958). In addition Barnhart published two articles: "The Individual Exclusion of Japanese Americans in World War II," *Pacific Historical Review*, XXIX (1960), 111–130, and "Japanese Internees from Peru," *Pacific Historical Review*, XXXI (1962), 169–178.

None of the authors had been original members of the project. Using Matson's 1953 M.A. thesis as an introduction[49] and relying largely on the wartime materials collected by the project, they essayed their own theory of the evacuation, which approximated that put forth by Bendetsen in *Final Report*, although they were highly critical of the assumptions on which the military justified its decisions.

A year later Stetson Conn, the civilian chief military historian of the United States, provided a definitive explication of the military aspects of "The Decision to Evacuate the Japanese from the Pacific Coast."[50] Conn demonstrated that, rather than being a military matter, the evacuation stemmed from political decisions made by the civilian heads of the army, Secretary of War Henry L. Stimson and his deputy, John J. McCloy, which went counter to the recommendations of the army's general staff. Conn also demonstrated that an obscure lawyer in uniform, Karl R. Bendetsen, and his chief, Provost Marshal General Allen W. Gullion, were important causal forces, along with General John L. De Witt, the West Coast commander, in the War Department infighting.

The wartime experience, in and out of concentration camps, has provided an important focus for Japanese American studies. Soon after the war, memoir accounts began to appear, and they continue to do so.[51] Two scholarly social-science treatments—Leonard Bloom and Ruth Reimer, *Removal and Return: The Socio-Economic Effects of the War on Japanese Americans,* and Leonard Broom and John I. Kitsuse, *The Managed Casualty: The Japanese-American*

---

49 "The Anti-Japanese Movement in California, 1890–1942" (M.A. thesis, University of California, Berkeley, 1953).

50 This appears in Kent Roberts Greenfield, ed., *Command Decisions* (New York, 1959), 88–109. A maturer version is his "Japanese Evacuation from the West Coast," in Stetson Conn, Rose C. Engleman, and Bryan Fairchild, *The United States Army in World War II: The Western Hemisphere: Guarding the United States and Its Outposts* (Washington, D.C., 1964), 115–149. See also Conn's chapter, "The Hawaiian Defenses After Pearl Harbor," pp. 197–222, in the same volume. Roger Daniels, *The Decision to Relocate the Japanese Americans* (Philadelphia, forthcoming, 1975), is an extended analysis of the decision-making process which reprints many of the key documents.

51 Toru Matsumoto, *Beyond Prejudice: The Story of the Church and Japanese Americans* (New York, 1946); Mine Okubo, *Citizen 12660* (New York, 1946); Monica Sone, *Nisei Daughter* (Boston, 1953); Daisuke Kitagawa, *Issei and Nisei: The Internment Years* (New York, 1967); Sue K. Embrey, ed., *The Lost Years, 1942–1946* (Los Angeles, 1972); Masie and Richard Conrat, *Executive Order 9066* (Los Angeles, 1972), a superb collection of wartime photographs with an unfortunate text; Estelle Ishigo, *Lone Heart Mountain* (Los Angeles, 1972); and Jeanne Wakatsuki Houston and James Houston, *Farewell to Manzanar* (Boston, 1973).

Family in World War II—collected valuable case histories but failed to achieve significant synthesis.[52] Robert W. O'Brien compiled a useful account of the efforts of the West Coast educational establishment to salvage the careers of Nisei college students and recounts some of the experiences of those students in midwestern and eastern colleges.[53] Allen H. Eaton examined the artistic activities in the camps in a well illustrated work.[54] Thomas W. Murphy evaluated the role of the Japanese American infantry in Europe, and, despite a certain lack of perspective, his work remains valuable.[55]

The work of professional historians, as usual, began to appear only later. In 1954 T. A. Larson provided a still unsurpassed account of how one western state, Wyoming, reacted to receiving a sizable shipment of Japanese relocatees.[56] In 1962 Leonard J. Arrington published a short study of the central Utah camp at Topaz, stressing its economic and social organization.[57] Two popularly written works of the late 1960s reexamined the whole topic. Allen R. Bosworth, a retired naval officer, added no new material in *America's Concentration Camps* (1967), but was the first to utilize the findings of Conn and other researchers in a full-scale treatment.[58] In *The Great Betrayal* Audrie Girdner and Anne Loftis contributed new and valuable information about the small minority of California

---

52 *Removal and Return* (Berkeley and Los Angeles, 1949); *The Managed Casualty* (Berkeley and Los Angeles, 1956). Leonard Bloom and Leonard Broom are the same person.

53 *The College Nisei* (Palo Alto, Calif., 1949).

54 *Beauty Behind Barbed Wire: The Arts of the Japanese in Our Relocation Camps* (New York, 1952).

55 *Ambassadors in Arms* (Honolulu, 1954).

56 *Wyoming's War Years* (Laramie, Wyo., 1954), 297–321.

57 *The Price of Prejudice: The Japanese-American Relocation Center in Utah during World War II* (Logan, Utah, 1962); Douglas W. Nelson, "Heart Mountain: The History of an American Concentration Camp" (M.A. thesis, University of Wyoming, 1970), should appear in print soon. Paul Bailey, *City in the Sun* (Los Angeles, 1971), is a less successful examination of the camp at Poston, Arizona. Gerald Schlenker, "The Internment of the Japanese of San Diego County during the Second World War," *Journal of San Diego History*, XVIII (1972), 1–9, is an example of the local history possibilities which should be emulated. We also badly need studies of the other camps and the assembly centers. State reactions have been explored in William Cary Anderson, "Early Reaction to the Relocation of Japanese in the State," *Arkansas Historical Quarterly*, XXIII (1964), 195–211, and Samuel T. Caruso, "After Pearl Harbor: Arizona's Response to the Gila River Relocation Center," *Journal of Arizona History*, XIV (1973), 335–346. Howard Sugimoto, "A Bibliographical Essay on the Wartime Evacuation of Japanese from the West Coast Areas," in Conroy and Miyakawa, eds., *East Across the Pacific*, 140–150, is a sophisticated analysis.

58 *America's Concentration Camps* (New York, 1967).

Caucasians who tried to ameliorate the lot of the relocatees.[59] A third full-scale treatment, Roger Daniels, *Concentration Camps USA*, further exploited Conn's research, related the evacuation to contemporary political and social developments, and demonstrated that there was a significant minority resistance movement among the "loyal" Japanese Americans. Rejecting earlier, monocausal explanations for the decision to evacuate, Daniels argued that political decisions by civilians, in and out of uniform, were more significant than a largely fictitious "military necessity," and that a racist ideology was much more important than economics.[60]

Partially because of the great attention paid to the evacuation, and the amazing recovery which the Japanese American community has made from it, there have been a number of sophisticated attempts to evaluate that community. In a widely discussed article in the *New York Times*, sociologist William Petersen argued that the Japanese American experience should serve as a kind of model for social scientists who wish to discover, by analogy, why other "nonwhite" minorities had not achieved similar success.[61] Shortly thereafter, Harry H. L. Kitano, a social scientist on the faculty of the University of California, Los Angeles, and a graduate of the high school of the Topaz, Utah, relocation center, published *Japanese Americans*, which remains the finest single study of an East Asian immigrant group. After a brief historical survey and an analysis of community institutions and social deviance, Kitano found that the Japanese American experience gave "some optimism for the future

---

59 (New York, 1969).

60 *Concentration Camps USA: Japanese Americans and World War II* (New York, 1971).

61 "Success Story, Japanese American Style," *New York Times Magazine* (Jan. 9, 1966), 20 ff. This article also represents one of the earliest evidences of the retreat from advanced positions of racial egalitarianism by social scientists under the impact of the social turmoil of the later sixties. For example: "For all the well-meaning programs and countless scholarly studies focussed on the Negro, we barely know how to repair the damage that the slave traders started" (p. 21). "On a campus [Berkeley] where to be a bohemian slob is a mark of distinction, [Japanese American students] wash themselves and dress with unostentatious neatness" (p. 40). Warning against the argument by analogy, I have maintained elsewhere that the Japanese immigrants "were a small, self-confident group entering a fertile region with a rapidly expanding population. They came with almost all the skills and technological know-how necessary to reach the bottom rungs of the ladder of success. They brought with them the ethnic pride of a successfully emerging nation about to assume the leadership of a continent. They came at a unique time in the history of their two countries: their experience cannot be repeated." Roger Daniels, "Japanese Immigrants on a Western Frontier: The Issei in California, 1890–1940," in Conroy and Miyakawa, eds., *East Across the Pacific*, 87.

of race relations in American society."[62] Kitano also insisted that there were positive aspects of the evacuation, since in the camps "for the first time young Nisei were able to feel themselves in the majority, and run things."[63] A more detailed, though less analytical, history of the Japanese American community was provided by Bill Hosowaka. An editor of the *Denver Post,* he styled the Nisei as "quiet Americans" in a work that can be regarded as consensus oriented.[64] The most ambitious assessment of the Japanese American community was provided by William Petersen in a work distinguished by wide-ranging erudition and marred by ideological polemics.[65]

All of these surveys, however, have been written without a solid, monographic predicate having been laid. Despite their importance in agriculture, for example, we have no detailed studies of Japanese agricultural communities, although there is one excellent article surveying the Japanese contribution in California.[66] Similarly, we have no historical studies of any magnitude on Chinese community life. For the Japanese at least, there has been a beginning. William M. Mason and John A. McKinstry have published a most detailed scrutiny of the early Japanese community in Los Angeles, and John Modell, in an as yet unpublished dissertation, has studied the same topic on a broader scale.[67] The San Francisco Bay Area and the Pacific Northwest are still, from a historical point of view, *terra*

---

[62] *Japanese Americans: The Evolution of a Subculture* (Englewood Cliffs, N.J., 1969). Apart from its intrinsic merit, it is significant that this represents the first major work of scholarship in this field by a second-generation Asian immigrant. For a survey from a Japanese point of view, see Teruko Kachi, "The Japanese Americans: Their History and Culture," *Tsudajuku-Daigaku Kiyō,* II (1970), 21–47.

[63] Kitano, *Japanese Americans,* 74. His remarks about "Japanese nonresistance," 44–46, should be modified by Daniels, *Concentration Camps,* 104–129.

[64] *Nisei: The Quiet Americans* (New York, 1969).

[65] *Japanese Americans: Oppression and Success* (New York, 1971), esp. 217–220. For an elaboration of some of Petersen's basic notions, see the special number of the *Journal of Social Issues,* XXIX (No. 2, 1973), "Asian Americans: A Success Story?," edited by Stanley Sue and Harry H. L. Kitano.

[66] Masakasu Iwata, "Japanese Immigrants in California Agriculture," *Agricultural History,* XXXVI (1962), 25–37.

[67] William M. Mason and John A. McKinstry, *The Japanese of Los Angeles* (Contribution in History No. 1, Los Angeles County Museum of Natural History, 1969). This study ends in 1915, when the Japanese population was some 7,000. John Modell, "The Japanese of Los Angeles: A Study in Growth and Accommodation, 1900–1946" (Ph.D. dissertation, Columbia University, 1969); see also Modell's articles "The Japanese American Family: A Perspective for Future Investigation," *Pacific Historical Review,* XXXVII (1969), 67–81, "Class or Ethnic Solidarity: The Japanese American Company Union," *Pacific Historical Review,* XXXVIII (1969), 193–206, and "Tradition and Opportunity: The Japanese Immigrant in America," *Pacific Historical*

incognita. Biographies and autobiographies are almost nonexistent. The most useful personal document in print is a portion of the diary of Charles Kikuchi, one of the major informants for the University of California study.[68]

Although, as indicated earlier, Filipinos, East Indians, Koreans, and other Asian ethnic groups have immigrated to the United States, little of a historical nature has been published about them, and there is, as yet, no substantial literature to analyze. There is a little more about the Filipinos than about other groups. One is tempted to characterize their historiography with an aphorism: last imported, least studied. A few articles by sociologists, inclusion in books on Spanish-speaking minorities, and a scholarly symposium or two make up their bibliography.[69]

Review, XL (1971), 163–182. Other studies include Marvin E. Pursinger, "The Japanese Settle in Oregon, 1880–1920," *Journal of the West,* V (1966), 251–262, and Susie Sato, "Before Pearl Harbor: Early Japanese Settlers in Arizona," *Journal of Arizona History,* XIV (1973), 317–334.

[68] John Modell, ed., *The Kikuchi Diary: Chronicle from an American Concentration Camp: The Tanforan Journals of Charles Kikuchi* (Urbana, Ill., 1973).

[69] J. M. Saniel, ed., *The Filipino Exclusion Movement, 1927–1935* (Occasional Papers No. 1, University of the Philippines, Quezon City, 1967), is a symposium by American scholars. Earlier works include Bruno Lasker, *Filipino Immigration to the Continental United States and Hawaii* (Chicago, 1939); Emory S. Bogardus, "American Attitudes Toward Filipinos," *Sociology and Social Research,* XIV (1929), 59–69; Maximo C. Manzon, *The Strange Case of Filipinos in the United States* (New York, 1938); John H. Burma, *Spanish Speaking Groups in the United States* (Durham, N.C., 1954). Two eloquent memoir complaints about discrimination are Manuel Buaken, *I Have Lived With the American People* (Caldwell, Ida., 1948), and Carlos Bulosan, *Sound of Falling Light: Letters in Exile,* ed., Dorothy S. Feria (Quezon City, 1960). For the best account of the changing legal status of Filipino immigration, see Divine, *American Immigration Policy.* For an aspect of the anti-Filipino campaign, see James R. Lawrence, "The American Federation of Labor and the Philippine Independence Question, 1920–1935," *Labor History,* VII (1966), 62–69.

For the status of East Indians, see Gary R. Hess, "The 'Hindu' in America: Immigration and Naturalization Policies and India, 1917–1946," *Pacific Historical Review,* XXXVIII (1969), 59–79, and Joan M. Jensen, "Apartheid: Pacific Coast Style," *ibid.,* 335–340. Other aspects are treated in Arun Coomer Bose, "Indian Nationalist Agitators in the U.S.A. and Canada Till the Arrival of Har Dayal in 1911," *Journal of Indian History,* XLIII (1965), 227–239, and *Indian Revolutionaries Abroad, 1905–1922* (Patna, India, 1971); Lawrence A. Wenzel, "The Rural Punjabi of California: A Religio-Ethnic Group," *Phylon,* LX (1968), 245–256; and Don K. Dignan, "The Hindu Conspiracy in Anglo-American Relations During World War I," *Pacific Historical Review,* LX (1971), 57–76. I have read an early draft of a book by Joan M. Jensen, "Outcasts in a Savage Land: The East Indian in North America," which will mark a breakthrough in this field.

This essay does not treat Hawaii extensively or Canada at all, yet developments in these areas often had reciprocal influence on events throughout North America. Highly detailed ethnic bibliographies are being published by the University of Hawaii; see, for example, Nancy Foon Young, *The Chinese in Hawaii: An Annotated*

As far as comparative studies of East Asian immigrant groups are concerned, only the barest beginning has been made. Daniels and Kitano have surveyed the oppression practiced against non-European ethnics in California, and H. Brett Melendy has produced a useful synthesis which compares East Asian groups and contrasts their experiences in Hawaii with those on the mainland.[70]

* * *

Much of the acceleration in Asian American studies which the foregoing indicates has been due to the heightened emphasis which American society has given to minority rights in the very recent past. This has been particularly true on West Coast college campuses where, largely at the behest of a concerned minority of Asian American students, a number of Asian American study centers have arisen. Although these have been, at least in part, a mimetic response to the prior rise of black studies, they may well eventually produce students who will go on to do some of the basic research and writing that is so necessary for the continued development of this field. So far, the fruits have been meager; the articles published in their magazines generally contain more indignation than research.[71] Of greater value have been some quite useful bibliographies.[72] More important, perhaps, has been the creation of courses

Bibliography (Honolulu, 1973), and Arthur L. Gardner, *The Koreans in Hawaii: An Annotated Bibliography* (Honolulu, 1970). For Canada, an excellent survey is Andrew Gregorovich, *Canadian Ethnic Groups Bibliography* (Toronto, 1972), which contains useful sections on "Chinese," "East Indians," "Japanese," and "Orientals."

70 Roger Daniels and Harry H. L. Kitano, *American Racism: Exploration of the Nature of Prejudice* (Englewood Cliffs, N.J., 1970); H. Brett Melendy, *The Oriental Americans* (New York, 1972). See also Robert F. Heizer and Alan F. Almquist, *The Other Californians: Prejudice and Discrimination under Spain, Mexico, and the United States to 1920* (Berkeley and Los Angeles, 1971), an anthropological approach whose scanty section on Asian Americans is flawed by error; and Ivan H. Light, *Ethnic Enterprise in America: Business and Welfare Among Chinese, Japanese and Blacks* (Berkeley and Los Angeles, 1972), a sociological treatise which argues that the comparative failure of blacks to establish businesses is largely due, not to oppression, but to the absence of rotating credit associations which were present among Chinese and Japanese.

71 Good examples are the *Amerasia Journal* (March 1971+), published at Yale and UCLA, and *Asian Women* (Berkeley, 1971), published at the University of California, Berkeley.

72 The most ambitious is William Wong Lum, comp., *Asians in America: A Bibliography of Master's Theses and Doctoral Dissertations* (Asian American Research Project, University of California, Davis, 1970), with two supplements. See also Harry H. L. Kitano, with E. Jung, C. Tanaka, and B. Wong, *Asian Americans: An Annotated Bibliography* (Asian American Study Center, UCLA, 1971).

at a number of universities and a growing concern for Asian American studies as a field.[73] If even a tiny proportion of the students now enrolled in these courses eventually do some serious research, the potential impact on this still largely undeveloped field could be enormous. The most obvious need is for a reversal of past trends so that the new focus will become the oppressed rather than the oppressors.

Since the initial publication of this essay, the following have come to my attention. Nancy Farrar, *The Chinese in El Paso* (El Paso, Texas, 1972) and Doug and Art Chin, *Up Hill: The Settlement and Diffusion of the Chinese in Seattle, Washington* (Seattle, Wash., 1973) are two pamphlets which give useful local accounts. Stanley Sue and Nathaniel Wagner, eds., *Asian-Americans: Psychological Perspectives* (Palo Alto, Calif., 1973) is a collection of essays, largely reprints, bearing on psychosocial aspects of the Asian American experience. Two 1974 books that contain useful chapters on the Chinese experience are Richard E. Lingenfelter, *The Hardrock Miners: A History of the Mining Labor Movement in the American West, 1863–1893* (Berkeley and Los Angeles, 1974), "Union Against the Chinese," pp. 107–127, which is particularly good on developments outside of California; and W. Eugene Hollon, *Frontier Violence: Another Look* (New York, 1974), "Not a Chinaman's Chance," pp. 80–105, which describes impressionistically the varieties of violence Chinese Americans suffered. Jeffery Paul Chan, Frank Chin, Lawson Fusao Inada, and Shawn Wong, eds., *Aiiieeeee! An Anthology of Asian American Writers* (Washington, D.C., 1974) is a pathbreaking collection marred by editorial matter that is often jejune. Arthur A. Hansen and Betty Mitson, eds., *Voices Long Silent: An Oral Inquiry into the Japanese Amer-*

---

[73] The new concern for Asian American studies as a teaching field is reflected in two articles in recent publications by the National Council for the Social Studies: Lowell K. Y. Chun-Hoon, "Teaching the Asian American Experience," in James A. Banks, ed., *Teaching Ethnic Studies: Concepts and Strategies* (Washington, D.C., 1973), 119–147, and Roger Daniels, "The Asian American Experience," in William H. Cartwright and Richard L. Watson, eds., *The Reinterpretation of American History and Culture* (Washington, D.C., 1973), 139–148. Among the more useful teaching materials, with an exclusive or heavy Asian American content, are three anthologies: Amy Tachiki, Eddie Wong, and Franklin Odo, eds., *Roots: An Asian American Reader* (Asian American Studies Center, UCLA, 1971); George E. Frakes and Curtis B. Solberg, eds., *Minorities in California History* (New York, 1971), and Roger Daniels and Spencer C. Olin, Jr., eds., *Racism in California: A Reader in the History of Oppression* (New York, 1972).

ican Evacuation (Fullerton, Calif., 1974) is a publication of the Japanese American Oral History Program at California State University, Fullerton, which contains, in addition to four interviews and a bibliography of its collection, two analytical articles, one of which is the best account yet of the Manzanar Riot.

Conflict and the Web of Group Affiliation in San Francisco's Chinatown, 1850-1910

Stanford M. Lyman

The author is professor of sociology in the Graduate Faculty of the New School for Social Research.

ALTHOUGH THE EARLY HISTORY of the Chinese in America has been explored by many authorities, most attention has been focused on the anti-Chinese movement. The structure and operations of Chinese associations established in the Oriental ghettos of the West have received scant and stereotyped treatment.[1] The net effect of these analyses has been a perfectly correct but one-sided image of victimization unrelieved by any analytical accounts of the organizational activity or associational creativity of the Asian victims.

Most of the contemporary reports on nineteenth-century Chinatowns that treat the basic types of traditional Chinese organizations —clans, *Landsmannschaften*, and secret societies—betray a Sinophobia deeply embedded in the general racism of that era. It is not

---

[1] See, e.g., George F. Seward, *Chinese Immigration, in Its Social and Economical Aspects* (New York, 1881), 223–242, 261–291; Mary Coolidge, *Chinese Immigration* (New York, 1909), 401–422; Carl Glick, *Shake Hands with the Dragon* (New York, 1941), 34–44, 81–92, 244–245; S. W. Kung, *Chinese in American Life: Some Aspects of their History, Status, Problems, and Contributions* (Seattle, 1962), 76–78, 197–227; Calvin Lee, *Chinatown, U.S.A.* (Garden City, 1965) 28–37, 82–128; Betty Lee Sung, *Mountain of Gold: The Story of the Chinese in America* (New York, 1967), 130–186; Roger Daniels, "Westerners from the East: Oriental Immigrants Reappraised," *Pacific Historical Review*, XXXV (1966), 378–384.

surprising that scholars of a later generation, seeking to redress this racist balance, would concentrate on the popular tribunals, prejudicial reports, and painful pejorative heaped upon the hapless Chinese. Moreover, in seeking to overturn the obloquy and slander of a whole people, sympathetic American scholars have tended to engage in a selective perception reflecting their own less venal outlook. Clans became "family associations," *Landsmannschaften* were transformed into "benevolent societies," and the activities of the once feared secret societies were said to be vastly exaggerated, if not wholly fabricated. To these liberal-minded scholars Chinese immigrants were white men with yellow skins.

In fact, the first six decades of Chinese settlement in San Francisco were distinguished by the fact that Chinese immigrants, beset with a hostile racist movement opposing their very presence in America,[2] built their own special community. This community—Chinatown —was remarkable for its fierce internal conflicts, its lack of solidarity, and its intensive disharmony. Popularly known as "tong wars," the violent battles in Chinatown actually involved clans, *Landsmannschaften,* and secret societies. These fights raged intermittently but frequently for sixty years. Then, in the years closing the first decade of the twentieth century, an era seemed to come to an end. The last major reorganization of the immigrants' prefectural associations—the absorption of the Yan Hoi group into the Sue Hing Association—occurred in 1909. Three years later secret society and merchant leaders—who had been at odds with one another for more than fifty years—formed the Chinese Peace Society in the hope that they could end tong wars in Chinatown. In 1911 the Republican Revolution ended dynastic rule in China and ushered in an era of class and cosmopolitan politics that also found expression in political and radical parties in the overseas Chinese colonies. By 1910 most of the immigrant Chinese laborers had been driven off the farmlands and out of most of the urban jobs in and around San Francisco and forced to work as well as live in Chinatown. An aging population that could not be replenished by immigration (forbidden since 1882) or by procreation—prevented by the enormous imbalance in the sex ratio—seemed in danger of extinction during

---

2 See Seward, *Chinese Immigration,* 292–310; Coolidge, *Chinese Immigration,* 26–336; Elmer C. Sandmeyer, *The Anti-Chinese Movement in California* (Urbana, 1939), 25–111; Stanford M. Lyman, *The Asian in the West* (Reno, 1970), 9–26.

the next half century.[3] But instead of disappearing, Chinatown in the years following 1910 became an established tourist attraction, dominated by its merchant and association leaders, exploiting the labor of its poorer elements, and hiding its fetid squalor under the show of its pagoda roofs, parades on Chinese New Year, and patriotic drives in behalf of the *Kuomintang*.[4] Yet, beneath the surface, the basic structure that had been established at such fearful cost during its first sixty years remained. It still does.

In this paper, the structure and operation of San Francisco's nineteenth-century Chinatown are presented in a schematic and sociological fashion. The argument can be stated quite succinctly: Nineteenth-century Chinatown was a complex, highly organized community whose associations were not in constant harmony with one another. Most important were the activities of the secret societies, whose competition for control of vice and whose political battles were fierce. As a result of intersociety conflicts and traditional modes of resolving them, violent altercations erupted repeatedly within the ghetto. Since these disputes were intramural, they acted as a further barrier to contacts with the larger society, placed many individuals under cross-pressures of loyalty to the several associations whose membership overlapped, and fastened on the Chinese community a pattern of antagonistic cooperation. Thus intracommunity conflict and cooperation acted together to help isolate the Chinese from the metropolis.

Chinese communities in the United States have enjoyed a measure of isolation and communal self-government far exceeding that

---

[3] Victor G. Nee and Brett de Bary Nee, *Longtime Californ': A Documentary Study of an American Chinatown* (New York, 1972), 272–273; Richard Dillon, *The Hatchet Men: The Story of the Tong Wars in San Francisco's Chinatown* (New York, 1962), 361; H. Mark Lai, "A Historical Survey of Organizations of the Left among the Chinese in America," *Bulletin of Concerned Asian Scholars*, IV (Fall, 1972), 10–19; Samuel Gompers, *Seventy Years of Life and Labor* (New York, 1925), I, 216–217, 304–305; II, 160–169; Herbert Hill, "The Racial Practices of Organized Labor—The Age of Gompers and After," in *Employment, Race and Poverty: A Critical Study of the Disadvantaged Status of Negro Workers from 1865 to 1965*, edited by Arthur M. Ross and Herbert Hill (New York, 1967), 365–402; Hill, "Anti-Oriental Agitation and the Rise of Working-Class Racism," *Society*, X (Jan.-Feb., 1973), 43–54; Carey McWilliams, *Factories in the Fields: The Story of Migratory Farm Labor in California* (Boston, 1939), 66–88; Lyman, *The Asian in the West*, 9–26, 65–80.

[4] Stanford M. Lyman, *Chinese Americans* (New York, 1974); Ivan Light, "From Vice District to Tourist Attraction: The Moral Career of American Chinatowns, 1880–1940," *Pacific Historical Review*, XLIII (1974), 367–394; Victor Nee, "The Kuomintang in Chinatown," *Bridge Magazine* I (May-June, 1972), 20–24.

of other ethnic communities.[5] One reason for the unusual separa-
tion of Chinatowns from regular public municipal controls was
their long period of electoral irrelevance to American politics.
Denied naturalization and the franchise for nearly a century, the
Chinese, unlike European immigrants, were not the objects of any
local ward politician's solicitations. Left to themselves—except
during anti-Chinese campaigns—the Chinese organized their own
benevolent, protective, and governmental bodies. In effect, the
Chinese community in America is more like a colonial dependency
than an immigrant settlement in an open society. The relationship
between the ghetto community and metropolitan authorities bears
a close resemblance to that which prevailed in the British, Dutch,
and French colonies in Oceania and Southeast Asia.[6] The "mayor
of chinatown,"[7] a person whose authority is tacitly acknowledged
by civic officials in the United States, is, in most respects, nothing
less than an American equivalent of the *Kapitan China,* an official
who represented the Chinese inhabitants of the European colonies
in Southeast Asia.[8]

Inside a Chinatown like that which developed in San Francisco,
a merchant class soon became the ruling elite.[9] Because commercial
success was so closely tied to social acceptance and moral probity
in America, this elite enjoyed good relations with public officials.
Chinatown merchants controlled immigrant associations, dispensed
jobs and opportunities, settled disputes, and acted as advocates for
the Chinese sojourners before white society.[10] The power of these

---

5 Thus, there has never been a "mayor of Little Tokyo" in the United States, nor
have European immigrant *Landsmannschaften* ever secured such a broad span of
power over their communities as that of the Chinese *hui kuan.* See Stanford M. Lyman, "The Structure of Chinese Society in Nineteenth Century America" (Ph.D.
dissertation, University of California, Berkeley, 1961), 272–276.

6 See C. S. Wong, *A Gallery of Chinese Kapitans* (Singapore, 1964).

7 Stewart Culin, "Customs of the Chinese in America," *Journal of American Folk-
Lore,* III (July-Sept. 1890), 193.

8 According to the system of colonial administration developed in the British,
Dutch, and French colonies in Southeast Asia, a *Kapitan China* was the representative of the Chinese inhabitants. He served on the various advisory councils, and
usually represented the interests of the dominant clan, speech, or secret societies
within the Chinese community. Usually he was elected by the Chinese societies and
approved for appointment by the European colonial administration, but the method
of securing this office varied. See, for example, J. M. Gullick, *The Story of Kuala
Lumpur* (Singapore, 1956), 16–25, 64–79; W. E. Willmott. *The Political Structure of
the Chinese Community in Cambodia* (New York, 1970), 111–126, 141–160.

9 For early evidence, see "Letter of the Chinamen to his Excellency Gov. Bigler,"
dated San Francisco, April 29, 1852, in *Littel's Living Age,* XXIV (July 3, 1852), 32–34.

10 See "New Rules of the Yeung Wo Ui Kum" and "Sze Yap Company," reprinted
in William Speer, "Democracy of the Chinese," *Harper's Monthly,* XXXVII (Nov.

merchants rested on a traditional foundation. They governed Chinatown through the complex interrelationships of clans and *Landsmannschaften,* or mutual aid societies.[11] Opposition to this system of authority came primarily from members of secret societies. Eventually secret society leaders infiltrated the legitimate associations and a mercantile power structure emerged uniting the purveyors of legal and illegal goods and services.

Clans

One of the most important of the legitimate associations was the clan, an organization which traces its origins to the lineage communities of southeastern China.[12] Although descent in the lineage community was usually carefully recorded so as to exclude all except direct descendants, such meticulousness was impossible to maintain in the fast-changing social conditions of the overseas colonies. There the surname alone established identity, and clan brothers assumed their blood relationship on the basis of their common name.[13] Moreover, practical considerations often superseded loyalty to ideals of lineal purity, producing combinations of clan names and the admission of different surnames into the same association.[14] Real or assumed kinship provided the basis for clan solidarity, while "practical reasoning" resolved those questions which tended to engender disunity.[15]

1868), 836–848; A. W. Loomis, "The Six Chinese Companies," *Overland Monthly*, I (Sept. 1868), 221–227; "Address of the Chinese Six Companies to the American Public," April 5, 1876, in "Report of the Joint Special Committee to Investigate Chinese Immigration," 44 Cong., 2 sess., *S. Rept. 689* (Feb. 27, 1877), 39; Pun Chi, "A Remonstrance from the Chinese in California to the Congress of the United States," 1855, in William Speer, *The Oldest and Newest Empire: China and the United States* (Hartford, 1870), 575–581.

11 *Landsmannschaften* is perhaps the only appropriate term to describe the several kinds of mutual aid societies established by Chinese in America. These societies originated in China as dialect groups founded by rural Chinese who had migrated to China's cities. See Ping-ti Ho, *Chung-Kuo hui kuan shih-lun* (Taipei, 1966).

12 See Maurice Freedman, *Lineage Organization in Southeastern China* (London, 1958).

13 Herbert A. Giles, "The Family Names," *Journal of the Royal Asiatic Society, North China Branch*, XXI (Aug. 1886), 255–288; Leong Gor Yun, *Chinatown Inside Out* (New York, 1936), 54–66.

14 Leong Gor Yun, *Chinatown Inside Out*, 59; W. E. Wilmott, "Chinese Clan Associations in Vancouver," *Man*, LXIV (1964), 33–37.

15 For example, in the United States and Canada there are two distinct clans using the surname "Wong." The characters forming the surname of the two clans are quite distinguishable in written script, but their Anglicization is the same, that is, the English term "Wong." There are members of both clans in each clan organization.

Overseas clans were organized by prominent ghetto merchants who assumed many of the duties and responsibilities that lineage communities had been responsible for in China. In place of the territorially compact village, the overseas clan was organized around a leading merchant's store.[16] The merchant usually exerted leadership in his clan, established a hostelry above the store for his kinsmen, and provided aid, advice, comfort, and shelter. The clan provided the boundary of the incest taboo, and marriage was prohibited among persons bearing the same surname.[17] Clans further served to remind the sojourner of his obligations to village and family in China, and, in the absence of lineage authorities, overseas clan leaders acted *in loco parentis*.[18]

In addition to their assumption of traditional lineage authority, clans afforded an opportunity for commercial monopoly. Just as certain clans in China kept trade secrets confined to their members and restricted the entrance of upstarts,[19] so the overseas clans organized brotherhoods in trade, manufacture, and types of labor. The Dear clan, for example, operated San Francisco Chinatown's fruit and candy-stores; the Yee and Lee clans owned better-class restaurants and supplied most of the cooks in domestic service. Because they varied in location and membership, the clans could (and still can) be classified according to their economic and community dominance.[20] Thus, the Lees are most prominent in Philadelphia; the Toms in New York City; the Loys in Cleveland; the Ongs in Phoenix. In some Chinatowns more than one clan is conspicuous by its size. Thus, the Fongs and Yees both predominate in Sacramento as do the Moys and Chins in Chicago. Small Chinatowns probably sprang up on the basis of a single clan, and in the

---

16 Stewart Culin, *China in America: A Study of the Social Life of the Chinese in Eastern Cities of the United States* (Philadelphia, 1887), 10.

17 Sir George Thomas Staunton, trans., *Ta Tsing Leu Lee; Being the Fundamental Laws, and a Selection from the Supplementary Statutes of the Penal Code of China; Originally Printed and Published in Pekin in Various Successive Editions . . .* (London, 1810), 114.

18 See the letters from a mother in China to her son in California and to his clan brothers, in A. W. Loomis, "The Old East in the New West," *Overland Monthly*, I (Oct. 1868), 362.

19 Max Weber, *The Religion of China: Confucianism and Taoism*, trans. Hans H. Gerth (Glencoe, 1951), 86–91.

20 Chinese Chamber of Commerce, *San Francisco's Chinatown: History, Function and Importance of Social Organization* (San Francisco, 1953), 3.

smaller towns of the Rocky Mountain areas there have rarely been more than four clans.[21]

Hui Kuan

In addition to clans, immigrant Chinese, during the first decade of their sojourn in America (1851–1862), established five *hui kuan*, organizations which were functionally similar to but structurally different from the clan.[22] The overseas *hui kuan*, similar to its urban counterpart in China,[23] unites all those who speak a common dialect, hail from the same district of origin, or belong to the same ethnic group. In many ways it is similar to those immigrant aid societies (*Landsmannschaften*) formed by Europeans in America; however, the scope of *hui kuan* controls and the diversity of its functions far exceed those of its European counterparts. For example, wherever Chinese groups settled, their local *hui kuan* served as caravansary, credit and loan society, and employment agency.[24] It also acted in a representative capacity, speaking for its members to other *hui kuan* and to white society as well.[25] In addition, it provided arbitration and mediation services for its members, settling disputes and adjudicating issues that might otherwise erupt in open violence, or, among a people who trusted public law more than the Chinese, might have found their way into the municipal courts.[26] As a combined eleemosynary, judicial, representative, and mutual aid society, the *hui kuan* exercised a wide span of control over its members. Precisely because of its multiplicity of functions, the *hui kuan* could command allegiance. To the individual Chinese who

---

[21] Leong Gor Yun, *Chinatown Inside Out*, 54–66; Chinese Chamber of Commerce, *San Francisco's Chinatown*, 3; Mary Chapman, "Notes on the Chinese in Boston," *Journal of American Folk-Lore*, V (Oct.-Dec. 1892), 324; Rose Hum Lee, "The Decline of Chinatowns in the United States," *American Journal of Sociology*, LIV (1949), 422–432.

[22] Cf. Maurice Freedman, "Immigrants and Associations: Chinese in Nineteenth-Century Singapore," *Comparative Studies in Society and History*, III (1960), 25–48.

[23] Ping-ti Ho, "Salient Aspects of China's Heritage," in *China in Crisis*, ed. Ping-ti Ho and Tang Tsou (Chicago, 1968), Vol. I, Book 1, 32–33.

[24] Otis Gibson, *The Chinese in America* (Cincinnati, 1879), 49–51; "Report of the Joint Special Committee to Investigate Chinese Immigration," 24; Lyman, "The Structure of Chinese Society," 283–308.

[25] Lyman, "The Structure of Chinese Society," 314.

[26] Fong Kum Ngon [Walter N. Fong], "The Chinese Six Companies," *Overland Monthly*, XXIII (May, 1894), 524–525; Speer, "The Oldest and Newest Empire," 836–848.

refused it fealty, it could withhold financial aid, order social ostracism, render a punitive judgment in a suit brought before its tribunal, and arrange for false charges and incriminating testimony in public courts.[27]

The *hui kuan* confederated in 1858, i.e., during the first decade of Chinese settlement in San Francisco. At first composed of five prominent *Landsmannschaften*,[28] the confederation expanded because of the addition of new speech groups, the disintegration and reformation of already established *hui kuan,* and the admission, after much pressure, of secret societies and other associations.[29] The consolidated federation of *hui kuan* commanded at least the grudging allegiance and obedience of the Chinatown masses during the latter half of the nineteenth century, and it also earned the respect of many urban whites. Popularly called the Chinese Six Companies[30] in San Francisco, the Chinese Consolidated Benevolent Association acted as an unofficial government inside Chinatown and was the most important voice of the Chinese immigrants speaking to American officials.

As a spokesman group the Chinese Consolidated Benevolent Association has frequently protested against the legal impositions and social indignities heaped upon Chinese immigrants in America,

---

27 Loomis, "The Six Chinese Companies," 221–227; Gibson, *The Chinese in America,* 339–343; Leong Gor Yun, *Chinatown Inside Out,* 49–50; "Report of the Joint Special Committee to Investigate Chinese Immigration," 95.

28 *Hui kuan* formed, dissolved, and reconstituted themselves throughout the first sixty years of Chinese settlement. The Canton Association, formed in 1851, reconstituted itself as the Sam Yup Association in the same year; the Sze Yup Association, formed in 1851, dissolved over internal disputes into the Hop Wo Association (also incorporating the entire Yee clan, which had withdrawn from the Ning Yung Association) in 1862 and the Kong Chow Association in 1867; the Young Wo Association formed in 1852; the Sun On Association, formed in 1851, reconstituted itself as the Yan Wo Association in 1854; the Ning Yung Association, formed in 1853, suffered the loss of the Yee clan in 1862 but continued to represent immigrants from Toishan; the Sue Hing Association was formed during the years 1879–1882 by dissidents from the Hop Wo Association, while the Yan Hoi Association was founded in 1898, again by Hop Wo defectors; the Look Yup Association was established in 1901 by a coalition of groups from the Sam Yup Association and the Kong Chow Association; in 1909 the Yan Hoi Association was absorbed by the Sue Hing Association. The structure remained stable thereafter for forty-two years; in 1951 the Fa Yuan Association formed as a splinter from the Sam Yup Association. See the historical chart made by Him Mark Lai in Nee and Nee, *Longtime Californ',* 272–273.

29 William Hoy, *The Chinese Six Companies* (San Francisco, 1942), 5, 28, 59–62; Chinese Chamber of Commerce, *San Francisco's Chinatown,* 5; Leong Gor Yun, *Chinatown Inside Out,* 6–9; Culin, *China in America,* 28.

30 Although the number of *hui kuan* increased beyond six, that number has been stereotypically associated with the confederation in San Francisco.

and on occasion it has requested judicial extraterritorial rights over those Chinese likely to be accused of crimes. Among its more significant proclamations and protests were the "Letter of the Chinamen to his Excellency Governor Bigler" in 1852; the "Reply to the Message of His Excellency, Governor John Bigler" in 1855; a "Remonstrance from Chinese in California to the Congress of the United States" in 1868; a "Memorial from the Six Chinese Companies: an address to the Senate and House of Representatives of the United States" in 1877; and, in 1916, a protest to the President of the United States over the onerous burden of America's exclusionist immigration practices.[31]

However, despite its growth in status, the Consolidated Benevolent Association did not have much success in preventing the passage of or revoking already existent discriminatory laws.[32] Neither did it succeed in establishing exclusive jurisdiction over Chinese criminals or in stopping the mobs that attacked Chinatowns throughout the latter decades of the nineteenth century.[33] For many years the Chinese spokesmen could not overcome the charge —leveled against them by anti-Chinese demagogues—that they held the people they claimed to represent in unlawful serfdom.[34] On the other hand, they were not always able to command complete obedience. For example, in 1893, when they ordered Chinese not to register in accordance with a newly enacted immigration act, and subsequently lost their appeal against the act in the courts, they encountered open resistance in Chinatown.[35] To most Chinese, the

---

31 See footnotes 9 and 10 *supra*; see also Speer, *The Oldest and Newest Empire*, 578–581; Gibson, *The Chinese in America*, 315–323; J. S. Tow, *The Real Chinese in America* (New York, 1923), 118–119.

32 The legislation is summarized in Lucille Eaves, *A History of Labor Legislation in California* (Berkeley, 1909), 105–195; Ira B. Cross, *A History of the Labor Movement in California* (Berkeley, 1935), 73–130; Coolidge, *Chinese Immigration*, 55–82; Sandmeyer, *The Anti-Chinese Movement in California*, 40–77; Lyman, "The Structure of Chinese Society," 383–386; Lyman, *The Asian in the West*, 23–24; Robert F. Heizer and Alan F. Almquist, *The Other Californians: Prejudice and Discrimination under Spain, Mexico, and the United States* (Berkeley, 1971), 154–177.

33 For Chinese merchant elites' abortive attempts to obtain extraterritorial rights over Chinese immigrant criminals, see Speer, *The Oldest and Newest Empire*, 579–580, 600–601; Gibson, *The Chinese in America*, 315–323. For unchecked mob actions in Chinatown, see Lyman, *The Asian in the West*, 12–16, 19–23.

34 See, for example, Richard Hay Drayton, "The Chinese Six Companies," *The Californian Illustrated Magazine*, IV (Aug. 1893), 472–479.

35 *Fong Yue Ting* v. *U.S.*, 149 U.S. 698 (1893). It was this decision, sustaining the Geary Act and requiring all Chinese in the United States to register with the collector of internal revenue, that sparked a rebellion against Chun Ti Chu, the Six

consequence of failure to register—deportation—was simply too grave. Eventually, however, after the worst phase of the anti-Chinese movement was over, and with the aid of white apologists who exaggerated its community services and charitable deeds, the confederated *hui kuan* achieved recognition as the sole spokesman for Chinese in America.[36] But recognition by white America was not matched by appreciation from the inhabitants of Chinatown. The latter often grumbled about the exploitative power of the combined *hui kuan* and occasionally revolted, without success, against its excesses.[37]

The community dominance of the Consolidated Benevolent Association was rooted not only in its traditional authority, but also in its control over debts, labor, commerce, and disputes.[38] The bulk of Chinese immigrants were debtors, and their obligations were owned or supervised by the *hui kuan* merchants. Moreover, the *hui kuan* acted as a general collection agency and creditor for its more affluent members. In addition, it charged its members entrance and departure fees and insisted that all debts be cleared before an immigrant returned to China. The *hui kuan* also provided the organizational base for a rotating credit system that became the principal source of capital for entrepreneurship and business development in Chinatown. Its power to give or withhold needed money served as a source of anger among those who suffered from its onerous exactions or its outright refusal to make needed loans.[39]

Companies' president. Chun had provoked the case by ordering Chinese to refuse to register. Thousands of Chinese might have been deported had not Congress, under pressure from the employers of Chinese, hastily enacted the McCreary Amendment, extending the deadline for registration another six months. See Drayton, "The Chinese Six Companies," 472–493; Fong, "The Chinese Six Companies," 525–526; Coolidge, *Chinese Immigration*, 209–233.

36 Coolidge, *Chinese Immigration*, 409–411; Nee and Nee, *Longtime Californ'*, 228–249; James T. Lee, "The Story of the New York Chinese Consolidated Benevolent Association," *Bridge Magazine*, I (May-June 1972), 15–18; James T. Lee, "The Chinese Benevolent Association: An Assessment," *ibid.*, (July-Aug. 1972), 15–16, 41, 43, 46–47.

37 See Loomis, "The Six Chinese Companies," 222–223; Gibson, *The Chinese in America*, 341–343.

38 For a complete discussion, see Lyman, "The Structure of Chinese Society," 288–328.

39 Gibson, *The Chinese in America*, 339–341; "Report of the Joint Special Committee to Investigate Chinese Immigration," 24; Hoy, *The Chinese Six Companies*, 23; Ivan Light, *Ethnic Enterprise in America: Business and Welfare among Chinese, Japanese, and Blacks* (Berkeley, 1972), 81–100.

The *hui kuan* appear to have supervised contract labor among the immigrants and also to have provided an organizational basis for craft and commercial guilds.[40] Although apologists for the Chinese denied that the *hui kuan* had anything to do with the labor system that existed among the sojourners, there is evidence that the *hui kuan* operated the "credit-ticket" system (by which Chinese borrowed money to come to America), acted as subcontractors for white labor recruiters, and may have supplied the bosses for Chinese labor gangs deployed in various parts of the country.[41]

The pattern of both labor and business organization in Chinatown reflected the *hui kuan's* interest. Common laborers, service workers, and skilled operatives were organized according to their dialect or their district of origin in China.[42] Crafts and commercial establishments were similarly organized so that district and linguistic group monopolies over labor and business prevailed in every major Chinatown. Stores and restaurants in Chinatown were allocated space according to a traditional property right system under the control of the *hui kuan*. The property right system protected group monopolies from excessive competition and the entrance of upstarts.[43]

---

40 "Chinese Immigration: Its Social, Moral and Political Effects," *Report to the California State Senate of Its Special Committee on Chinese Immigration* (Sacramento, 1878), 70; *Proceedings of the Numismatic and Antiquarian Society of Philadelphia*, Nov. 7, 1895 (Philadelphia, 1899), 99–100; Fong, "The Chinese Six Companies," 523–524; H. C. Bennett, "The Chinese in California, Their Numbers and Influence," *Sacramento Daily Union* (Nov. 17, 1869), 8; Chinese Chamber of Commerce, *San Francisco's Chinatown*, 5; Loomis, "The Six Chinese Companies," 226; Coolidge, *Chinese Immigration*, 406–407; Rose Hum Lee, *The Chinese in the United States of America* (Hong Kong, 1960), 146, 385–386.

41 Seward, *Chinese Immigration*, 136–158; Coolidge, *Chinese Immigration*, 48–51. Cf., for example, the "Agreement Between the English Merchant and Chinaman" (1849), a contract for transporting Chinese to California. Subsequent translations have pointed out that the "English" merchant was in fact an American. The contract will be found in the Wells Fargo Bank Historical Collection, San Francisco; see also "Letter of the Chinamen," 32–33; Persia Crawford Campbell, *Chinese Coolie Emigration to Countries within the British Empire* (London, 1923), 27–36, 150–151; Rhoda Hoff, *America's Immigrants: Adventures in Eyewitness History* (New York, 1967), 74–75; "Chinese Immigration: Its Social, Moral, and Political Effects," 70; Fong, "The Chinese Six Companies," 523–524; "Japanese and Other Immigrant Races in the Pacific Coast and Rocky Mountain States," 61 Cong., 2 sess., *S. Doc. 633* (1911), 391–399; Thomas W. Chinn, ed., *A History of the Chinese in America: A Syllabus* (San Francisco, 1969), 11–21; Albert Rhodes, "The Chinese at Beaver Falls," *Lippincott's Magazine*, XIX (June, 1877), 708–714.

42 Chinese Chamber of Commerce, *San Francisco's Chinatown*, 5; Thomas W. Chinn, *A History of the Chinese in America*, 47–54.

43 Rose Hum Lee, *The Chinese in the United States*, 385–386; Leong Gor Yun, *Chinatown Inside Out*, 36–39.

Perhaps the most important power of the consolidated *hui kuan* was jurisdictional in nature.[44] Mention has already been made of the mediation and arbitration service provided individual clans and *hui kuan*. When an individual felt wronged in his original suit or when disputes arose among associations, an appeal could be lodged with the tribunal of the confederated *hui kuan*. The Benevolent Association was thus the supreme organ for settlement of disputes. So long as the Chinese were either denied the right to testify in public courts or unwilling to employ the American legal system,[45] the merchant elite of Chinatown exercised an awesome authority. Persons who were not in good standing with their clan or *hui kuan* could be refused a hearing. Those who openly revolted against the Chinatown establishment might be stripped of their property, boycotted, ostracized, or, in extreme cases, given even more violent treatment.[46]

Secret Societies

Clans and *hui kuan* were traditional and lawful societies in China and in the overseas colonies; secret societies were traditional in China, but they usually became criminal or subversive associations. Nineteenth-century migrants from Kwangtung included not a few members of the Triad Society, China's most famous clandestine association.[47] Active in rebellions and crime for centuries

---

[44] Loomis, "The Six Chinese Companies," 223; Fong, "The Chinese Six Companies," 524–525; Culin, "Customs of the Chinese in America," 193; Speer, "Democracy of the Chinese," 836–848.

[45] In 1854 the statute prohibiting Negroes and Indians from testifying for or against Caucasians was extended by the California Supreme Court to ban Chinese testimony as well. *People* v. *Hall,* 4 Cal. 399 (1854). See also *Speer* v. *See Yup,* 13 Cal. 73 (1855); *People* v. *Elyea,* 14 Cal. 144 (1859). The statute was revised to admit the testimony of Negroes in 1863, but Mongolians, Chinese, and Indians remained under the ban until January 1, 1873, when the revised California statutes admitted witnesses to the courts regardless of color or nationality. See Chinn, *A History of Chinese in California,* 24; Heizer and Almquist, *The Other Californians,* 47, 129–130, 229–234; Coolidge, *Chinese Immigration,* 75–76. However, during this period Chinese mounted numerous civil rights cases in the courts where testimony against whites was not a factor. The traditional Chinese opposition to employing public courts predates the coming of Chinese to America. See Sybille van der Sprenkel, *Legal Institutions in Manchu China* (London, 1962), 80–111.

[46] "Report of Special Committee to the Honorable, the Board of Supervisors of the City and County of San Francisco," in Willard B. Farwell, *The Chinese at Home and Abroad* (San Francisco, 1885), 51–58.

[47] For nineteenth-century reports on the Triad Society, see Jean Chesneaux, *Secret Societies in China in the Nineteenth and Twentieth Centuries,* trans. by Gillian Nettle (Ann Arbor, 1971), 1–135; Chesneaux, ed., *Popular Movements and Secret*

in China, the Triad Society provided the model for the secret societies that sprang up overseas.[48] In some settlements, such as those in rural British Columbia, where clans and *hui kuan* had failed to form, secret societies became the sole community organization.[49] The secret societies enrolled members according to interest, rather than by kin or district ties, and in one recorded instance in 1898 admitted an American journalist.[50] From the beginning of Chinese settlement in America the secret societies, popularly known as *tongs*,[51] have remained a significant part of Chinatown's organizational structure.

The scope of operations of secret societies was wide, but confined for the most part to Chinatown. On the basis of available data, their activities may be classified according to their political, protest, criminal, and benevolent character.

Political Activities. Secret societies in the Chinese community of the United States and other areas of immigrant settlement did not seek to alter, oppose, or subvert the national political structure of their host countries. They did, however, attempt to influence the course of political events in China. For the most part, their political activities failed, but in the establishment of Dr. Sun Yat-sen's re-

---

Societies in China, 1840–1950 (Stanford, 1972), 1–144; Gustave Schlegel, *Thian Ti Hwui: The Hung-League or Heaven-Earth-League—A Secret Society with the Chinese in China and India* (Batavia, 1866); William Stanton, *The Triad Society or Heaven and Earth Association* (Shanghai, 1900); J. S. M. Ward and W. G. Stirling, *The Hung Society or the Society of Heaven and Earth* (3 vols., London, 1925); Mervyn Llewelyn Wynne, *Triad and Tabut: A Survey of the Origin and Diffusion of Chinese and Mohammedan Secret Societies in the Malay Peninsula, A.D. 1800–1935* (Singapore, 1941), 1–151, 202–352; Leon Comber, *An Introduction to Chinese Secret Societies in Malaya* (Singapore, 1957); Comber, *Chinese Secret Societies in Malaya: A Survey of the Triad Society from 1800 to 1900* (Locust Valley, 1959); Wilfred Blythe, *The Impact of Chinese Secret Societies in Malaya: A Historical Study* (London, 1969); W. P. Morgan, *Triad Societies in Hong Kong* (Hong Kong, 1960).

48 Stewart Culin, "Chinese Secret Societies in the United States," *Journal of American Folk-Lore*, III (Jan.-Mar. 1890), 39–43; Culin, "The I Hing or 'Patriotic Rising,' a Secret Society among the Chinese in America," *Proceedings of the Numismatic and Antiquarian Society of Philadelphia for the Years 1887–1889*, III (Nov. 1887), 51–57.

49 Stanford M. Lyman, William Willmott, and Berching Ho, "Rules of a Chinese Secret Society in British Columbia," *Bulletin of the School of Oriental and African Studies*, XXVII (1964), 530–539.

50 *San Francisco Call*, Jan. 9, 1898.

51 See Stanford M. Lyman, "Chinese Secret Societies in the Occident: Notes and Suggestions for Research on the Sociology of Secrecy," *Canadian Review of Sociology and Anthropology*, I (May, 1964), 79–102.

public in 1911 their efforts were significant. Sun found considerable support for his anti-Manchu movement among the overseas Chinese and especially within the secret societies.[52] A founder of two revolutionary societies himself, Sun joined or participated with many others and persuaded them to give money and, on a few occasions, men to the cause.[53] On his trip to the United States in 1904 he worked with the *Chih-kung T'ang*, an overseas branch of the Triad Society, because "there was at the time no other organization which could claim membership all over America."[54] Purposefully vague about the precise nature of his revolutionary aims, Sun did not openly challenge the secret societies' interest in restoring the Ming Dynasty.[55] Ultimately he prevailed over several rival insurrectionist groups by organizing his own revolutionary party and by gaining the support of Christian and non-Christian Chinese, a few prominent whites, and most of the secret societies.[56] So successful was Sun's movement in America—the money for the new republic was printed in San Francisco's Chinatown—that by 1910 he seriously considered transferring his headquarters from Japan to the United States.[57]

Protest. As was the case in China, secret societies provided the organizational base and the muscle for protest against individual or collective oppression. However, the secret societies in the United States did not direct their actions against white racism, Sinophobic legislation, or anti-Chinese mobs. Rather, their attention was con-

---

[52] Sun Yat-sen, *Memoirs of a Chinese Revolutionary* (London, n.d.), 190–193.

[53] A romanticized account of the recruitment and training of Chinese youths for service in the revolution will be found in Carl Glick, *Double Ten: Captain O'Banion's Story of the Chinese Revolution* (New York, 1945). See also Ta-Ling Lee, *Foundations of the Chinese Revolution, 1905–1912* (New York, 1970), 104–109; Carl Glick and Hong Sheng-Hwa, *Swords of Silence: Chinese Secret Societies—Past and Present* (New York, 1947), 94–235; Harold Z. Schiffrin, *Sun Yat-sen and the Origins of the Chinese Revolution* (Berkeley, 1968), 243–244, 334–338; Philip P. Choy, "Gold Mountain of Lead: The Chinese Experience in California," *California Historical Quarterly*, I (1971), 271.

[54] Ta-Ling Lee, *Foundations of the Chinese Revolution*, 106.

[55] James Cantlie and Sheridan Jones, *Sun Yat Sen and the Awakening of China* (New York, 1912), 132–134.

[56] Schiffrin, *Sun Yat-sen and the Origins of the Chinese Revolution*, 331–334.

[57] For a discussion and a photograph of the money printed in San Francisco, see Alexander McLeod, *Pigtails and Gold Dust* (Caldwell, 1947), 148–150. On the proposed move of Sun's headquarters from Tokyo to San Francisco, see K. S. Liew, *Struggle for Democracy: Sung Chiao-jen and the 1911 Chinese Revolution* (Berkeley, 1968), 79–80.

centrated on the power elite of Chinatown. The secret societies provided a check on clan and *hui kuan* exploitation and control over the sojourners.

There is evidence to suggest that the more notorious toughs and thugs employed by the secret societies in the United States were recruited from those who revolted against or were alienated from the merchant elite oligarchy of the *hui kuan*. Elmer Wok Wai, severely disturbed by the way of life in his broken family and bereft of clan protection, ran away from home at fifteen, became a gunman for the *Hop Sing Tong,* and served seventeen years in prison before he went to work as a domestic servant for a white family.[58] Mock Wah, certain that his inability to secure a favorable hearing before the Chinese Six Companies' tribunal stemmed from the fact that he came from a weak clan, established the *Kwong Duck Tong*.[59] Num Sing Bark, a scholar and intellectual from China, founded the *Hip Sing Tong* to take revenge on those powerful Chinatown clans that he blamed for his failure in business.[60]

Business failure because of Chinatown's clan and *hui kuan* monopolies also led Wong du King and Gaut Sing Dock to join secret societies, while an unsuccessful suit before the tribunal of the Chinese Consolidated Benevolent Association caused Yee Low Dai to form the *Suey Sing Tong* and to take by force what he could not obtain by law.[61] Hong Ah Kay, a notorious gunman for the *Suey Sing Tong,* entered the society only after losing both his father and his mistress through clan and *hui kuan* machinations.[62] Two tong leaders were apparently alienated intellectuals. Kung Ah Get of the San Jose chapter of the *Hip Sing Tong* was a self-educated and illiterate orator of considerable eloquence, while another *Hip Sing* leader, Ton Back Woo, was an erstwhile military student in China who had passed only the first of his examinations before adverse circumstances forced him to emigrate to New York City.[63] Just as the secret societies of China recruited those Chinese who had fallen

58 Veta Griggs, *Chinaman's Chance: The Life Story of Elmer Wok Wai* (New York, 1969).

59 St. Clair McKelway, *True Tales from the Annals of Crime and Rascality* (New York, 1951), 153–169; Eng Ying Gong and Bruce Grant, *Tong War!* (New York, 1930), 27–30.

60 Gong and Grant, *Tong War,* 30–31.

61 *Ibid.,* 31–33, 112–130.

62 *Ibid.,* 39–54.

63 *Ibid.,* 122–130, 161–162.

or been forced out of the traditional ascriptive associations, so the clandestine lodges among the Chinese in America gathered their members from among those angered by and ostracized from Chinatown's more powerful clans and *hui kuan*.[64] However, unlike the situation in China, where bandit dynasties had occasionally been established, a tong bandit could not hope to utilize his overseas tong connections to become an emperor.[65] He might occasionally participate from afar in China's political upheavals, but usually he spent his days looking after the society's criminal operations and fighting in its many feuds.

Criminal Activities. Provision of illegal goods and services—opium, gambling, and prostitution—became the economic base for secret societies.[66] A few early efforts of the clans and *hui kuan* to subvert tong business operations were successful. However, American authorities refused the merchant leaders' requests for extraterritorial rights over Chinese criminals in America.[67] Later, after 1882—the precise date is not clear—secret society leaders were admitted to the ruling elite of Chinatown; thereafter, the strong opposition of the secret societies to traditional authorities was gradually replaced by attempts to hide and to regulate vice operations. By 1913, secret society members held positions in the Chinese Peace Society, which had been established to end internecine fights in Chinatown.[68]

The criminal activities of the secret societies were nearly impervious to American agencies of law enforcement. Policemen on the Chinatown detail were easily bribed.[69] Moreover, the widespread police practice of vice control, rather than total abolition,

---

[64] Lyman, "The Structure of Chinese Society," 246–251.

[65] According to Wolfram Eberhard, the founders of the Han Dynasty (206 B.C.–220 A.D.), the Later Liang Dynasty (907–922 A.D), and the Ming Dynasty (1368–1644) were secret society bandit leaders. Eberhard, *Conquerors and Rulers: Social Forces in Medieval China* (Leiden, 1956), 89–106.

[66] "Chinese and Japanese Labor in the Mountain and Pacific States," *Reports of the United States Industrial Commission on Immigration*, XV, Part 4 (Washington, D.C., 1901), 773–792; Stewart Culin, "The Gambling Games of the Chinese in America," *Publications of the University of Pennsylvania Series in Philology, Literature, and Archaeology*, I (1891), 1–17.

[67] Speer, *The Oldest and Newest Empire*, 603–604.

[68] Hoy, *The Chinese Six Companies*, 11, 22–23; Lee, *The Chinese in the United States of America*, 156–160; Gong and Grant, *Tong War*, 211; C. N. Reynolds, "The Chinese Tongs," *American Journal of Sociology*, XL (1935), 623; Dillon, *The Hatchet Men*, 361.

[69] "Chinese and Japanese Labor in the Mountain and Pacific States," 777; Reynolds, "The Chinese Tongs," 622.

led them into tacit cooperation with the secret societies.[70] In some cases a Chinese tong leader used both the police and the courts to his own advantage. For example, Fong Ching, popularly known as "Little Pete," regularly informed the police about vice operations in San Francisco's Chinatown. After the arrest of the malefactors, he would reopen their establishments under police protection, the reward for being an informer.[71] The municipal courts could also be subverted by tong machinations. Tong gunmen could count on perjured testimony to be presented in their behalf and on the effective bribery of court interpreters as well.[72] Indeed, according to a set of instructions taken from a secret society thug in British Columbia in 1887, the tong promised its "salaried soldiers" protection against conviction in the courts, and, should that fail, the society further guaranteed financial aid for the convicted felon and for his family while he served his prison sentence, and burial and other death benefits should he die while working in behalf of his secret society.[73]

Benevolent Activities. The charitable and fraternal activities of the secret societies were confined to aiding their own members. As the societies prospered they erected elaborate halls in Chinatown which not only reflected their affluence, but also were used for fraternal and charitable purposes. For example, when the Chinese Society of Free Masons, a euphemism for the Triad Society,[74] opened a new building in San Francisco in 1907, a local newspaper reported that one of its floors would house destitute widows and orphans because "care will be taken of all those in any way connected with the lodge, who have been overtaken with misfortune."[75]

---

70 Gong and Grant, *Tong War*, 59–65.

71 Richard H. Dillon, "Little Pete, King of Chinatown," *California Monthly*, LXXIX (Dec. 1968), 42–58.

72 A set of instructions to a "salaried soldier" of a secret society, captured in Victoria, B.C., Canada in 1899, indicates that perjured testimony would be made available for any secret society thug who was charged with a crime committed as part of his societal duties. "Chinese and Japanese Labor in the Mountain and Pacific States," 771; a case of such perjury is reported in Oscar T. Shuck, "Seniors of the Collected Bar—Frank M. Stone," *History of the Bench and Bar of California* (Los Angeles, 1901), 938–942.

73 "Chinese and Japanese Labor in the Mountain and Pacific States," 771; see also Dillon, *The Hatchet Men*, 167–205.

74 See Lyman, *The Asian in the West*, 34–38.

75 "Fine New Home for Chinese Free Masons," *San Francisco Examiner*, Oct. 6, 1907.

Mutual aid was also a feature of rural lodges of the secret societies, but charity was chastened by a cautious regard for the small treasury available and by the fear that interlopers would presume upon the tong's benevolence. A set of secret society rules from a lodge in the Fraser River area illustrates the conservatism and apprehensions of the small isolated chapters. The society provided a bunkhouse, arbitration and mediation services, and sickness and death benefits, but, perhaps in keeping with the womanless condition of the miners, no funds were provided for expenses related to childbirth, marriage, or funerals.[76] A partial exception to this rule seems to have been made in the case of secret society thugs. There is evidence that at least one such thug was promised a $500 death benefit, free medical care, a subvention of $10 per month, and a flat fee of $250 plus the cost of transportation back to China in case of permanent disability.[77] The rural chapters, beset by local problems and worried about interlopers from San Francisco's Chinatown, took care to protect their jurisdiction from frauds. A British Columbia lodge rule read: "Headmen from San Francisco intending to establish a forum for teaching disciples whether in the town or in the mining areas must hold a license from the *Chih-kung T'ang*. Anyone without such a license pretending to be a Headman will be prosecuted."[78] Penury and fear seemed to place significant limitations on mutual aid and benevolence within the secret societies.

Conflict and the Web of Group Affiliation in Chinatown. Chinese communities were highly organized, but organizations rested on different and in some cases contradictory foundations. The aims of the clans, *hui kuan,* and secret societies often clashed, and their peaceful competition not infrequently gave way to violence. Chinese immigrants frequently fell out with one another in quarrels over women, money, or politics. Sometimes these disputes escalated into group conflicts. Although the term "tong war" suggests that the violent altercations within America's Chinatowns were confined to the several secret societies, in fact these struggles included all three of the basic types of associations. For many decades the in-

---

[76] Lyman, Willmott, and Ho, "Rules of a Chinese Secret Society in British Columbia," 535.

[77] "Chinese and Japanese Labor in the Mountain and Pacific States," 771.

[78] Lyman, Willmott, and Ho, "Rules of a Chinese Secret Society in British Columbia," 536.

ternal conflicts among the Chinese sojourners isolated them from the larger society and bound them together in an antagonistic cooperation.

Violent conflicts in Chinatown arose for the most part out of four major kinds of situations: rival aspirations for control of the illegal commerce in drugs, gambling, and prostitution; transplantation of mainland civil wars or revolutions to the overseas Chinatowns; revolts of the poor against the merchant oligarchy of Chinatown; and rival claims to a woman. The first is illustrated by the unfortunate career of Fong Ching, a secret society leader whose daring plan to take control of vice in San Francisco's Chinese quarter resulted in the formation of a coalition of tongs to oppose his scheme and, finally, in his assassination in a Chinatown barbershop.[79] The second by the Weaverville War (1854), the California version of China's Hakka-Punti War (1855–1868).[80] The third by the war between the wealthy Yee clan and the On Yick Tong, a secret society composed largely of underpaid workers.[81] The last has countless illustrations. The shortage of women among the overseas Chinese led many of the young male immigrants to resort to prostitutes, most of whom were Chinese girls brought to America under contract as indentured domestic servants and put to work in the brothels that dotted San Francisco's Chinatown.[82]

At the turn of the century, several powerful secret societies fought one another for monopoly of vice operations in Chinatowns throughout the United States.[83] The worst of these fights occurred in San Francisco and New York, although branches and chapters in smaller Chinese settlements also took part. Since stakes in these battles were high, the fighting was fierce. Ultimately the less powerful secret societies were destroyed or co-opted into the larger ones. The outcome of these struggles was the admission of secret society leaders into the councils of the confederated *hui kuan* and a consolidation of crime and vice in Chinatown under the control of a restive secret society oligopoly.

---

79 Dillon, "Little Pete, King of Chinatown," 52–55.

80 Jake Jackson, "A Chinese War in America," and H. H. Noonan, "Another Version of the Weaverville War," in *Trinity 1957: Yearbook of the Trinity County Historical Society* (Weaverville, 1957), 5–12.

81 Gong and Grant, *Tong War*, 194–202.

82 Lyman, *The Asian in the West*, 29–31.

83 Gong and Grant, *Tong War*, 50; Drayton, "The Chinese Six Companies," 427–477; Dillon, *The Hatchet Men*, 241–340.

Although secret societies were at first opposed by clan and *hui kuan* leaders, the latter's efforts to stamp them out failed. Buoyed by their success in vice, the secret societies challenged the right of the clan-*hui kuan* elites to dominate Chinatown. In the late 1880s a violent struggle broke out between the Suey Sing Tong and the Wong Clan in San Francisco;[84] a few years later another bloody fight between the Yee Clan and the On Yick Tong ended the armed truce that characterized Chinatown after the Suey Sing-Wong fight had ended.[85] In another bloody fight in 1893 the secret societies sought to end *hui kuan* authority in Chinatown. After a financially exhaustive and abortive attempt by San Francisco's Six Companies to test the constitutionality of the Geary Act, several secret societies combined in a violent and vituperative campaign to persuade the rank and file Chinese to renounce their allegiance to the confederation of *hui kuan*.[86] That effort failed, but secret society leaders were soon established within the power structure of Chinatown.[87]

Not all the fights in Chinatown were related to local matters. Another source of violence in the Chinese communities of San Francisco and elsewhere were the rivalries between lineage communities and ethnic groups in southeastern China that were carried overseas by the emigrants.[88] A local incident might spark the renewal of a feud that had originated in the homeland. Thus, the Hakka-Punti war was fought not only in Kwangtung between 1855 and 1868, but also in Malaya as the Larut War of 1872–1873 and in the United States as the Weaverville War of 1854.[89] In the American phase of this war, the *Sam Yap Hui Kuan,* composed of Cantonese, fell out with the *Yan Wo Hui Kuan,* which represented the Hakka group, at China Camp and at Weaverville, California. In one battle at Kentucky Ranch, some 900 "soldiers" of the Yan Wo met 1200 of the Sam Yap "army" and fought until the latter were victorious.[90] Both groups secured military assistance from local white Californians.

---

84 Gong and Grant, *Tong War,* 50–54.

85 *San Francisco Chronicle,* Nov. 11, 1909, Feb. 7, 1910.

86 Drayton, "The Chinese Six Companies," 475–476.

87 Hoy, *The Chinese Six Companies,* 23–26.

88 Wynne, *Triad and Tabut,* 7–15, 49–113, 202–351.

89 E. J. Eitel, "Outline History of the Hakkas," *The China Review,* II (1873–1874), 160–164; Wynne, *Triad and Tabut,* 59–61, 260–280.

90 In addition to the sources cited in footnote 80, *supra,* see McLeod, *Pigtails and Gold Dust,* 53–56; Joseph Henry Jackson, *Anybody's Gold: The Story of California's Mining Towns* (San Francisco, 1970), 210–223.

After 1900 not a few of the so-called "tong wars" in America's Chinatowns were among rival factions seeking to overthrow the Manchu dynasty. Although Dr. Sun was able to unite the warring factions in many overseas areas, including the United States, these united fronts did not last long. Disputes among societies supporting different leaders and ideologists broke out before and after the Chinese Revolution of 1911.[91] Because the secret societies were essentially criminal and rebellious rather than political and revolutionary, these fights also coincided with local struggles for power, wealth, and women.

Some of the conflicts in San Francisco's Chinatown were primitive class conflicts. They represented the inarticulate, nonideological revolts of poor Chinese against a system which they resented and did not control. One example of this premodern class struggle is found in the war between the Yee Clan and the On Yick Tong.[92] Ostensibly begun because of an argument over a prostitute, the bloody fight also reflected the resentment of the secret society members toward the Yee clan because of its wealth, status, and power. The clan was composed of many prosperous merchants, and its treasury allegedly contained hundreds of thousands of dollars. In sharp contrast the On Yick group consisted primarily of laborers, cooks, and restaurant workers, who lived in the Chinatowns of Stockton, San Francisco, and Portland. In this "war," as in most such fights, the merchants were eventually victorious.

Still another source of hostility in San Francisco and elsewhere was the extreme imbalance in Chinatown's sex ratio, a situation which helps explain the numerous fights that broke out over women.[93] These quarrels between suitors were often used as a pretext to reopen old feuds, or as a justification for violent seizure of power. Not only did such fights break out between rival suitors but also between lovestruck men and the brothelkeepers who held girls under contract.[94] Sometimes a young Chinese would offer to buy up a girl's contract, and if he was refused he would

---

91 Stewart Culin, "The I Hing or 'Patriotic Rising,'" 51–57; Liew, *Struggle for Democracy*, 68–103, 172–190; Glick and Hong, *Swords of Silence*, 160–190, 255–262.

92 Gong and Grant, *Tong War*, 194–202; *San Francisco Chronicle*, Nov. 11, 1909, Feb. 7, 1910.

93 Lyman, *The Asian in the West*, 27–31; John E. Bennett, "The Chinese Tong Wars in San Francisco," *Harper's Weekly*, XLIV (Aug. 11, 1900), 746–747.

94 H. H. Bancroft, "Mongolianism in America," *Essays and Miscellany* (San Francisco, 1890), 356; Gibson, *The Chinese in America*, 139–140; Farwell, *The Chinese at Home and Abroad*, 8–14.

kidnap her. The brothelkeeper would call on his secret society protectors to recover the girl, and the kidnapper would enlist the aid of his clan or *hui kuan*. The resulting struggle would be short, bloody, and usually fatal for the couple.[95] So long as the shortage of females in Chinatown remained acute, and it remained so until the late 1920s, rivalries and feuds over women continued to generate wars among associations.

*   *   *

This analysis of the first six decades of organizational life inside Chinatown permits a concluding discussion that is both sociological and historical. In the first sixty years of their settlement in San Francisco, Chinese immigrants, hard-pressed by the anti-Chinese movement, still managed to forge a community in the strange and hostile environment of the West. It was a traditional community, transplanting to the urban overseas Chinatown many of the institutions and customs of imperial China. Thus clans, *hui kuan,* and secret societies emerged among the immigrants as the principal organizations promoting, respectively, familial solidarity, mutual aid, and organized crime and rebellion. In the new Chinatowns these traditional associations vied with one another for the allegiance of the immigrants, overall community domination, and, in the case of the *hui kuan,* the jurisdictional right to speak for all the Chinese in the city.

The organizational developments and internecine fights that took place in Chinatown from 1850 to 1910 indicate that forming an overseas Chinese community was not an easy task. Principles of clan solidarity, barriers of language and dialect, allegiance to rebellious secret societies, and their own competitive interest in making enough money to permit retirement in China divided the loyalties of the Chinese immigrants. Yet during the same period the depredations of anti-Chinese mobs, the difficulties and indignities imposed by restrictive immigration legislation, the occupational discrimination created by state and local laws prohibiting or limiting the employment of Chinese, and the active opposition of the American labor movement to the Chinese workingman all seemed to call for a community united in the face of its enemies.

---

[95] *San Francisco Chronicle,* Nov. 11, 1909, Feb. 7, 1910; Dillon, *The Hatchet Men,* 227.

What emerged out of this condition of pressures from without the ghetto and divisions within was a pattern alternating between order and violence. By 1910 this pattern had assumed a complex but recognizable sociological form: that of the community whose members are bound to one another not only because of external hostility but also because of deadly internal factionalism.[96]

Both community order and interassociation conflict developed patterns and rituals in Chinatown. When order did prevail in the Chinese quarter, it was grounded in the community's institutions of law, arbitration, and conflict resolution. Most of the disputes within and among clans, *hui kuan*, and secret societies were settled by arbitration, and many appeals were amicably resolved by the tribunal of the confederation of *hui kuan*. Of course, some litigants did not accept the judgments of the tribunals. In some cases angry losers to a suit would withdraw from the association, join or found a new *hui kuan* or secret society, or rebel against the established authority in Chinatown.[97] But any system of law and order implies, if it does not generate, resistance and rebellion. Although the desire for order in Chinatown was strong during the nineteenth century, conflict was more in evidence. Even during the peaceful periods, ghetto life more nearly resembled an armed truce than a harmonious community.

If order in Chinatown was governed by traditional law, the violence in the ghetto had a definite ritual to it. In accordance with Chinese custom, no interassociation feud began without a ceremonial exchange of insults and the posting of a *chun hung*, i.e., a declaration of war.[98] Thus, the Weaverville War of 1854 began with the antagonists hurling carefully worded abusive statements at one another followed by a challenge to fight. In another case, that of the abortive attempt to overthrow the president of San Francisco's Consolidated Benevolent Association in 1893, the secret societies posted a properly worded and insulting *chun hung* on the bulletin boards and store windows of Chinatown.[99] The mode of fighting and the designation of those who would be permitted to

[96] For the formal theory upon which this section of the paper is based, see the two essays by Georg Simmel, *Conflict and the Web of Group Affiliation*, translated by Kurt H. Wolff and Reinhard Bendix (Glencoe, 1955), 11–195.

[97] Lyman, "Structures of Chinese Society," 364–377.

[98] Examples of these declarations of war will be found in McLeod, *Pigtails and Gold Dust*, 53–54.

[99] Drayton, "The Chinese Six Companies," 475.

engage in armed violence were also carefully regulated. The secret societies maintained their own bands of "salaried soldiers," and, although the evidence is not so clear, the clans and *hui kuan* probably did the same.[100] According to the instructions given to one thug by his secret society, he was forbidden to use weapons except in service to the tong.[101] In any fight the number of casualties on each side was carefully enumerated, and a crude version of the *lex talionis* seems to have governed the taking of life. A fight was brought to an end by diplomatic negotiations carried out by representatives of the belligerent parties and, often enough, presided over by a neutral mediator. The end of a "tong war" was solemnized by the signing of a treaty of peace and followed by a ceremonial banquet.[102] These rules, codes, and rituals provided a measure of stability to the wars and even curbed, but did not altogether eliminate, violence.[103]

San Francisco's Chinatown witnessed both a considerable amount of conflict and an increasingly complex web of group affiliation in the years between 1850 and 1910. On the one hand, the intramural struggles for wealth, women, and power certainly did not lend themselves to peaceful relations among the immigrants. On the other hand, the fabric of group affiliation was woven more tightly[104] as wars generated the need for allies and a system of collective security. And throughout this period of intracommunity conflict, the *hui kuan* leaders presented themselves to municipal authorities, state legislators, and congressional investigators as the spokesmen for the entire Chinese community.[105]

Viewed from the perspective of a sociology of conflict, Chinatown in the years between 1850 and 1910 appears to be an extremely complex example of the thesis first developed by Georg Simmel

---

[100] Dillon, *The Hatchet Men*, 167–206; McLeod, *Pigtails and Gold Dust*, 238–252.

[101] "Chinese and Japanese Labor in the Mountain and Pacific States," 771.

[102] Lyman, "The Structure of Chinese Society," 352–354.

[103] The last major tong war appears to have been fought in 1933. Glick, *Shake Hands with the Dragon*, 265. Twenty-five years later a dispute between the Hop Sing Tong and the Bing Kung Tong threatened to erupt in violence, but after months of negotiations the matter was settled peacefully. *San Francisco Examiner*, Jan. 3, 1958, May 3, 5, 7, and 9, 1958; *San Francisco Chronicle*, Jan. 3 and 4, 1958.

[104] The number of secret societies in San Francisco rose and fell as wars continued in the period between 1880 and 1910. See Dillon, *The Hatchet Men*, 243–367. The *hui kuan* experienced a great number of factional disputes resulting in group defections, establishment of new *Landsmannschaften*, and finally a grudging recognition of the rights of secret societies. Nee and Nee, *Longtime Californ'*, 13–124, 228–252.

[105] Lyman, "The Structure of Chinese Society," 204–221.

and elaborated by Edward Alsworth Ross and Lewis Coser.[106] As Coser states it: "It seems to be generally accepted by sociologists that the distinction between 'ourselves, the we-group, or in-group, and everybody else, or the others-groups, out-groups' is established in and through conflict."[107] The social organization of San Francisco's Chinatown was comprised of a number of we-groups, each one of which looked at the others as an out-group. At times these we-groups were arrayed against one another in deadly combat. Yet, at other times, for example, when the Chinese immigrants as a whole felt threatened by white American racism, these opposed groups would postpone or put aside their differences and appear to form a united front.[108] The oscillation between intramural wars and the semblance of solidarity required in the face of a common enemy must have modified the strength and character of the Chinese associations, although, one must add, the evidence for this statement is not readily available.

The intramural conflicts probably added to the already considerable isolation of the Chinese community from the larger society. Feuds among clans, tong wars, and fights to depose the headmen of the Consolidated Benevolent Association must have seemed incomprehensible to most white Americans, who were not informed about traditional Chinese modes of organization or conflict resolution. These wars did generate a widespread stereotype of Chinatown that included lurid stories about opium dens, sing-song girls, hatchet men, and tong wars.[109] The real Chinese society was difficult to discern behind this kind of romantic illusion.

However, if intramural conflicts isolated Chinatown from the metropolis, they also very probably challenged the complex structures of solidarity inside the ghetto. Although we need much more evidence than we now have, including such documents as the bi-

---

106 Simmel, *Conflict and the Web of Group Affiliation*, 11–195; Lewis Coser, *The Functions of Social Conflict* (Glencoe, 1956); Edward A. Ross, *Principles of Sociology* (New York, 1920), 162.

107 Coser, *The Functions of Social Conflict*, 35; Ross, *Principles of Sociology*, 162.

108 One of the finest examples of this solidarity was shown when hundreds of Chinese, under the direction of the Consolidated Benevolent Association, went to jail to protest San Francisco's lodging house ordinance. See *Ho Ah Kow v. Matthew Nunan*, 5 Sawyer 552 (1879); McLeod, *Pigtails and Gold Dust*, 199–212.

109 See William Purviance Fenn, *Ah Sin and his Brethren in American Literature* (Peking, 1933), 1–131; Dorothy B. Jones, *The Image of China and India on the American Screen, 1896–1955* (Cambridge, 1955), 13–42; Colin Watson, *Snobbery with Violence: Crime Stories and Their Audience* (New York, 1971, 109–129.

ographies and papers of many ordinary Chinatowners, it is not unreasonable to suppose that feuds and fights among associations were the occasions for discovering and testing group loyalty. Clan, *hui kuan,* and secret society leaders very likely made demands of allegiance, service, and money on their members during times of hostilities in the ghetto. And it seems equally reasonable to suppose that, at different times and in different situations, the ordinary clan, *hui kuan,* or secret society member was variously disposed to regard his own association with warm feelings, fierce patriotism, troublesome annoyance, and even, perhaps, nagging fear. Yet in times of fighting, there was no mass exit of Chinese from Chinatown. At the very least, then, it would appear that the ordinary Chinese immigrant acquiesced in the difficulties imposed by his ghetto situation, and, at the most, some must have joined feverishly in support of their associations.

Simmel pointed to the fact that enmities and reciprocal antagonisms maintain established systems by encouraging a balance among their components.[110] The conflicts in Chinatown seem to bear out his observation in two distinct ways. First, the very fact that fights were confined to the ghetto and limited to matters affecting its Chinese denizens helped to establish and maintain the boundaries of the ghetto community. Chinese clans feuded with one another and not with white American families or Irish or any other ethnic group's clans. The *hui kuan* established its merchant oligopoly in Chinatown and not throughout the city, and the primitive class conflicts against its economic domination took place inside the Chinese quarter. The secret societies organized vice and crime in the ghetto and not elsewhere, and their gang wars were also confined to Chinatown. Moreover, the fights that broke out among the associations were aimed at issues and elements that were physically, socially, and politically located inside Chinatown (or, on occasion, in China). It is true that occasionally outsiders—police, clergy, diplomats, and the representatives of the Chinese government—became involved in the wars in Chinatown. But outsiders served only in an *ad hoc* capacity; their services were employed to balance the power of one or another of the contending factions.

The second sense in which Chinatown conflict provided for bal-

---

110 Simmel, *Conflict and the Web of Group Affiliation,* 17–28.

ance in the community arises from the fact that it was not directed at the absolute obliteration of opponents.[111] It must be remembered that hardly any struggle in Chinatown ever ended with unconditional surrender or total annihilation. The balance of power among contending parties prevented such an outcome. And this balance established the precarious stability in the community's structure. When peace treaties were signed, each party recognized the rights of the other to exist and to continue in the competition for women, wealth, and power. Chinatown was thus something of a Hobbesian cockpit, except that no fight ever escalated into a war of all against all or ended with a genocidal "final solution." We may speculate that the condition of long-term armed watchfulness probably generated an interest in the conservation of the existing institutions, since any party had an interest in knowing just who was representing any other body of Chinese and how many persons he represented. Thus, community conflict and group maintenance complemented one another. Conflict in Chinatown generated the need for groups to form and cohere; groups found added sources of *esprit de corps* in the conflicts that erupted. Conflict and group affiliation were the warp and woof of the first six decades of the Chinese community.

---

111 Cf. *ibid.*, 25–26.

Chinese Immigration through Communist Chinese Eyes: An Introduction to the Historiography

Shih-shan H. Ts'ai

The author is a member of the history department in the University of Arkansas.

Following the successful Communist revolution of 1949 in China, the diplomatic histories written on the mainland, with the exception of a few studies on Sino-Russian relations, were characterized by xenophobia.[1] In their studies of Sino-British, Sino-French, and Sino-Japanese relations, Communist Chinese historians not only intended to help their countrymen "understand more fully the aggressive nature of imperialism and the causes of China's poverty and backwardness," but also to educate the Chinese "in love of their country."[2] Since the United States played such an important role in the "China tangle" of the 1940s, studies of American "aggression" against China proved especially attractive to Communist Chinese scholars. The outbreak of the Korean War in 1950, in

---

[1] For other discussions of Communist Chinese historiography, see *Chinese Studies in History and Philosophy*, I (1967), 1–94; Albert Feuerwerker and Sally Cheng, *Chinese Communist Studies of Modern Chinese History* (Cambridge, 1961). Some of the material in the latter study has been compressed into article form by Feuerwerker in "China's History in Marxian Dress," *American Historical Review*, LXVI (1961), 323–353. See also Harold Kahn and Albert Feuerwerker, "The Ideology of Scholarship: China's New Historiography," *China Quarterly*, XXII (1965), 1–13; and Shih-shan H. Ts'ai, "Sino-American Relations through Communist Chinese Eyes: A Study in Comparative Interpretation" (M.A. thesis, University of Oregon, 1967).

[2] Liu Ta-nien, "New Approach to History," *China Reconstructs*, XI (1962), 27.

particular, touched off intensive academic research on Sino-American relations. Among the topics that received special attention was Chinese immigration to the United States in the nineteenth century.

During the last decades of the Ch'ing dynasty (1644–1911), there were a few reports on Chinese immigration prepared by such famous Chinese scholars as Hsieh Fu-ch'eng, Cheng Kuan-yin, and Liang Ch'i-ch'ao.[3] For the most part, however, the Chinese did little serious historical research on immigration, perhaps because of the tradition of dynastic histories, inward-looking intellectual patterns, and disdain which persisted until the late nineteenth century for those who had left their homeland. The rising national consciousness of the early twentieth century further focused attention on events in China rather than on the experiences of the overseas Chinese, while the revolutionary unrest and factionalism of the period after 1911 made difficult the completion of broad historical studies. Serious research on immigration had to wait until World War II when Ch'en Li-t'eh, a Sorbonne-trained historian, became one of the first Chinese scholars to investigate the subject.[4] Since 1949, however, both Communist and non-Communist Chinese scholars have produced valuable publications.[5] American scholars, on the other hand, have been interested in Chinese immigration ever since it became a diplomatic as well as a domestic problem of the United States in the late nineteenth century.[6]

---

[3] Hsieh was a Chinese envoy to Great Britain. His comments on immigration were printed on November 14, 1893, in the Shanghai Shen-pao, one of the earliest sociopolitical Chinese newspapers. Cheng was a very popular writer in the late Ch'ing period. His observations and essays were collected and edited by Wu Hsiang-hsiang, Sheng-shih wei-yen [Critical Comments During Prosperous Ages] (2 vols., Taipei, 1965). For his remarks on Chinese immigration to the United States, see volume II, pp. 20–24.

[4] Ch'en Li-t'eh, Chung-kuo hai-wai yi-min shih [A History of the Chinese Emigration] (Shanghai, 1946). Ch'en's book is by no means detailed, but its brief account of Chinese emigration since the seventh-century T'ang dynasty, particularly its chapter on the coolie trade, is very useful.

[5] This paper intends to discuss all of the Communist works available outside of mainland China. Among the important non-Communist publications are Wu Shan-yin's Mei-kuo hua-chiao pai-nien chi-shih [A History of One Hundred Years' Overseas Chinese in the United States] (Hong Kong, 1954); Chang Ts'un-wu's Chung-Mei kung-yueh fang-chao [Agitation of the Sino-American Exclusion Treaty] (Taipei, 1965); Kao Teh-kun's Pi-lu hua-chiao shih-hua [The Story of Overseas Chinese in Peru] (Taipei, 1966); and Li Ch'ang-fu's Chung-kuo jir-min shih [A History of Chinese Emigration] (Taipei, 1966).

[6] The more important American works on Chinese immigration include George F. Seward, Chinese Immigration in Its Social and Economic Aspects (New York, 1881);

Though they came to the subject at different times, Communist Chinese as well as American scholars have tended to focus on the same three aspects of the problem: the motives and processes of Chinese immigration;[7] the background of a series of treaties and laws by which the United States managed the immigration; and the reasons for the anti-Chinese movement. The most significant difference between the two groups of scholars is methodological, the Americans preferring behavioral analyses of the causes of the anti-Chinese movement and the Chinese tending to emphasize American malevolence in terms of how many Chinese were killed or how many houses in Chinatown were burned. Not surprisingly, the Chinese historians mix this approach with a Marxist economic interpretation.

But while Communist Chinese scholars may have fallen behind historiographically so far as sociological or sociopsychological interpretation is concerned, the literary quality and vividness of their accounts do not suffer by comparison. Certainly, no American work is a match for A Yin's *Fang-Mei hua-kung chin-yueh wen-hsueh chi* [*An Anti-American Literary Collection on the Exclusion of Chinese*

Ira M. Condit, *The Chinaman As We See Him* (New York, 1900); Mary Roberts Coolidge, *Chinese Immigration* (New York, 1909); Elmer Clarence Sandmeyer, *The Anti-Chinese Movement in California* (Urbana, 1939); Alexander McLeod, *Pigtails and Gold Dust* (Caldwell, Idaho, 1947); S. W. Kung, *Chinese in American Life* (Seattle, 1962); Gunther P. Barth, *Bitter Strength* (Cambridge, 1964); Betty Lee Sung, *Mountain of Gold: The Story of the Chinese in America* (New York, 1967); Stuart Creighton Miller, *The Unwelcome Immigrant: The American Image of the Chinese, 1785–1882* (Berkeley, 1969); Stanford M. Lyman, *The Asian in the West* (Reno, 1970); Alexander P. Saxton, *The Indispensable Enemy: Labor and the Anti-Chinese Movement in California* (Berkeley, 1971); Stanford M. Lyman, "The Structure of Chinese Society in Nineteenth Century America" (Ph.D. dissertation, University of California, Berkeley, 1961); Paul Crane and Alfred Larson, "The Chinese Massacre," *Annals of Wyoming*, XII (1940), 47–55, 153–161; Jules A. Karlin, "Anti-Chinese Outbreak in Seattle, 1885–1886," *Pacific Northwest Quarterly*, XXXIX (1948), 103–130; Patricia Ourada, "The Chinese in Colorado," *Colorado Magazine*, XXIX (1952), 273–284; Jules A. Karlin, "The Anti-Chinese Outbreak in Tacoma, 1885," *Pacific Historical Review*, XXIII (1954), 271–283; and Roy T. Wortman, "Denver's Anti-Chinese Riot, 1880," *Colorado Magazine*, XLII (1965), 275–291.

7 Various motives were involved in the immigration of more than a hundred thousand Chinese to the Pacific Coast of the United States by 1875. In addition to Chinese internal problems, such as overcrowding, poverty, war, and other catastrophes, external influences were equally important. Although American historians generally concur that the demand in the United States for labor was the major motivating force of Chinese emigration, they are aware of other factors, such as the discovery of gold in California and the promotion and competition of the Pacific steamship companies. See Coolidge, *Chinese Immigration*, 17; Sandmeyer, *Anti-Chinese Movement*, 15; and Barth, *Bitter Strength*, 61–62.

Laborers].[8] A Yin is the pseudonym of Chien Hsing-ts'ung, a specialist in the history of the literature of the late Ch'ing dynasty and a scholar who has long been active in Chinese literary circles. Among other accomplishments, he has edited a series of anthologies designed to show Chinese patriotism in the face of foreign aggression.[9] A Yin selected most of the items for his *Anti-American Literary Collection* from Dr. Sun Yat-sen's library in Canton. His selections include Liang Ch'i-ch'ao's essay, "About the Treaty which Excluded the Chinese Laborers," plus a sampling of fiction, poems, songs, and journalistic accounts. Among the latter are *The Golden World, Ashes after Catastrophe, Tears of the Overseas Chinese,* and other works that stress the harsh experiences of early Chinese immigrants in the United States. A representative item in A Yin's anthology is *Bitter Society,* a touching novel about how the "pigs" (Chinese coolies) were kidnapped and forcibly carried to Peru and Cuba by American ships. Written in the early 1860s, *Bitter Society* is based on the testimony of survivors who, after returning to China, reported how they were seized and imprisoned in barracoons, treated inhumanely in the transport ships, and forced to toil in the foul guano pits on islands off the coast of Peru. Another vivid writer who also incorporates portions of *Bitter Society* into his narrative is Liu Ta-nien, one of the most productive Communist Chinese historians and a man who served as associate editor of *Li-shih yen-chiu* [*Historical Research*] before the Proletarian Cultural Revolution.[10]

---

8 A Yin, *Fang-Mei hua-kung chin-yueh wen-hsueh chi* (Shanghai, 1960). Hereafter this work will be cited as *Anti-American Literary Collection.*

9 His works include *Ya-p'ien chan-cheng wen-hsueh chi* [*A Literary Collection on the Opium War*] (Peking, 1957); *Chung-Fa chan-cheng wen-hsueh chi* [*A Literary Collection on the Sino-French War*] (Peking, 1957); *Chia-wu Chung-Jih chan-cheng wen-hsueh chi* [*A Literary Collection on the Sino-Japanese War*] (Peking, 1958); and *Keng-tzu shih-pien wen-hsueh chi* [*A Literary Collection on the Boxer Incident*] (Peking, 1959). A Yin has been the chief editor of a number of magazines, including the *T'ai-yang yueh-pao* [*Sun Monthly*] and the *Hai-feng chou-kang* [*Sea Wind Weekly*]. At one time he served in the Communist New Fourth Army and directed a famous historical drama, *Chung Ch'ang Wang.* During World War II, he was appointed the president of Ta-t'ung University and in 1949 he took over the cultural administration of Tientsin. In 1955 he was elected vice secretary general of China's Literature and Arts' Association.

10 Liu Ta-nien, *Mei-Kuo chin-hua shih* [*A History of American Aggression against China*] (Peking, 1951). In August 1949, North China University published Liu's study under the title, *Concise History of American Aggression against China.* In 1951, when the Korean War was at its height, Liu revised and enlarged his study into the present volume. Liu's writing is heavily footnoted. He documents his book not only

Several Communist Chinese historians discuss the coolie trade to Latin America as part of their overall treatment of Chinese immigration.[11] Painstakingly exploring the involvement of American merchants in this traffic, they exert every effort to advance their main theme—American aggression against China. Ch'ing Ju-chi, a prominent anti-American historian and the author of a lengthy work, *Mei-kuo chin-hua shih* [*A History of American Aggression against China*], devotes two long chapters to the coolie traffic.[12] He puts the responsibility for the kidnapping of Chinese coolies on Caleb Cushing of the United States and Ch'i-ying of the Ch'ing government, the two men who in 1844 drafted the Treaty of Wanghia. Article twenty-six of the treaty stipulates that "Merchant vessels of the United States [,] lying in the waters of the five ports of China open to foreign commerce, will be under the jurisdiction of the officers of their own government, . . . without control on the

---

with Chinese and American official papers, monographs, and articles, but also with a number of Japanese works. In 1954 Liu was appointed secretary of the Chinese Academy of Science. In May 1955, he was named a member of the research committee of the Philosophy and Social Sciences Department of the Academy. Ten years later, in May 1965, he headed the Chinese delegation to Pakistan's fifteenth historians' conference in Karachi. During that conference, he presented a paper entitled "How to Evaluate Asian History?" in which he ridiculed Walter Lippmann, former Secretary of State Dean Acheson, and Western "capitalist" historiography. For more details about Liu, see the *Jen-min jih-pao* [*People's Daily*], July 8, 1965, Oct. 23–25, 1966.

11 The Chinese who came to the United States were technically not "coolies" or bond laborers, while those who went to Latin America were. For nearly a century the term "coolie"—which has the connotation of "servitude, slavery or peonage"—has been used loosely in the United States to designate only Chinese laborers. Yet the history of the term "coolie" gives no sanction to such usage. Although some American businessmen were involved in the Latin American coolie trade, the Chinese who came to the United States were free emigrants who had come on their own. Three laws enacted by the United States government in 1847, 1849, and 1862 stated that the American shippers could carry bond laborers from China to Latin America but not from any Chinese port to the United States. See the report of the House Committee on Commerce, April 16, 1860, in *H. Rept. 443*, 36 Cong., 1 sess. (1860), serial 1069, p. 3; Daniel Cleveland to Ross Browne, July 27, 1868, in *Papers Relating to the Foreign Relations of the United States, 1868* (Washington, D. C., 1869), 541; and Li and Pao to U. S. Commissioners, Oct. 7, 1880, in *Papers Relating to the Foreign Relations of the United States, 1880* (Washington, D. C., 1881), 173. Also, see Hosea Ballou Morse, *The International Relations of the Chinese Empire* (3 vols., London, 1910 & 1918), II, 166; Coolidge, *Chinese Immigration*, 41; McLeod, *Pigtails and Gold Dust*, 71.

12 Ch'ing Ju-chi, *Mei-kuo chin-hua shih* [*A History of American Aggression against China*] (2 vols., Peking, 1952 & 1956). Not too much is known outside of mainland China about Ch'ing's academic and political background. Judging from the sizeable bibliography cited in his study, the excellent English knowledge he shows in his translations, and the detailed historical events he utilizes for his arguments, he may have had American training.

part of China."[13] This article, Ch'ing argues, not only allowed
Americans to kidnap Chinese laborers and to protect the Chinese
crimps who helped American coolie dealers steal peasant boys, it
also deprived the Chinese government of the jurisdiction needed to
stop such practices.[14]

The practices used to obtain Chinese coolies are recorded in
documents published by the United States government, and Communist Chinese historians do not fail to cite them. One fourth of
Chu Shih-chia's *Mei-kuo p'o-hai hua-kung shih-liao* [*Historical
Materials Concerning America's Persecution of Chinese Laborers*]
consists of U. S. documents describing American roles in this traffic.
Chu, a Columbia University Ph.D., has devoted his life to the collection and publication of Sino-American historical documents.[15]
To illustrate the fortunes of Chinese coolies, he extracted a para-
graph from John E. Ward's correspondence to Secretary of State
Lewis Cass in 1860:

When a Chinaman has been kidnapped or stolen, he is taken to the first
vessel and asked if he wishes to emigrate. Should he answer in the negative, the captain, with great apparent honesty, declares he cannot receive
him. His captors then leave the ship with him, and he is held in the
water, or tied up by the thumbs, or cold water is trickled down his
back, or some other torture inflicted, until he consents to go, when he
is taken to the next ship, and the same question repeated, "Are you
willing to emigrate?" If his reluctance to become an exile is still un-
subdued, he is again returned to his captors, and this process repeated
until a consent is wrung from him, when he is received as one of the
"willing emigrants."[16]

13 Hunter Miller, ed., *Treaties and Other International Acts of the United States*
(Washington, D. C., 1931), IV, 567.

14 Ch'ing, *American Aggression against China*, I, 96–97.

15 Chu Shih-chia, *Mei-Kuo p'o-hai hua-kung shih-liao* [*Historical Materials Concerning America's Persecution of Chinese Laborers*] (Shanghai, 1958), hereafter cited
as *America's Persecution of Chinese Laborers*. In October 1939, Chu obtained a position in the U. S. Library of Congress, Asiatic Division, and compiled a list of Chinese
gazetteers. In 1942, he published his study, *A Catalog of Chinese Local Histories in
the Library of Congress* (Washington, D. C., 1942). During his stay in Washington,
Chu also copied a large number of important Sino-American diplomatic communications and memorials in the National Archives. These documents now appear as the
important parts of his two anti-American books, *America's Persecution of Chinese
Laborers* and *Shih-chiu shih-chi Mei-kuo chin-hua tang-an shih-liao hsuan chi* [*Selected Archival Materials on American Aggression against China in the Nineteenth
Century*] (2 vols., Shanghai, 1959).

16 Chu, *America's Persecution of Chinese Laborers*, 22–23; cf. "Chinese Coolie
Trade," *H. Ex. Doc. 87*, 36 Cong., 1 sess. (1860), serial 1057, p. 29.

Chu Shih-chia accuses the United States government of being an accomplice in these outrages, claiming that "American diplomats in China were in collusion with American merchants in seducing the Chinese coolies." "American captains," Chu states, "bought and sold Chinese coolies like slaves."[17] They could usually buy a Chinese coolie from his captor for eight Mexican silver dollars and sell him for more than a hundred Mexican dollars.[18]

Most Chinese scholars agree that the coolie trade began in the late 1840s. According to Ch'ing Ju-chi's account, American merchants initiated this traffic at Amoy (one of the five treaty ports) in 1847, only three years after the signing of the Treaty of Wanghia. From that date to 1853, over twelve thousand Chinese coolies were brought to Latin America.[19] It should be noted here that published U.S. documents contain statistics on the number of Chinese coolies who were carried to the New World under the flag of the United States, and the Communist historians have used these statistics correctly. For example, Ch'ing points out that at Swatou, an illegal port (i.e., not one of the five treaty ports), the coolie trade for 1855 was as follows:[20]

Ships		Tonnage	Coolies
American	5	6,592	3,050
British	3	3,821	1,938
Chilean	1	500	250
Peruvian	3	1,860	1,150
Total	12	12,773	6,388

From 1847 to 1862, moreover, American coolie traders almost monopolized the traffic between Macao and Havana. And from 1847 to 1859 the number of Chinese coolies carried by American shippers to Cuba alone averaged over six thousand a year.[21]

However, these statistics do not tell the whole story of American involvement in the coolie trade. There is also evidence that the treatment of the Chinese coolies transported to Latin America was

17 Chu, *America's Persecution of Chinese Laborers*, 3, 4, 8.
18 Ch'ing, *American Aggression against China*, I, 98.
19 *Ibid.*, 97.
20 *Ibid.*, 98; cf. Peter Parker to William L. Marcy, Feb. 12. 1856, in "Slave and Coolie Trade," *H. Ex. Doc. 105*, 34 Cong., 1 sess. (1856), serial 859, p. 73.
21 Ch'ing, *American Aggression against China*, I, 97–98; cf. "Coolie Trade." *H. Rept. 443*, 36 Cong., 1 sess. (1860), serial 1069, p. 28.

inhuman, and this evidence provides Communist Chinese historians with the rationale for their attacks on American traders and government officials. As a congressional report of 1856 testifies, American ships were usually badly equipped and overcrowded. Food was poor and sanitary facilities were lacking. Of the 450 coolies on board the American ship *Waverly*, bound from Swatou to Callao, Peru, in late 1855, nearly three hundred perished by suffocation. During the period from 1847 to 1860, there were 7,782 deaths among the 50,880 Chinese coolies shipped to Cuba in American ships. Many coolies could not endure the treatment they received. Some of them committed suicide, while the militant ones who instigated mutinies were usually captured and put on trial by Chinese authorities.[22]

After discussing the coolie trade, Communist Chinese historians usually shift their attention to the reasons for Chinese immigration to the United States. Uniformly they contend that America's need for labor was the most important external inducement to immigration. "In the forties of the nineteenth century," Ch'ing Ju-chi writes, "a big Mexican territory was annexed to the United States. . . . In order to cultivate and exploit this newly obtained western land and the resources, to develop a modernized industry, to build a transcontinental railway . . . the United States needed labor badly. Naturally, she looked to the numerous hardworking, resourceful and good quality Chinese people for help."[23] Chu Shih-chia agrees: "American capitalists, in order to exploit Chinese laborers, whipped them to dig gold mines, to build railroads, to cultivate barren land and do all kinds of manual work like farming, planting. The answer to the question of why industry and agriculture developed so fast in western America was to be found in the Chinese laborers' sweat and blood exploited by American capitalists."[24]

Writing earlier than Ch'ing and Chu, Chang Jen-yu, another anti-American historian and the author of *Mei-ti p'ai-hua shih* [*A History of Imperialistic American Exclusion against the Chinese*], asserts that the U. S. suggested the principle of free immigration in the 1868 Burlingame Treaty because "the United States needed the

---

22 H. N. Palmer to William L. Marcy, Nov. 9, 1855, in "Slave and Coolie Trade," *H. Ex. Doc. 105*, p. 71, *passim*; "Coolie Trade," *H. Rept. 443*, p. 28; and Ch'ing, *American Aggression against China*, I, 99–101.

23 Ch'ing, *American Aggression against China*, II, 508–509.

24 Chu, *American Persecution of Chinese Laborers*, 4.

Chinese laborers and American businessmen wanted to trade with the Chinese."[25] Liu Ta-nien makes the same point: "American capitalists were aware of the fact that Chinese labor was cheap. Therefore, they used all kinds of fraud and propaganda to bring Chinese laborers to the United States."[26]

Communist Chinese historians also devote considerable attention to American laws and riots aimed at the Chinese immigrants. They have collected a varied and substantial number of sources on America's anti-Chinese "crimes," drawing from such materials as American scholarly works, Chinese and American official correspondence, historical fiction, poems, songs, contemporary Chinese and American newspapers, diaries, and memorials to the Chinese emperors. Ch'ing Ju-chi utilizes published American archival materials and works of sympathetic American scholars, especially Mary Roberts Coolidge's *Chinese Immigration,* to condemn American Sinophobes.[27] Liu Ta-nien, on the other hand, relies primarily on Wang Yen-wei's *Ch'ing-chi wai-chiao shih-liao* [*Historical Documents of Ch'ing Diplomacy*],[28] an invaluable collection of late Ch'ing archival materials. Liu documents his book, for example, with the memorials of Chang Chi-tung, governor-general of Liang-kwang, and with petitions written to the Ch'ing government by the Chinese in the United States. These firsthand accounts graphically describe the hardships that the immigrants faced in the New World.[29]

The numerous attacks on Chinese immigrants in the 1880s and the prejudicial legislation led to diplomatic exchanges between China and the United States. Perhaps the best study of the legal and diplomatic aspects of the controversy over the status of the Chinese in the United States is Chang Jen-yu's *A History of Imperialistic American Exclusion against the Chinese.* Chang maintains that both the United States and Ch'ing governments were responsible for the numerous anti-Chinese outrages and discrim-

---

25 Chang Jen-yu, *Mei-ti p'ai-hua shih* [*A History of Imperialistic American Exclusion against the Chinese*] (Peking, 1951), 18, hereafter cited as *American Exclusion against the Chinese.* Little is known about Chang's academic training. He uses very hostile language in condemning America's exclusion policy.

26 Liu, *American Aggression against China,* 56–57.

27 Ch'ing, *American Aggression against China,* II, 508–519.

28 Wang Yen-wei, ed., *Ch'ing-chi wai-chiao shih-liao* [*Historical Documents of Ch'ing Diplomacy, 1875–1911*] (218 vols., Peking, 1932–1935).

29 Liu, *American Aggression against China,* 56–60.

inatory laws. He accuses the United States of unilaterally violating the spirit of the Sino-American Treaty of 1880 when it passed the Scott Act in 1888, and he condemns the Ch'ing government for failing to adopt a firm and consistent policy to protect the Chinese in the United States.[30] Throughout his book, Chang documents his study of the anti-Chinese riots and laws with the official protests lodged with the United States government by Chinese envoys. He also cites published U. S. and Chinese documents, including Envoy Chen Lan-pin's protest over the Denver, Colorado, riot (1880); Envoy Cheng Tso-ju and Envoy Chang Yin-huan's protests over the massacre at Rock Springs, Wyoming (1855); and Wu Ting-fang's opposition to General Elwell S. Otis's application of the Geary Act and other exclusion laws in the Philippines in 1899.[31]

While serving at Washington, these Chinese envoys kept diaries and some of them—for example, Chen Lan-pin's *Shi-Mei chi-lueh* [*Diary of My mission to the United States*] and Tsuei Kuo-yin's *Shi-Mei-Jih-Pi jih-chi* [*Diary when Serving in the United States, Spain, and Peru*]—were later published.[32] Among other things, the diaries provide valuable insights into the diplomatic negotiations between the Chinese diplomats and American officials. Thanks to these diaries, A Yin is able to include in his *Anti-American Literary Collection* part of Envoy Chang Yin-huan's *San-chou jih-chi* [*Diary of the Three Continents*] which was presented to the emperor in 1890. In his diary, Envoy Chang Yin-huan recorded that, following the delivery of his protest (August 16, 1887) over the Snake River Massacre, he and Secretary of State Thomas Bayard got into a hot debate. Bayard reportedly explained that the United States government could not create a special "Chinese Bureau" for the protection of the Chinese laborers. "Why then," Chang asked, "did the United States want to make exclusion laws specially aimed to discriminate against all the Chinese who reside in the United States and also to shut out the emigration into this country?" Chang seemed to be pleased with this exchange, for he also recorded in his diary: "Bayard was very embarrassed and he could not reply to most of my questions."[33]

In addition to diplomatic exchanges, Communist scholars also

---

30 Chang, *American Exclusion against the Chinese,* 23–28.

31 *Ibid.,* 35–37, 48.

32 Portions of the diaries of Chen and Tsuei can be found in Wang Hsi-chi, ed., *Hsiao-fang-hu-chai yu-ti ts'ung ch'ao* [*Collection of Essays on Chinese and Western Geography, Politics and Others*] (26 vols., Taipei, 1962 & 1964), XII, 57–67.

33 A Yin, *Anti-American Literary Collection,* 585–586.

pay attention to broader perspectives of the Chinese immigration issue. Chu Shih-chia's *America's Persecution of Chinese Laborers* contains a long preface in which he traces the Chinese laborers' ill fortune in America from 1860 to 1905. His documentary materials are grouped under four headings: (1) "American criminal acts of kidnapping and defrauding Chinese laborers" (mainly from published U.S. documents); (2) "America's persecution of Chinese laborers" (largely from the Ch'ing Tsungli Yamen Archives in Peking); (3) "The attitude of the Ch'ing government towards American persecution of Chinese laborers" (largely from *Historical Documents of Ch'ing Diplomacy*); and (4) "The Chinese people's boycott of American goods" (documents from such contemporary Chinese newspapers as the *Pei-jing jih-pao* [*Peking Daily*]).

Besides gathering a considerable number of documents in his book, Chu Shih-chia had also carefully examined the Chinese and English texts of the immigration treaty of 1880. He finds that the Chinese were misled by the American negotiators—James B. Angell, John F. Swift, and William H. Trescot. Article I of the treaty stipulates that, "whenever in the opinion of the Government of the United States, the coming of Chinese laborers to the United States, or their residence therein, affects or threatens to affect the interests of that country, . . . the Government of China agrees that the Government of the United States may regulate, limit, or suspend such coming or residence, but may not absolutely prohibit it . . . ."[34] But Chu says that in the original Chinese text there is no such word as "suspend." Chu is correct, and his contention can be verified by an examination of *Hsin-ts'uan yueh-chang ta-chuan* [*A New Compilation of Treaties*], a reliable semiofficial Ch'ing publication. The Chinese text of the treaty of 1880 does mention "regulate" and "limit," but does not say "suspend."[35] Chu charges that the treaty of 1880 marked the end of the free migration guaranteed by Burlingame's treaty of 1868. From 1882 onward, the United States Congress, using the treaty of 1880 as a pretext, passed a series of exclusion laws against the Chinese, most notably the Scott Act of 1888 and Geary Act of 1892.

Besides discussing treaties, diplomatic exchanges, riots, and dis-

---

34 Charles I. Bevans, ed., *Treaties and Other International Agreements of the United States of America, 1776–1949* (Washington, D. C., 1971), VI, 686.

35 Here Chu does not document his claim (see his *America's Persecution of Chinese Laborers*, 5), but the Chinese text of the Immigration Treaty of 1880 can be found in Lu Fang-shih, ed., *Hsin-ts'uan yueh-chang ta-chuan* [*A New Compilation of Treaties*] (Shanghai, 1908), XII, 10.

criminatory laws against the Chinese, Communist scholars also attempt to explain the reasons behind the anti-Chinese movement. American scholars have attributed the hostility against the Chinese to a number of factors—a national fear of inundation by the Chinese, labor surplus, standards of workmanship, differences in living customs, the maneuverings of wily politicians, racial prejudice, and even the altruistic efforts of Americans to obtain liberty for Chinese coolies.[36] Communist Chinese scholars, in contrast, place the blame entirely on America's economic depression of the early 1870s, a cyclic "disease" of capitalism. "In 1872," writes Chu Shih-chia, "depression hit the United States so hard that industrial manufactories shut down, commerce decreased its activities, and the unemployed increased." Following this, "Denis Kearney, the opportunistic political agitator, . . . organized the Workingmen's Party and propagated the idea that American unemployment was caused by the immigration of Chinese laborers."[37] In the same vein, A Yin says: "During the depression, the Chinese laborers still could maintain their living because they had a lower living standard. The American capitalist class and government, in order to divert American laborers from the target of their struggle, attributed all the evils of unemployment to the Chinese."[38] In other words, according to A Yin and Chu, Chinese laborers were made to bear the blame for American depression and unemployment.

In corroboration of this Marxist interpretation, Communist Chinese historians have called attention to the importance of class struggle and have played down the claims of Rodman W. Paul and other American scholars who attribute the hostility to racism.[39] In the early 1870s, asserts Chu Shih-chia, many American workers,

---

36 Gunther Barth has offered a rather provocative explanation for the anti-Chinese movement. His view is that the Chinese immigrants were not free laborers. In order to liberate the bonded Chinese coolies from the control of despotic Chinese merchants and to extend American liberty to them, Americans launched the anti-Chinese campaign. (See Barth's *Bitter Strength*, 213). Criticizing Barth's view, Wolfram Eberhard of the University of California, Berkeley, writes, "Unfortunately, all of his [Barth's] source material is in English . . . . The remarks indicate that exclusive use of Chinese sources, if they were systematically collected and analyzed, might yield a completely different picture from the one Barth has presented." *American Historical Review*, LXX (1965), 1244.

37 Chu, *America's Persecution of Chinese Laborers*, 4.

38 A Yin, *Anti-American Literary Collection*, 6.

39 Rodman W. Paul, "The Origins of the Chinese Issue in California," *Mississippi Valley Historical Review*, XXV (1938), 182; also, see Sandmeyer, *Anti-Chinese Movement*, 109; Coolidge, *Chinese Immigration*, 55.

because of their lack of strong class consciousness, were beguiled and incited to act against their Chinese working brethren by the American capitalist class. "They were misled to believe that the influx of Chinese laborers rather than their being cruelly exploited by the capitalist class caused their unemployment."[40] According to Ch'ing Ju-chi, A. Whitney Griswold's *The Far Eastern Policy of the United States* (New Haven, 1938), Stanley K. Hornbeck's *The United States and the Far East* (Boston, 1942), Foster R. Dulles's *China and America* (New York, 1946), and other capitalist-oriented works failed to recognize the basic truth in the century-long Sino-American relationship: "The American laboring class was always friendly and sympathetic to the Chinese workers." It was the capitalist class that made trouble for both the Chinese and American laborers. Ch'ing believes that his responsibility as a historian is to expose the "criminal acts" of the American capitalist class and to help reunite the "exploited and oppressed" American and Chinese peoples.[41]

Liu Ta-nien's ideological argument is even more explicitly Marxist. "Owing to the development of American capitalism," Liu writes, "a cyclic economic depression inevitably happened. At the moment the surplus of labor caused ceaseless and tremendous unemployment. As a result, the American capitalist class did evil for good. Using the same sneaky tactics they employed to induce Chinese laborers to America, they incited white laborers against Chinese laborers. They blamed unemployment—one of the crimes of capitalism—on Chinese competition with the American laboring class. By doing this, they could, on the one hand, destroy the cooperation of the international labor class and, on the other hand, make Chinese laborers the scapegoats to redeem the crimes of American capitalism."[42]

Since Communist China and the United States have been mutually hostile for over two decades, it is not surprising that Communist Chinese historians have used the often tragic subject of Chinese immigration to condemn the "aggressive crimes" of the United States and to expose American "treachery." Although they approach this problem in a somewhat exaggerated tone and in the expected doctrinaire Marxist manner, they nevertheless deserve careful at-

---

40 Chu, *America's Persecution of Chinese Laborers*, 4.
41 Ch'ing, *American Aggression against China*, preface, 1–5.
42 Liu, *American Aggression against China*, 57.

tention. Chu Shih-chia's two books of selected archival materials are among the most important Sino-American historical documents prepared by any Chinese. Ch'ing Ju-chi's lengthy work must also be ranked as a leading Sino-American diplomatic history in the Chinese language. A Yin's *Anti-American Literary Collection* is an invaluable addition to the literature on Chinese immigration. Admittedly, the authors of these works often support their ideological viewpoints with materials well known in the United States, but they nonetheless provide useful insights into Ch'ing attitudes toward Chinese immigrants in the United States—attitudes which American scholars have not thoroughly investigated. They also introduce students of nineteenth-century Sino-American diplomacy to such important Chinese-language materials as the archival holdings in the Tsungli Yamen, *Historical Documents of Ch'ing Diplomacy*, memorials, diaries, and newspapers.[43] Though we might not accept their Marxist analyses, we must recognize that the Communist Chinese researchers have added a considerable array of new data to the study of Chinese immigration.

---

[43] Of course, there are also many valuable non-Communist publications in Taiwan and Hong Kong.

Class or Ethnic Solidarity: The Japanese American Company Union

John Modell

The author is a member of the history department in the University of Minnesota.

THE CONFLICTS which beset the maturing second-generation Japanese Americans were even more intense than those which so often have faced second-generation groups in the United States. The Nisei had inherited from their parents a remarkable drive to succeed in the face of hardships, but they had also learned the American definition of success, by which standard the accommodation made by their parents could not be considered satisfactory. Suspicious and hostile white Americans had years before put the ambitious Japanese immigrants in their place by means legal and extralegal. The coming of age of the new generation can be dated, for the 1930s saw the proportion of adult Japanese males born in the United States increase from one in fifteen to one in three. Nowhere was the quiet drama of maturation played with deeper feeling or significance than in Los Angeles, the Japanese American metropolis, where—in contrast to the continental United States as a whole —Japanese population increased during the depression decade. By 1940, the 36,866 Japanese in the country, alien and native-born, constituted 29 percent of the national total.[1]

To date, writings on the Japanese Americans have tended to con-

---

[1] Eighty-nine percent of the Japanese in the continental United States were found on the Pacific coast, 74 percent in California. The nearest competitor to Los Angeles County as a Japanese American center was King County (Seattle), Washington, which in 1940 had only about one-fourth as many Japanese as did Los Angeles County. U.S.

centrate on what was done to them by hostile whites and to deal primarily with those periods in which the hostility was most obtrusive.[2] Accordingly, the 1930s have usually been treated as an interlude between the agitations which brought about the closing off of immigration from Japan in 1924 and the removal of the Japanese Americans from the Pacific coast in 1942. Yet the period offers a case study of a group striving for identity in the face of racism and in the face of an older, and no longer satisfying, image of itself. The most insightful earlier studies, notably those of Bloom and Riemer, McWilliams, and Thomas, have glimpsed the Nisei struggle.[3] But their emphasis has been on the relocation period and their scope too broad to examine in detail the deeply ambivalent attitude which the Nisei had toward white-American institutions.[4]

Without straying far from their assigned status, Japanese immigrants had created for themselves a viable and often thriving economy by working marginal fields abandoned or ignored by whites in search of easier profits elsewhere. In Los Angeles County, the Japanese economy was based solidly upon the growth, distribution, and sale of small fruits and vegetables. The proud record of Nisei educational attainment rested upon the fact that 99 percent of the celery and 95 percent of the strawberries in Los Angeles County were grown by Japanese.[5]

Bureau of the Census, Sixteenth Census, 1940, *Characteristics of the Nonwhite Population by Race* (Washington, 1943), 7; Sixteenth Census, 1940, *Population*, II, pt. 1, 630; House Select Committee Investigating National Defense Migration, "Fourth Interim Report," 77 Cong., 2 sess., *H. Rept. 2124* (1942), 96–98.

[2] Roger Daniels, reviewing the historiography of Oriental immigration to America, has noted a "concentration on the excluders rather than the excluded," a function of the apparent assumption that "Asians were somehow outside the canon of immigrant history. Other immigrant groups were celebrated for what they had accomplished; Orientals were important for what was done to them." Daniels, "Westerners from the East: Oriental Immigrants Reappraised," *PHR*, XXXV (1966), 375.

[3] Leonard Bloom and Ruth Riemer, *Removal and Return* (Berkeley, 1949); Carey McWilliams, *Prejudice—Japanese-Americans: Symbols of Intolerance* (Boston, 1944); and Dorothy Swaine Thomas, *The Salvage* (Berkeley, 1952). An exception to the general tendency to ignore Nisei developments in the 1930s was Edward K. Strong, who early in that decade studied the progress of the Nisei generation from the point of view of an educationist in *Vocational Aptitudes of Second-Generation Japanese in the United States* (Stanford University, California, 1933) and in *The Second-Generation Japanese Problem* (Stanford University, California, 1934).

[4] Leonard Bloom (with John I. Kitsuse), however, subsequently elaborated his insights into the Nisei dilemma in a valuable theoretical discussion of "The Validation of Acculturation: A Condition to Ethnic Assimilation," *American Anthropologist*, LVII (1955), 44–48.

[5] Sixteenth Census, *Characteristics of the Nonwhite Population by Race*, 105; Sixteenth Census, *Characteristics of the Population* (Washington, 1942), II, pt. 1, 632;

Nisei were on the whole decidedly loyal and obedient to their parents and, as youths, participated in their economy. They had learned, however, that jobs of high prestige which brought them into contact with whites on an equal basis were goals appropriate to American citizens. But the patterns established by their parents seemed to impose themselves upon the Nisei. Suspicion of each race for the other continued to evoke its complement. The separate Japanese social and economic structure remained vigorous and the safest recourse for Nisei denied other opportunities by discrimination.

For Los Angeles Nisei, the bitterest symbol of their frustration was the fruitstand. Nisei in need of jobs had long availed themselves of retail produce work as a relatively sure resort, where the ethnic stereotype they carried would be an advantage rather than a hindrance. By the late 1930s the trade had become the symbol, moreover, which immediately embraced 20 percent of the working Nisei who toiled on the stands.[6] The manifold pressures upon the Nisei were focused with particular intensity there, perhaps the more so because of the incongruity between the mundane business and the heightened emotions of reflective participants.

The tasks of a Nisei fruitstand employee were neither unpleasant nor inspiring. The hours—up to seventy-two a week—were vexing to the Nisei fruitstand workers, but were generally accepted as the price that had to be paid for Japanese business to flourish. The very genius of the retail produce industry was that, like other Japanese American industries in Los Angeles, it allowed a ready translation of labor into cash. But over the years, many Nisei began to resent fruitstand work as a perversion of their hopes. One Nisei wrote in the English-language section of a local vernacular newspaper:

I am a fruitstand worker. It is not a very attractive nor distinguished occupation, and most certainly unappealing in print. I would much

---

Select Committee Investigating National Defense Migration, "Fourth Interim Report," 130 (acreage estimates supplied by Los Angeles County Agricultural Commission).

6 Fifteen hundred to 2,000 Nisei worked in retail produce in Los Angeles County before World War II. In addition to these workers, another 500 Nisei worked in groceries but not in produce. Females accounted for between a quarter and a third of the Nisei produce workers. Bloom and Riemer, *Removal and Return*, 18; Thomas, *The Salvage*, 603; Wartime Civil Control Agency, *Bulletin No. 10* (1942), 5.

rather it were doctor or lawyer . . . but my aspirations of developing into such [were] frustrated long ago by circumstances, . . . [and] I am only what I am, a professional carrot washer. . . . The little optimism that is left in me goads me on with the hope that when I have a few shekels saved that I can call my own, and only God knows when that may be, I will invest it in an enterprise which will be, through habit and familiarity rather than choice, most likely another market.[7]

The Japanese retail produce industry grew rapidly after the mid-1920s, when the first Nisei achieved their majority.[8] As long as the stands could multiply, family or community connections could provide hard-to-find jobs for younger Nisei, whose cheap and theoretically grateful labor in effect subsidized the new stands begun by their ambitious and experienced elders. Three developments simultaneously challenged the Japanese fruitstand in the 1930s, indicating three points of potential vulnerability in the economic system built upon it. The depression might cause a decline in the demand for produce; the new supermarket might provide overly stiff competition; and new trends in unionism might threaten the economic solidarity within the Japanese ethnic group.[9] The Japanese worried about all of these menaces. But most of all Japanese fruitstand entrepreneurs, and the leaders of both first- and second-generation groups, believed the greatest threat lay in the idea that workers—even Nisei workers—might have an interest distinct from that of

[7] Taishi Matsumoto, "The Protest of a Professional Carrot Washer," *Kashu Mainichi*, April 4, 1937. See also Thomas, *The Salvage*, 420–422.

[8] Figures on the growth of the retail produce trade among the Japanese in Los Angeles are contained in: Shichiro Matsui, "Economic Aspects of the Japanese Situation in California" (unpublished M. A. thesis, University of California, Berkeley, 1922), 53–54 (figures for 1922); W. T. Kataoka, "Occupations of Japanese in Los Angeles," *Sociology and Social Research*, XIV (1929), 54 (for 1929); *Rafu Shimpo*, Dec. 12, 1934 (for 1934); Thomas, *The Salvage*, 35 n.54 (for 1941, including a discussion of conflicting figures for this last date).

[9] Considering the generally depressed state of consumer indexes, the retail fruit and vegetable trade in Los Angeles initially held up remarkably well. But, by the mid-1930s, temporary small gains of retail produce outlets were halted as the new supermarkets made their first rapid inroads into the traditional market. Although no more than 129 Japanese in Los Angeles who were experienced workers reported to the Census Bureau in 1940 that they were out of work in retail produce, the figure reflected only a small part of the discomfort Nisei were feeling because of unemployment in the industry. No more than two-thirds of all Japanese workers in food retailing (mainly in produce) had worked a full twelve months in 1939, and periods of unemployment were long. Inexperienced men often could get no jobs at all. U. S. Bureau of the Census, Fifteenth Census, *Unemployment*, I, 162; Fifteenth Census, *Retail Distribution*, I, pt. 2, 192; U. S. Census of Business, 1935, *Retail Distribution*, II, 145; U. S. Bureau of Foreign and Domestic Commerce, *Consumer Market Data Handbook, 1936* ("Market Research Series," No. 15; Washington, 1936), R–53; U. S. Bureau of Foreign

their employers, even when those employers were Japanese. Such multiple threats to the delicate economic balance established by their parents revealed to Nisei the precarious position of their race in America. But they also suggested that in a period of change a way out might possibly be at hand.

Unionization in the late 1930s was anathema to the now-conservative Japanese leaders in Los Angeles. Early in the century California's Japanese agricultural laborers had frequently bettered their condition by striking against their Caucasian employers. Now, with many Japanese in entrepreneurial positions and dependent for their success upon abundant and cheap labor, the situation had changed. In dealing with Nisei workers, this older generation recalled fondly the paternalistic employer-employee relationship which predominated in Japan, and reacted with horror (shading into red-baiting) to the idea of Nisei joining unions.[10]

Nineteen thirty-seven was a year of resurgence for traditionally feeble organized labor in Los Angeles, where local boosters had proudly pointed to the great economic advantages of an open-shop city, and a high point throughout the state of organization in retail

and Domestic Commerce, *Consumer Market Data Handbook* (Washington, 1939), 30; U. S. Bureau of the Census, Sixteenth Census, *Census of Business*, I, pt. 3, 91; Sixteenth Census, *Population*, III, pt. 2, 205, 244–247; M. M. Zimmerman, *The Super Market* (New York, 1955), 48, 54, 60–65, 131; Rom J. Markin, *The Supermarket: An Analysis of Growth, Development, and Change* (Washington State University, Bureau of Economic and Business Research, College of Economics and Business, Bulletin No. 36; Pullman, Washington, 1963), 6–17; Lucius P. Flint, "The Los Angeles Super," *Chain Store Age* (Grocery Managers' Edition), XXVI (June, 1950), J34–J35.

10 Stuart Marshall Jamieson, "Labor Unionism in Agriculture" (unpublished Ph.D. dissertation, University of California, Berkeley, 1943), I, 123ff; Federal Writers Project [Oakland, California], "Oriental Labor Unions and Strikes, California Agriculture" (typescript, n.d.), *passim*, available in the library of the University of California, Berkeley; *Kashu Mainichi*, April 15, 1937; Togo Tanaka, "The Vernacular Newspapers," report for War Relocation Authority, typescript, 8, in the Japanese Evacuation and Resettlement Study Collection, folder A1.11, Bancroft Library, University of California, Berkeley. Industrial conflict within the group was profoundly antithetic to Japanese society in which considerable moral obligation went along with the hierarchical arrangement of economic and political power. Such a sense of obligation would render illegitimate the very notion of industrial conflict. Talcott Parsons, in comparing Japan with the West, noted that "moral conflict [in Japan] is a matter of being caught between conflicting obligations, not of conflict between principles and pressure of practical necessity as it is predominately with Occidentals." Unionization, in heightening class solidarity across ethnic lines, was thus troubling to the first generation on grounds that transcended the simply selfish. Parsons, "Population and the Social Structure of Japan," in *Essays in Sociological Theory* (rev. ed.; New York, 1964), 283; James C. Abegglen, *The Japanese Factory: Aspects of Its Social Organization* (a publication of the Center for International Studies, Massachusetts Institute of Technology; Glencoe, Ill., 1958).

sales and clerical occupations.[11] In this generally hopeful climate, a new and vigorous organization, Retail Food Clerks, Local 770, undertook a concerted attempt to organize the Los Angeles retail food industry. Local 770 received its charter from the usually unaggressive Retail Clerks International Protective Association, AFL, in early 1937.[12]

Under the stewardship of Joseph De Silva, the Retail Clerks diverged from the tradition of the statewide AFL, which years before had led the pack in harassing the Japanese immigrants. The California AFL tradition, stemming from San Francisco, had seen in the Japanese a threat to the employment of the white workingman and to the racial integrity of white California. The Retail Food Clerks, however, arrived at a time when Japanese immigration had long ago been halted and at a place where labor had been only a cheering section for San Francisco anti-Orientalism. At this time the Los Angeles AFL was generally playing an opportunistic game with the Japanese, retaining their essential antipathy but lowering the official barriers to Japanese membership "sufficiently so that . . . they could be taken into our unions" in those industries where their numbers made their organization imperative.[13]

Local 770, of course, was mainly intent upon establishing what it called an "American" standard of living for white workers. If Nisei workers were willing to throw in their lot with the "American" workers—and this meant primarily adherence to a high wage-and-

---

[11] California Department of Industrial Relations, Division of Labor Statistics and Law Enforcement, *Biennial Statistical Report to the Legislature, 1939–40*, pp. 48, 55; Richard Norman Baisden, "Labor Unions in Los Angeles Politics" (unpublished Ph.D. dissertation, University of Chicago, 1958), 160–166; Louis B. Perry and Richard S. Perry, *A History of the Los Angeles Labor Movement, 1911–1941* (Berkeley, 1963), 442–491.

[12] Michael Harrington, *The Retail Clerks* (New York, 1962), 6–8, 46–53; *Retail Clerks International Advocate*, XL (March, 1937), 19; Lee Quick, "History of Local 770," *Voice of 770*, 1 (Jan., 1942), 14–15.

[13] Roger Daniels, *The Politics of Prejudice* (Berkeley, 1962), *passim*. A perusal of issues of the *Los Angeles Citizen*, official newspaper of the Los Angeles Central Labor Council published during times of statewide anti-Japanese agitation, indicates the less rabid nature of that sentiment in the southern city. Although prior to 1937 some Japanese had been admitted to membership in various AFL locals in Los Angeles (some of which, like the Japanese and Oriental Hotel and Restaurant Workers' Union, Local 646, were segregated), their experiences did not greatly modify the suspicion of most Japanese for the AFL. *Rafu Shimpo*, Sept. 13, 17, 1933; *Los Angeles Citizen*, July 2, 23, Sept. 17, 1937. Quotation from John Buzzell in House Special Committee on Un-American Activities, "Investigation of Un-American Propaganda Activities in the United States," 78 Cong., 1 sess. (1943), 9287.

hour standard—benefits would be shared by both groups of workers, and 770 would treat the Nisei as natural allies. But to the extent that the Nisei sought special treatment for the Japanese portion of the industry, they were to be condemned as enemies of American labor. Since white-run concerns could not concede a substantial advantage in labor costs to their Japanese competitors without suffering losses in trade, Local 770 believed that, if it was to organize the white portion of the industry, it could not ignore the Japanese.

Before 770 had a chance to move, the alarmed Japanese launched a preemptive attack. In early 1937, some 450 Nisei fruitstand workers established a union of their own, called the Southern California Retail Produce Workers Union. President and leading force of the union was a Nisei, Thomas Hiromu Yamate, a buyer. Membership was limited to Japanese workers in retail produce and was to include them all. The SCRPWU emphasized its community responsibility by immediately incorporating, thereby making itself open to legal suit. All mention of strikes and even of collective bargaining was omitted from its stated purposes. The SCRPWU was only "to assist" the workers "in obtaining adequate compensation for their services." Within two weeks and without any controversy, recognition came from the all-Japanese Retail Market Operators' Association.[14] Though the Nisei union was not—as 770 repeatedly charged—a company union pure and simple, its characteristics were distinctly similar. The immediate interest of the Nisei worker was decidedly of secondary importance; when necessary, the union would suppress his grievances in order to assert ethnic solidarity in the face of changes which went far beyond the ethnic group and far beyond the produce industry. Never could the union credibly define its relationship to management as even potentially one of con-

---

14 When the SCRPWU subsequently engaged in litigation, it alleged that its articles of incorporation not only provided for collective bargaining, but also promised "to protect the interests of every kind of the members of this Union and to maintain and advance the standard of living for each member." "Articles of Incorporation of Southern California Retail Produce Workers Union," filed August 3, 1937 (but dated May 28, 1937), California, Secretary of State, Corporation Number 172,404; *Makita et al. v. Three Star Produce Co., Ltd.*, Superior Court, Los Angeles County, Docket no. 431,741 (1939), "Brief of Plaintiff," 2; *Rafu Shimpo*, May 16, 17, and 27, 1937; *Kashu Mainichi*, May 17, 1937; *Doho*, Sept. 1, 1938; *Los Angeles Citizen*, May 21 and Sept. 17, 1937; Senate Committee on Education and Labor, "Hearings on Violations of Free Speech and Rights of Labor," 76 Cong., 2 sess. (1940), 24354–24355. All references to these hearings, except where otherwise specified, are to memos and letters subpoenaed from the files of The Neutral Thousands, a Los Angeles antilabor group, and printed as exhibits (henceforth these hearings are designated as SCEL, "Hearings").

flict. Rather, ethnic consensus was sought, so that a unified effort might hold off 770.

Local 770 shortly set out to attack frontally what it considered its two major obstacles: the chain groceries and the Japanese produce merchants. The initial attack upon the parallel ethnic union structure was itself two-pronged. One prong was aimed at the Japanese employers and was intended to convince them that present arrangements would not bring industrial peace, even should Nisei employees fully accept them. The other prong was aimed directly at the Nisei worker.

On July 4, 1937, Local 770 addressed an open letter in the vernacular press to its "Dear Brothers and Sisters" in the Japanese fruitstands and concessions. Maintaining that the ethnic union was only of advantage to Japanese employers, the individual Nisei worker was challenged to place class interest above ethnic interest, thus supporting what 770 considered to be the American way.

> We believe that the Japanese and white workers should unite and work together. We recognize no national or racial difference. The "Company Union" that your employers have asked or told you to join, has been for the purpose of isolating and segregating the Japanese workers from the white . . . that they may, and can, keep you under their thumbs, . . . that they can, and will, work you longer hours for less pay. . . . If you are real Americans, why don't you fight for the American standard of living?

The rhetoric had no apparent effect on the Nisei. De Silva later attributed the failure of his recruitment effort to the "prejudice" most of the Japanese had towards the AFL, and their fear of "comingling" with whites.[15]

In the meantime, 770 was working directly on some of the larger Japanese employers of Nisei retail clerks, beginning by picketing the Three Star Produce Company, the largest chain of Japanese retail markets. When Teamsters respected the picket line, Three Star quickly capitulated, signing a contract with 770 which called for the union shop, higher wages, and shorter hours to go into effect at such time as 770 succeeded in gaining the adherence of half the

15 *Kashu Mainichi,* July 4, 1937; Joseph De Silva to John Modell, March 14, 1968; John Buzzell in House Special Committee on Un-American Activities, "Investigation of Un-American Propaganda," 9287; interview with O. I. Clampitt, Financial Secretary, Retail Clerks Local 1442, Santa Monica, California, March 23, 1968.

remaining Japanese retailers in Los Angeles.[16] But after an injunction was secured which removed the danger of further 770 picketing, few retailers were converted. The threat of economic strangulation, however, had evoked a general shudder in the Japanese community.

In December 1937, Yamate widened the conflict. When his ability to protect the Japanese industry was threatened by 770 picketing, he spoke out in a Los Angeles City Council meeting in favor of a proposed antipicketing ordinance, a measure intended by its sponsors to restore the previous feeble position of organized labor in Los Angeles.[17] What De Silva thought of workers who would support a step like this can easily be imagined. The conflict between the Japanese union and 770 had driven both to new and more extreme positions. Local 770 was readying arguments about the Japanese workers as well as their employers that were more than dimly reminiscent of the old brand of AFL anti-Orientalism. The Nisei group, for its part, had become a militantly antilabor organization, stressing ethnic ties to the exclusion of all others.

Even within the Japanese community, however, Yamate's union was under attack, most notably by confirmed foes of labor organization who earlier had supported his union as a prudent compromise. Prime exponent of this position was Susumu Hasuike, president of Three Star Produce, who believed himself a living example of the applicability of the classical American success story to Japanese Americans and who accordingly wished to free his genius of all trammels.[18] Beginning in April 1938, Hasuike threatened to discharge Three Star employees who made a point of their continued membership in the SCRPWU. The scarcity of jobs in the depression gave impact to this threat, and a few weeks later Hasuike forced a vote in which his 300 employees signified that they wanted

---

[16] *Los Angeles Citizen*, Nov. 26 and Dec. 3, 1937, Feb. 11, April 29, and May 13 and 20, 1938; *Rafu Shimpo*, Feb. 7, 1938; SCEL, "Hearings," 21244 (communication from John Buzzell, Los Angeles Central Labor Council, to SCEL), 24354–24356.

[17] *Los Angeles Times*, Dec. 11, 1937.

[18] Hasuike's favored self-image is reflected in the portrait of him in the sympathetic article on the Los Angeles Japanese community by Magner White in the *Saturday Evening Post*, published in 1939. In the article we see Hasuike, a young and ambitious immigrant, working his way up from a train-washer at nineteen, to a fruitstand owner (on a capital investment of $200) in 1920, to a capitalist in the trade (worth $20,000) four years later, and a large entrepreneur with properties grossing $3 million a year in 1939. Magner White, "Between Two Flags," *Saturday Evening Post*, CCXII (Sept. 30, 1939), 75.

nothing to do with the union. They knew, as Hasuike later told newspapers, that their employer knew best how to care for their welfare.[19]

Hasuike's actions and the rift in the Japanese community had the effect of weakening Nisei attachment to their ethnic union, which could not protect them against the Three Star owner. The failure of that economic solidarity in the Japanese community which Yamate had considered his strongest advantage and the *raison d'être* of his union drove him into the hands of those outside the ethnic community who were willing to lend assistance. By no accident, he found aid among strongly antilabor whites who had earlier been intrigued by his stand on the antipicketing ordinance.

The Neutral Thousands, a local organization devoted to making Los Angeles once again an open-shop haven by encouraging so-called "independent" unions, was enlisted. Yamate asked this group whether it might devise a way of bringing Hasuike around. What Yamate had in mind was undoubtedly economic pressure, for to some extent Hasuike was the prisoner of the white proprietors of markets in which most of the Three Star Produce concessions were located. The Neutral Thousands promised to try, and in return asked Yamate to secure signatures of SCRPWU members in order to get the antipicketing measure onto the ballot as an initiative.[20] Yamate readily agreed and offered also to deliver the endorsement for the initiative measure (once on the ballot) of the Nisei Voters League and of the Los Angeles chapter of the Japanese American Citizens' League.[21] Hasuike, however, could not be reached, and in September 1938, Yamate shifted ground and (in violation of the proposed antipicketing initiative) placed pickets around a few of the Three Star locations. Yamate declared that working conditions at Three Star were a "shameful blot" and brought civil suit against Hasuike, with the officers of Local 770 as codefendants, charging a conspiracy of the AFL union and the antiunion employer to destroy the Japanese union.[22]

19 *Rafu Shimpo*, May 4 and 10, 1938; SCEL, "Hearings," 24354–24356.

20 SCEL, "Hearings," 24417–24419, 24424, 24354–24357.

21 *Ibid.*, 24357–24359; *Kashu Mainichi*, Sept. 12, 1938. A local version was adopted by Los Angeles in September 1938, but a statewide version was defeated in November. Both denied the right to picket to all but employees of the struck concern and then only when a strike not over jurisdiction had been voted by a majority of employees in secret ballot. A copy of the ordinance is in SCEL, "Hearings," 20949.

22 The suit was brought in the name of three of the 80 employees whom Hasuike

Both sides believed that in the last analysis the disagreement hinged upon differing definitions of ethnic-group policy. Each, accordingly, asked the community to arbitrate the struggle and pitched its argument in terms of the broader issues at stake. These received a full and clear expression at the expense of bread and butter issues, which were mainly unspoken.

Hasuike explained his side in an open letter in the vernacular press. "The welfare of the Japanese community is at vital stake," he insisted. "We of the Three Star Company fail to understand why one Japanese organization that claims to be interested in community welfare is trying to attack, disrupt and tear down another Japanese business organization." Like other Japanese businesses—and in proportion to its great size—Three Star was fulfilling an essential community need. By "opening new outlets of employment for the Nisei," according to Hasuike, "a far more concrete and real contribution to the Nisei welfare and community progress" was being made.[23] Hasuike argued from the macroeconomic viewpoint that Three Star was bringing money into the Japanese community and generating new jobs. That these jobs were for "professional carrot washers" bothered Hasuike not at all, for this pursuit, at least in the macroeconomic sense, had sustained the Japanese of Los Angeles. Only selfishness had led SCRPWU members to ignore the economic rationality of Hasuike's message to the Japanese community.

Yamate, in reply, insisted that his union did not represent the interests of any one class, but rather that it served the entire ethnic community. "Order and reason" had been brought into "the fruit-stand industry," but without forgetting that "the circumstances and condition among the Japanese people, with a different traditional background from other races, called for a modified form of workers' organization." Yamate had fulfilled his responsibility as he saw it, but condemned "the selfishness of one man who cannot see that by giving Nisei a square deal he will be helping to build a bright future for the second generation in America. Who can better themselves when they must work twelve, thirteen hours every day?"[24]

had discharged. *Rafu Shimpo*, Sept. 2 and 4, 1938; *Kashu Mainichi*, Sept. 4, 1938; *Makita et al. v. Three Star Produce Co.*, "Brief of Plaintiff," *passim*.

[23] *Rafu Shimpo*, Sept. 7, 1938.

[24] *Kashu Mainichi*, Sept. 7, 8, and 9, 1938.

The conflict between Yamate and Hasuike ended with a vague truce about two weeks after the picketing began.[25] But soon De Silva resumed his attack. Accustomed to little Nisei cooperation, he now turned to a boycott, which he promoted with undisguised racial appeal. "DON'T BUY JAPANESE," read handbills put out by 770 over its name. "Support the organized RETAIL FOOD CLERKS. Do not contribute to unemployment, Low Wages. Long Hours [.] Do not let us compete with un-American standards of living [.]"[26]

His boycott was "not one of racial prejudice," De Silva explained, but was a "humanitarian action" designed to bring down the Nisei union which had "divided the workers so that they suffer and trust no one." He argued:

> The Japanese Association through its agent, the Company Union, has so incensed the Japanese workers against the American Labor movement, they have withdrawn into a world of their own. . . . These anti-labor merchants are practicing a dictatorship within our democracy, and are set to destroy, with keenest competition, the little we have accomplished.[27]

Though De Silva had insisted during the course of the boycott that "there is no discrimination nor feeling against the rank and file Japanese workers" and that Nisei employees were "free and welcome" to affiliate with 770, this was hardly the effect of the racial boycott.[28] In terms of its stated purpose the boycott was listlessly prosecuted and generally ineffective. Whatever its economic cost to Japanese merchants may have been, it was absorbed (along with the cost of a brief downturn in the business) by the Nisei workers, whose wages were reduced.[29]

The irony in the situation undoubtedly appealed at the time neither to the Japanese nor to members of 770, for what had oc-

---

[25] *Rafu Shimpo*, Sept. 17, 1938; *Doho*, Nov. 20, 1938.

[26] *Los Angeles Citizen*, Feb. 24, 1939; *Rafu Shimpo*, March 10 and 19, 1939. The last reproduces a photograph of one such broadside.

[27] *Los Angeles Citizen*, March 3, 24, and April 28, 1939.

[28] *Doho*, Sept. 20, 1939.

[29] Forlornly, Yamate complained to his allies at The Neutral Thousands that the passage of the antipicketing ordinance, which he had supported, had left the union weaponless in the face of employers. The union accepted a wage cut to a minimum of $20.25 for a 60-hour week for experienced men in 1939, agreed to settle for the same again in 1940, but managed a dollar-a-week raise in late 1940. Yamate to C. C. Rittenhouse, The Neutral Thousands, SCEL, "Hearings," 24361; *Rafu Shimpo*, Jan. 31, 1939, Feb. 1, Sept. 19, 1940.

curred was a classical self-fulfilling prophecy. Earlier experience
had taught the Japanese elders to fear the AFL and to stay safe within the ethnic economy. As a reflex, Nisei had been led to reject the
overtures of the Retail Clerks, which, though clearly tactical in purpose, had raised the possibility that the Nisei might develop there
a modicum of power against both whites and their parents' generation. This rejection in turn encouraged labor to recapitulate its
old patterns of denunciation of "un-American" Oriental labor,
which, again, cemented the Japanese community.

By late 1940, Yamate had retired from his post—quite without fanfare—and visited Japan, reportedly to "sell some rubber
patents." Members of his union had become more and more
troubled by the lack of militancy it showed despite the far more
satisfactory wage-and-hour scales won by white clerks. The situation
was pregnant with change. Officials of the Retail Clerks International, wishing to relieve De Silva of a burden and also of a chance
to increase his power, called upon the Nisei unionist, Robert K.
Sato, to take out a charter and organize the Nisei retail fruit-and-
vegetable workers.[30] Sato four years previously had briefly led an
ethnic union in wholesale produce similar to Yamate's, but had
quickly been co-opted by the independent Wholesale Produce
Drivers 630 (which subsequently affiliated with the Teamsters).
Sato had been able to bring his union into the 630 fold when the
president of Local 630 agreed to sign a pledge of nondiscrimination
and was by 1941 well esteemed by local unionists. In March 1941,
the Retail Clerks International leadership handed Sato a charter
establishing the "Fruit & Vegetable Store Employees' (Japanese)
Union, Local 1510," with jurisdiction over all Japanese employees
in retail fruit-and-vegetable stores in southern California.[31]

With both Yamate and De Silva out of the picture, members of
the ethnic union quickly and unanimously consented to its immediate demise and the transfer of membership lists (and two
officers) to Local 1510. Relieved at escaping the unsympathetic De
Silva, the Japanese merchants soon granted union contracts with

[30] Thomas, *The Salvage*, 422–423; *Rafu Shimpo*, Sept. 19, 1940; *Doho*, April 1 and
Aug. 14, 1941; *Retail Clerks International Advocate*, XL (May–June, 1941), 26; interview with Robert K. Sato, May 2, 1968.

[31] Interview with Sato, May 2, 1968; *Rafu Shimpo*, May 3, 11, 12, 15, 16, and June
4, 1937; *Kashu Mainichi*, May 12 and 15, 1937; *Los Angeles Citizen*, Sept. 3, 1937;
Charter of Local 1510, March 27, 1941; C. C. Coulter to Robert Sato, March 28, 1941.
These last two documents are in the possession of Robert K. Sato.

terms identical to those previously won by 770.[32] Membership in
1510 grew slowly, however, and certain Japanese merchants—
notably Hasuike—were reluctant to live up to the terms of their
contracts. Relations with 770 were strained and formal, and not
until two months after the birth of 1510 were "All Japanese Markets" taken off the Central Labor Council's unfair list. Just two
months before Pearl Harbor, 770 threatened unofficially to take
over its segregated fellow local if it continued to show tendencies
toward company unionism.[33]

Caste, though shaken by a concatenation of essentially uninter-
ested forces, had been left undisturbed. Japanese American workers
in retail produce remained in an all-Japanese local until the war,
apart from white workers and in some ways still competing as a
racial group.[34] Ethnic solidarity was maintained, but apparently at
the price of declining an opportunity of unknown value that was
briefly open to members of the group. The seriousness of labor's
invitation was never tested, and the possibly useful implications of
economic power and occupational concentration were left unex-
plored. When the war came and the ultimate caste definition was
applied to Japanese Americans, they had achieved no foothold in
American labor that might turn away the wrath of this traditional
foe. Neither, however, did the episode destroy the group's cohesion
which later helped the Japanese Americans, in a somewhat less
hostile postwar world, overcome the psychological and economic
dislocations caused by internment. For the immediate problem of
Japanese ethnic unionism, though, the relocation was—as it was
for many things—the final solution.

---

32 *Rafu Shimpo*, March 26 and April 6, 1941; *Kashu Mainichi*, April 2, 1941; *Doho*,
April 15, 1941.

33 *Rafu Shimpo*, April 27, 1941; *Doho*, June 1, Aug. 1, and Oct. 5, 1941; *Los Angeles
Citizen*, Aug. 8, 1941; Togo Tanaka, "Journal," Aug. 20, 1941, typescript, in Japanese
Evacuation and Relocation Study Collection, folder A17.06; De Silva to Modell,
March 14, 1968.

34 After the Japanese returned to the coast. Local 1510 was not revived, and the
many Japanese workers who returned to retail produce joined 770 as a matter of
course. In 1952 *all* Japanese members of 770 were in produce, experiencing thereby
a form of "segregation, which, though not limiting a group to low status work, nevertheless limits them to certain functions within an industry . . . [and thereby] effectively limits job opportunities." The prewar definition of the Japanese in Los Angeles
retail produce, thus, was perpetuated at least until 1952 despite the fact that the war
had accomplished union integration. Scott Greer, "The Participation of Ethnic
Minorities in the Labor Unions of Los Angeles County" (unpublished Ph.D. dissertation, University of California, Los Angeles, 1952), 59.

Japanese Americans: The Development of a Middleman Minority

Harry H. L. Kitano

The author is professor of social welfare and sociology in the University of California, Los Angeles.

Most social systems contain a variety of positions between the ruling elite at the top and the dominated at the bottom. Minority groups often occupy the lower-status positions, but under certain circumstances they may rise to a higher niche, and play, for example, the role of a middleman minority. This essay will examine the development of the middleman minority position of Japanese Americans in the United States.

Recent scholarship suggests that the middleman role may result from a wide variety of factors—for example, differences in race, nationality, or religion. One of the most commonly cited examples is the historic experience of the Jew in Europe, but other prominent examples of middleman minorities include the Indian in Africa and the Chinese in Southeast Asia.[1] Perhaps the best description of the characteristics and functions of a middleman minority has been provided by sociologist Hubert Blalock, Jr. According to Blalock, such a group rises above the status of other minorities because of a competitive advantage or because of a high adaptive capacity.[2] Its

---

[1] Victor Purcell, *The Chinese in Modern Malaysia* (Rev. ed., Singapore, 1960); Richard J. Coughlin, *Double Identity: The Chinese in Modern Thailand* (Hong Kong, 1960); and Edgar Wickberg, *The Chinese in Philippine Life, 1850–1898* (New Haven, Conn., 1965).

[2] Hubert Blalock, Jr., *Toward a Theory of Minority Group Relations* (New York, 1967), 79–84.

members often occupy a special occupational niche, and, if the social system remains structurally stagnant, they may become "perpetual minorities." Drawing on examples from peasant-feudal econ-
omies, Blalock finds that the middleman minority acts as a buffer
between a numerically small elite ruling group and the large group
of peasants at the bottom of many societies. This buffer is numerically insignificant and represents, in the words of Lewis Coser, a kind
of "political eunuch," since its power is largely dependent on the
goodwill and tolerance of the power elite.[3] A challenge to the power
elite may result in the loss of protection and approval. On the other
hand, the middleman minority often must contend with the wrath
and frustration of those positioned lower in the system. The middleman's generally higher status and income relative to the subordi-
nated masses belie his weak and vulnerable position. As sociologist
Gary Hamilton has observed, the middleman minority occupies a
paradoxical "weak money" position; although it possesses revenues
and resources out of proportion to its numbers, its members are
relegated to a low status and are allowed only minor political and
social privileges.[4]

The middleman also serves as a convenient scapegoat. Blalock, in
writing about the Jews in Europe, notes: "During periodic crises,
such as major depressions, peasant uprisings, or epidemics such as
the Bubonic Plague, the Jew has been turned upon in a kind of
temporary coalition between the other two groups."[5] Because most
middlemen minorities such as the Jews absorb stress, they can play
an important role in preserving the stability of a social system by
serving as ready objects to drain off frustration and aggression. They
can also become the pawns or mediators in power struggles between
the upper and lower groups; they can provide a ready source of revenue; they can perform certain needed but distasteful economic functions; and they may be used to staff petty official roles that cannot
be entrusted to the masses.

Given such a vulnerable position it is difficult to understand why
a group of people would be content to serve as a middleman minority. Perhaps the best answer is that they have no choice, and are

---

3 Lewis A. Coser, "The Political Functions of Eunuchism," *American Sociological
Review,* XXIX (1964), 880–885.

4 Gary Hamilton, "Pariah Capitalism: A Paradox of Power and Dependence" (1972),
unpublished manuscript in possession of the author.

5 Blalock, *Toward a Theory of Minority Group Relations,* 82.

trapped in a social structure which shapes their adaptations. Drawing on this notion, several scholars have proposed models to explain the appearance of minorities in middleman positions. Blalock, for example, suggests that the answer may be found in the culture of a foreign group.[6] At first the group may develop competitive resources which permit a degree of upward mobility. Desperately wanting to succeed, its members rise above some of the other pariah groups, but they soon reach a ceiling. The barriers may be self imposed (for example, the group is reluctant to assimilate); but, more often, mobility is limited by a combination of the ethnic group culture and dominant group discrimination. The discrimination may be based on such variables as race, nationality, and religion, though race appears to be the dominant reason in the United States.[7] Therefore, the minority finds that, although it has arisen above the lower levels, it has been prevented from rising to the top, and has become a middleman minority. This model can be labeled *finding a place in the structure* to emphasize that social position is shaped by ethnic group interaction with the majority group. It reflects a dynamic and fluid process in which positions change as the participants themselves change.

Another model has been suggested by Gary Hamilton, who emphasizes the relationship between the economic role of the minority and the political power of those in authority. Although it too stresses the process that occurs in the development of a middleman minority, it also focuses upon the relatively fixed nature of certain occupational roles so that one can speak of ethnicized professions. The roles are maintained primarily through the political power of the dominant group, but the minority also receives benefits, such as control or monopoly over certain occupations and a status higher than the masses. This model accentuates the planned role of the middleman in the economic structure.[8] There may be an active recruitment as well as careful socialization and training for these roles. Such a development is closely linked to colonialism and European capitalism. While Blalock's model seems to approximate more closely the situation in the United States, Hamilton's appears to fit the situation

---

[6] *Ibid.*, 79–84, 120–121.

[7] Roger Daniels and Harry H. L. Kitano, *American Racism: Exploration of the Nature of Prejudice* (Englewood Cliffs, N.J., 1970).

[8] Hamilton, "Pariah Capitalism," *passim.*

under African and Asian colonialism. In the United States, most immigrant groups started at the bottom and some have worked their way up to the middleman position. In a more traditional colonial system, however, there has been a greater tendency to recruit and socialize groups into relatively fixed middleman positions. There are many examples of natives themselves being trained in Europe for the middle positions.[9]

Several interrelated factors are important in understanding the development and maintenance of a middleman minority. They include a) the visibility of the group, including its cultural styles and networks; b) the structure and response of the host culture; and c) the power relationships within that system. The degree of rigidity among these factors is related to the clarity of the position; conversely the degree of openness limits the development of any fixed role. We emphasize that the middleman concept will seldom achieve a perfect "fit" with any group in the United States, but can serve as a useful analytical tool for understanding the experiences of selected immigrants. We are also limiting the term to group phenomena.

It is the purpose of this paper to compare the experiences of the Japanese migrating to two areas, Hawaii and California, as a means of illustrating the middleman concept. All immigrant groups pass through various positions as they adapt to a new country so that length of stay, acculturation, and social position are intimately related. However, it is our observation that the Japanese in Hawaii are different from their cohorts in California. For example, the Japanese in Hawaii were never a small, scattered minority in a vast land but were a large, almost majority group on a few concentrated islands; they entered into a more racially tolerant society than their peers in California and they were one of a large number of imported nationality groups. Further, they were close enough to Japan so that homeland influences were much stronger than on the mainland.

Close observers generally agree that there are behavioral and

---

[9] A newspaper article appearing in the Washington, D.C., *Evening Star* on January 12, 1972, page B-11, points out the dilemma facing one Nigerian youngster who left his country to attend Eton College and is now faced with the question of "Who am I?" Does he belong to Nigeria, or England, or neither?

cultural differences between the groups. There is even a special Japanese vocabulary to differentiate between them—the *kotonk* for the mainlander and the *Buddahead* for the Japanese from Hawaii.[10] The general theme is that the Californian is overly concerned about surface appearances, too materialistic, too careful about impressing the majority groups, too acculturated, and, in one word, too "haolefied" (white).

Because of their numbers and relative cohesion it was inevitable that the Japanese in Hawaii would eventually gain some degree of power and achieve a wider dispersion in terms of occupation, political representation, and social status than their brothers and sisters in California. However, before concentrating on the Hawaiian-Californian comparison, a general background of the Japanese will be presented.

There is much written material about the Japanese in the United States. Although the literature deals with different time periods and is written from a variety of perspectives, it is in essential agreement on several points. Japanese immigration was relatively small; although there was an initial period of welcome, this soon changed to hostility and overt discrimination; and, in spite of the barriers, the Japanese achieved upward mobility, especially in professions requiring a strong educational background.[11]

An important consideration in the development of a middleman position appears to be the characteristics of the ethnic group itself. What that group brings to the interaction initially determines where its members fit into society and how they adjust. The Issei immigrants to both Hawaii and California were products of the Meiji era of Japan (1868–1912). The people of this period are currently the beneficiaries of a "heroic reputation," inspired partly by the nostalgia of older intellectuals for the "good old days." Terms such as loyal, hard working, honest, stoic, patient, patriotic, selfless, and persevering are closely associated with the people of the Meiji era. They were members of a vertical social structure where there

---

10 Dennis Ogawa, *Jan Ken Po* (Honolulu, 1973), 17.

11 See, for example, Hilary Conroy, *The Japanese Frontier in Hawaii* (Berkeley, 1953); Roger Daniels, *The Politics of Prejudice* (Berkeley, 1962); Yamato Ichihashi, *Japanese in the United States* (Stanford, Calif., 1932); Andrew W. Lind, *Hawaii's People* (3rd ed., Honolulu, 1967); Harry H. L. Kitano, *Japanese Americans: The Evolution of a Subculture* (Englewood Cliffs, N.J., 1969); and Bradford Smith, *Americans from Japan* (Philadelphia, Pa., 1949).

was limited upward mobility and where the group, rather than the individual, was considered of most importance.[12] Thus, one important characteristic of these Japanese—and a characteristic closely related to the middleman position—was their ability to understand and adapt to their places in the social structure. Family and bloodlines—as reflected in the "*i e* system," age, education, and sex —were all interrelated and established clear role positions. These Japanese married primarily within their own group, and they shared feelings of superiority towards non-Japanese, especially those from other Asian countries. Very few Japanese immigrants achieved, or expected to achieve, leadership or elite roles in either their home society or in the new country. On the other hand, very few would have been content to remain in the lowest positions. Thus, a combination of their values (hard work, thriftiness), their expectations (to rise, but not too high), their visibility (nonwhite), and their organization (family and community system) set the stage for their encounter with the United States.

The first major encounter occurred in Hawaii. Although 148 Japanese laborers came to Hawaii in 1868, significant Japanese immigration began after 1886. By 1890, some 12,610 Japanese were listed in the census, and by 1900 there were 61,111. This influx occurred during a period when large plantations were emerging in Hawaii. The white planters who came to dominate society were a mixture of Europeans and Americans drawn together by their relatively common culture. Many of them were "skilled artisans, professionals or tradesmen and hence enjoyed positions of prestige and affluence within the emerging economy of the Islands."[13]

The planters developed an economy that required a large, controllable labor force. Because the native population did not fit their labor needs, they had from the beginning looked for other populations—at first, the Chinese—to do the necessary manual labor. Soon, however, they had become fearful that there might be an "oversupply of this class of immigrants" and a "consequent loss of control over labor in general."[14] They then turned to the Portuguese, who were recruited chiefly between 1878 and 1887, and eventually to Germans, Koreans, Puerto Ricans, Norwegians, Russians, Micronesians, Melanesians, Filipinos, Scots, and Japanese in varying num-

---

[12] C. Nakane, *Japanese Society* (Berkeley and Los Angeles, 1970).
[13] Lind, *Hawaii's People*, 20.
[14] *Ibid.*, 27.

bers to man different positions in the plantation economy. With few exceptions, the nonwhite populations filled the lowest positions in the economic system.

The Japanese were initially welcomed because they worked hard, were thrifty, and learned to communicate in English. By 1910 (see Table 1), they constituted forty-two percent of Hawaii's population. Despite their large numbers, however, none were able to secure positions of power and prestige. These were reserved for the white elite. "Whether as the early tradesmen who could supply the natives with the foreign artifacts," writes Andrew Lind, ". . . or as missionaries who taught and advised on all matters . . . or as the planters . . . the Haoles [whites] expected and, for the most part, received a status superior to that of most natives and of all the immigrant labor groups."[15]

TABLE I

Proportion of Japanese in Hawaii
and in California by Decade

Year	Percentage of Japanese in Population of Hawaii	California
1900	39	.01
1910	42	.02
1920	43	.02
1930	38	.02
1940	37	.01
1950	37	.01
1960	32	.01
1970	28	.01

Source: U.S. Dept. of Commerce, Bureau of the Census, *Japanese, Chinese and Filipinos in the United States, 1970* (Washington, D.C., 1973).

Plantation strategy was to obtain maximum productivity from the laborers and to maintain a high degree of social control. One effective technique was to separate various nationality groupings into competing labor camps. Segregation and competition served as spurs to production and limited intergroup contact over racial and nationality lines. Wages were low (albeit higher than in the workers' native lands); the company store, the lack of alternative opportunities, and racial discrimination were means of maintaining a dependent supply of workers to work on the plantations.

The middleman positions on the plantation were filled by the

---

[15] *Ibid.*, 32.

overseers or *lunas,* usually white. They were the buffers between the masses of laborers on one side and the elite owners on the other. They absorbed much of the hostility, and, even today, memories of the brutality and autocratic styles of certain *lunas* are remembered.[16] A good insight into plantation life has been provided by Kazuo Miyamoto in his autobiographical novel, *Hawaii, End of the Rainbow.* Miyamoto graphically describes the grueling and monotonous labor under harsh, demanding *lunas* in the "Hawaiian paradise."[17] His story also contains a theme that is typically Issei—that hardship and sacrifice will eventually benefit the second generation children. The term *kodomo no tame ni* (for the sake of the children) reflected the ethos of a group that viewed family line as an important factor in their lives.

Most Japanese, like the members of most other ethnic minorities, were not content to remain as plantation laborers. Since the Japanese constituted a numerically large force, their collective actions posed a threat to the ruling white elite. A major crippling strike in 1909, followed by another in 1920, served notice that the Japanese worker expected better treatment and that his desire for upward mobility was a strong one.[18] One "solution" to curtail their possible influence was to limit the number of Japanese immigrants. The Gentlemen's Agreement of 1907–1908 between Japan and the United States restricted the flow of immigrant laborers, while the immigration law of 1924 formally ended Japanese immigration.

The immigration restrictions and the hostility on the plantations contrast sharply with Hawaii's popular tradition of racial tolerance. It is true that the early settlers, including the missionaries, were extremely tolerant of race, and that the initial outside contacts were guided by the business and market place in such a way as to minimize race prejudice. Nevertheless, it is equally true that the large landowners, primarily whites, manipulated the native rulers for their own benefit and imported thousands of ethnics for their labor. Many Japanese returned home after their disappointing sojourn in Hawaii, but the greater proportion remained and eventually be-

---

16 Recently in Hilo, many Japanese Americans told me stories about the Scottish bosses who were particularly noted for their "toughness."

17 Kazuo Miyamoto, *Hawaii, End of the Rainbow* (Rutland, Vt. and Tokyo, 1964), 101–104.

18 Ernest C. Wakukawa, *A History of the Japanese People in Hawaii* (Honolulu, 1938), 169.

came the dominant ethnic group in Hawaii. Still others, perhaps 40,000, left for California and the West Coast in search of better economic opportunities.[19]

In California, as in Hawaii, the Chinese preceded the Japanese. Significant Chinese immigration began about the time that gold was discovered in 1848, and although there was a short period of early welcome, by 1852 there was already a strong anti-Chinese sentiment. Nonetheless, many Chinese were employed to fill the labor vacuum caused by the gold rush and the scarcity of women domestics, and others eventually worked on the railroads. The anti-Chinese forces denounced the Chinese for being unassimilable, for practicing heathen customs, and for lowering wages and depressing the standard of living. Their defenders emphasized the desirability of their labor and also alluded to the undesirable ways of the Irish, who in the 1870s constituted the largest immigrant group in California, outnumbering the Chinese 75,000 to 60,000.[20]

By the time of the major Japanese immigration to California, the Chinese problem had been "solved" through a combination of harassment, intimidation, and immigration restrictions. Significant Japanese migration to the mainland began after 1890, and, by 1900, there were 85,000 Japanese in the United States. California was the principal mainland attraction; in 1900 there were 10,151 Japanese living there, and by 1930 that number had increased to 97,456. Nevertheless, they never constituted even one percent of the California population.[21]

As in Hawaii, the early Japanese immigrants started at the bottom of the ladder, working as laborers on the railroads, in the canneries, in logging, and in the mining, meat packing, and salt industries.[22] But the most attractive occupation was in agriculture where they worked as laborers and with the expectation that they would eventually own land. The idea of upward mobility and eventual equality for the Japanese was difficult for American racists to tolerate. At one stage the Japanese filled the role of ideal laborer—single, male, young, mobile, and hard working—but as they sought to move upward, to raise a family, to acquire land, and to achieve parity

19 Lind, *Hawaii's People*, 30.
20 Daniels and Kitano, *American Racism*, 41.
21 Kitano, *Japanese Americans*, 15.
22 *Ibid.*

with whites they aroused the suspicions and hostility of the majority group. Land ownership was restricted through the passage in 1913 of the California Alien Land Act, which provided that Japanese aliens could lease agricultural land for only three years and that lands already owned or leased could not be bequeathed. In 1920 an amended alien land law deprived the Japanese of the right to lease agricultural land. Other legislation interdicted marriage with whites, restricted immigration, and discriminated against Japanese in a host of other ways.[23]

For those Japanese who still managed to "pull themselves up," there were limited middleman positions available in agriculture, small businesses, and service trades. In agriculture many tried to circumvent the land laws by looking for white friends who might agree to purchase land for them. The situation was similar to the experiences of the Chinese in the Philippines during the eighteenth century. Some Chinese requested baptism as Catholics so that their Spanish "sponsors" could be counted upon as creditors, bondsmen, and protectors. The arrangement could be profitable for the godparent, especially if he acquired a protege with moneymaking talents.[24]

Another common arrangement was for a Japanese to lease agricultural lands or other property from a white landowner. He would work the land, hire fellow ethnics and other laborers to harvest the crops, and then pay off the man on top. But since many could not become the direct landowner, the hard work, ingenuity, and productivity were primarily for the benefit of others.

The alien land laws provide an interesting example of what we term the "Rashomon effect." The concept is drawn from the famous Japanese movie in which various actors report on a single event from their own perspectives. Since individuals respond to stimuli primarily from their own experiences and needs, their reactions to "social facts" may differ. For example, some non-Japanese scholars have examined land ownership figures and concluded that the Japanese in California were not adversely affected by the alien land laws. On the other hand, the findings of some ethnic scholars, including those of myself, suggest that the legislation had damaging effects on the Japanese community. Among other things, it lowered

---

23 *Ibid.*, 18.
24 Wickberg, *The Chinese in Philippine Life*, 191–192.

expectations, raised serious questions about the future of the Japanese in California, and heightened feelings of inferiority and difference at a time when the melting pot ethos was a part of the American dream.[25]

My father faced a typical situation. Although he would have preferred to own his own property, he felt that it was wiser to make other arrangements. He leased a hotel; the vulnerability of his position was clearly demonstrated during World War II when the Japanese were sent to the wartime relocation centers. His lease was canceled (he could not live up to the terms of the lease while incarcerated), and everything he had put into the property was lost.

One of the popular occupational areas in both California and Hawaii was the small, independent business. These usually involved a grocery, small hotel, or restaurant, where there was no need for a large capital investment. The establishments were typically family based and used labor intensive practices. They remained competitive by remaining open the year round and drew much of their business from the surrounding ethnic and other minority communities.[26] The sociologist, Edna Bonacich, writes that this type of small business is critical in explaining the middleman economic position. Because of the structure of the business and its high dependence on family and other ethnic members, the chances for rapid growth and development are limited.[27] This was especially true in California where dependence on ethnic clientele kept most businesses small.

The Japanese had other characteristics that were associated with middleman minorities. They resisted marrying non-Japanese; they established their own language and cultural schools; they maintained their own churches; and except for affairs that directly affected their group, they avoided an involvement in local politics. Bonacich attributes the persistence of these features to an early sojourner orientation.[28]

There were several factors that aided Japanese entrance into the American economic system. One was the vertical arrangement.

---

25 Harry H. L. Kitano, *Race Relations* (Englewood Cliffs, N.J., 1974), 6–10.

26 Kitano, *Japanese Americans*, 57–59; see also Ivan Light, *Ethnic Enterprise in America: Business and Welfare among Chinese, Japanese and Blacks* (Berkeley, Calif., 1972), 11–17.

27 Edna Bonacich, "A Theory of Middleman Minorities," *American Sociological Review*, XXXVIII (1973), 583–594.

28 *Ibid.*

whereby most phases of a business operation remained primarily within the group. For example, the entire process of raising, harvesting, packing, distributing, and selling vegetables was under the control of Japanese Americans. Another resource was the *tanomoshi*, which served as a sort of cooperative bank to provide a ready supply of capital to its members. The peak period for these occupational and economic structures was in the years before World War II.[29]

Events during World War II illustrated the vulnerable Japanese position, especially in California. The Japanese became scapegoats for some of the early American battlefield reverses; their property was confiscated or sold at depressed prices; and they were herded behind barbed wire. Even citizenship was insufficient protection, since all persons of Japanese ancestry, whether citizens or aliens, were placed in the relocation camps. Interestingly enough, there was no mass detention of the Japanese in the much more sensitive area of Hawaii.[30]

The numerically significant Japanese in Hawaii were vital to the economy of the islands; their size precluded any thought of a mass evacuation as it would have strained the logistical capabilities of the U.S. Navy. On the other hand, the visible, small, scattered Japanese in California were easily uprooted and placed in concentration camps. The small business, leased-land type of economy could be swiftly absorbed with no great loss to the overall system, although the Japanese contributions to agriculture (especially in the area of vegetables) were temporarily missed.

The rather remarkable story of the Japanese Americans after World War II has prompted some to call them America's most successful minority. After release from the concentration camps in the mid 1940s, their rise has been steady. By 1970, median Japanese family income was over $13,000 so that, as a group, they have clearly risen above the basement. Associated with this rise has been their high achievement in education and entrance into professions.[31]

However, even though upward mobility has been common, it is the hypothesis of this paper that it has taken place primarily into middle and professional positions. Japanese secretaries are in high

29 Kitano, *Japanese Americans*, 18–20.

30 *Ibid.*, 30–45.

31 U.S. Dept. of Commerce, Bureau of the Census, *Japanese, Chinese and Filipinos in the United States, 1970* (Washington, D.C., 1973), 44.

demand because they work hard and are productive; public school teaching, which was virtually closed until the 1950s, has opened up; and many Japanese are in the Civil Service. Contract gardening and agriculture remain popular, with the major shift being a closer identification with management than with labor.[32]

Perhaps the most impressive statistic is the move into the professional category. In 1970, the modal occupational category for the Japanese in California was professional.[33] In contrast, the Japanese in Hawaii were spread out much more evenly in terms of occupation.[34]

Other data from the census of 1970 illustrate the degree of economic "success" for the Japanese American in California and Hawaii. The mean family income was $13,370 in California and $14,618 in Hawaii.[35] Only 7.7% of the group had incomes below the poverty level in California, while an even lower 4.8% fell into this category in Hawaii.[36] Housing patterns also reflect the increased affluence and mobility. The pre-World War II ghettos have been replaced by a move to the suburbs and middle-class areas. By 1970, the median value of homes owned by Japanese Americans in California was $25,400 and in Hawaii, $34,000.[37] However, it should also be noted that the cost of living in Hawaii and in California are among the highest in the country.

Part of the reason for the socioeconomic rise of Japanese Americans is due to educational achievement. In 1960 the Japanese in California had the most years of schooling among all groups.[38] And in 1970, the median number of school years completed was 12.3 in Honolulu and 12.6 in Los Angeles.[39]

Our examples of mobility center primarily around the areas of education, income, and occupation. There is little question that the Japanese have risen above the lower levels of the American system, but the question in dealing with the middleman concept is,

---

32 Kitano, *Japanese Americans*, 52–59.
33 U.S. Dept. of Commerce, Bureau of the Census, *Japanese, Chinese and Filipinos*, 40.
34 *Ibid.*
35 *Ibid.*
36 *Ibid.*, 44.
37 *Ibid.*
38 Kitano, *Japanese Americans*, 48.
39 U.S. Dept. of Commerce, Bureau of the Census, *Japanese, Chinese and Filipinos*, 11.

have they gotten to the top? Or, more realistically, has the ethnic group achieved a more random distribution in the social system? These questions are important because one symptom of a middleman minority is the rise from the bottom, but to limited positions in the middle.

Another hypothesized characteristic of a middleman minority is its differential status on a number of variables, as was mentioned earlier in the discussion of the "weak money" paradox. The middleman minority may achieve success on certain indicators, such as income and education, but may still rank low in other areas, such as social status and power.

In Los Angeles, the Japanese (as well as other Asian Americans, blacks, Chicanos, and Jews), even if they have overcome the barriers of education and income, are generally excluded from the "country club" and elite settings where much of the power and social status is concentrated.[40] The situation in Hawaii is different. For example, the current mayor of Honolulu, a white, is married to a Japanese woman; moreover, according to Dennis Ogawa of the University of Hawaii, there are Japanese names on the membership rolls of the high status island clubs.[41]

But social status is not the only problem area. Progress in the way that Japanese Americans are depicted in the mass media (for example, movies and television) remains minimal. Many of the old stereotypes persist, and there is little exposure of Japanese Americans (or other Asians), except as exotics, menials, or as products of an alien culture. Aside from an occasional "Flower Drum Song," Asian performers find little steady employment, so that type casting in the cook-houseboy-loyal follower image remains. When there is an opportunity for an Asian "hero," the role is often given to a Caucasian.[42]

For whatever reasons, it is our observation that many Japanese

---

[40] Kitano, *Race Relations*, 124.

[41] Interview with Dennis Ogawa, associate professor of American studies, University of Hawaii, July 9, 1974. According to Professor Ogawa, the admission of Japanese Americans to the exclusive clubs may reflect a policy of tokenism, but it also reflects the increased power of the Japanese on the islands. See also Frederick Samuels, *The Japanese and the Haoles of Honolulu* (New Haven, Conn., 1970), 112–113, for a discussion of the Pacific Club, which in 1968 quietly admitted two Asian Americans and ended a 117-year policy of limiting membership to Caucasians.

[42] The most recent example is that of the television program, "Kung Fu," in which David Carradine plays the role of the Asian. The various non-Asian Charlie Chans are an example from the past.

Americans in Hawaii and California have retained their conservative orientation. The less-than-equal perspective brought over from
Japan appears to have survived in modified form in spite of the
change in generations. The feeling that the "top" and most prestigious positions are reserved for whites dies hard. The "best houses,"
the "best looking people," and the most envied life styles were the
province of the dominant group for so long that these perceptions
have become the realities. The quest to be accepted by the group
in power led to a strategy of high achievement, conformity, productivity, and a rise above the basement, but in such a way as not
to threaten the status of the dominant group. However, the recent
emphasis on ethnic identity and ethnic pride is no doubt affecting
this orientation.

In most of the above areas, the Japanese in Hawaii and California
were essentially similar. However, there are differences in a number of critical areas. For example, the Japanese in Hawaii are in a
dominant position, whereas this is not the case with their cohorts
on the mainland. Since the groups were initially similar, an analysis
of such factors as visibility, discrimination, and power may provide
clues to explain the differential development.

Visibility has been an important middleman factor in other settings. The Chinese in the Philippines and the Indian in Africa
were visible. The Jews in Europe were also visible, not because of
race (although they were considered an inferior race by the Nazis),
but because of religion, occupation, and culture. It is debatable
whether the Japanese in Hawaii were more visible (through sheer
numbers, but in the context of multi-Asian groups) than in California (where Asians stand out by being such a small minority).
Therefore, visibility, although important in understanding the
different experiences of Japanese in Hawaii and California, is not
the most important factor in explaining the differences between
Japanese in the two areas.

Discrimination has been another important factor. For example,
the Chinese and Indians in foreign lands had great difficulty in
obtaining citizenship and access to equal opportunities. Similarly,
the initial immigrant Issei did not acquire citizenship until 1954,
and they faced the constant barriers of racism encountered by most
Japanese for a greater portion of their history. The acquisition of
citizenship through birth by the Nisei was an extremely important

step in modifying the effects of discrimination. Associated with discrimination are prejudice, disadvantage, stereotyping, and isolation. All combine to create relatively fixed positions for a minority. It is possible to argue that, in relative terms, the Hawaiian experience was less traumatic than the California experience so that it is an important factor in describing a middleman position. The differential treatment of the Japanese in the two areas during World War II is a case in point.

But the most important factor in changing any position is power. The Chinese in the Philippines, the Jews in Europe, and probably all middleman minorities, known or unknown, are caught in powerless positions. The causes of the powerlessness may vary—for example, lack of citizenship, limited resources, or small population —but whatever the reason, the acquisition of power is the sine qua non for change. The Japanese in Hawaii had numerical superiority, so that once these numbers could be organized, there was an opportunity for change. It was the Nisei, especially after their experiences during World War II, who were able to challenge the political status quo. They were numerically strong; they were citizens; and they had ties based on ethnicity, culture, nationality, and kinship. They were well educated; and many had volunteered and fought valiantly in the United States armed forces (in segregated units under white officers). By the time Hawaii became a state, the Japanese American was no longer content to settle for a second-class status.

In his autobiography, Senator Daniel Inouye recalled the 1954 campaign where a young inexperienced group of Nisei war veterans and their allies began their challenge of the long entrenched Republican political machine. Individuals who were in that original group included John Burns, eventually to be governor; Spark Matsunaga of the 100th Infantry Battalion and currently senior member of the Hawaiian delegation to the U.S. House of Representatives; Masato Doi of the 442nd Infantry Regiment, chairman of the city council and eventually a circuit judge.[43] The success of the Japanese American political breakthrough in Hawaii since the early 1950s has been one of major proportions. Currently, Senator Daniel Inouye and Representatives Spark Matsunaga and Patsy Mink are Japanese Americans in the United States Congress.

---

[43] Daniel K. Inouye, *Journey to Washington* (Englewood Cliffs, N.J., 1967), 242–245.

The number of Japanese Americans in the Hawaiian state government is high. For example, according to the 1971–1972 edition of the *Who's Who in Government in Hawaii,* there were eleven Japanese Americans in the state senate, and Japanese Americans comprised over fifty percent of the membership of the state house of representatives. The attorney general was Japanese American, and Japanese Americans headed the Departments of Budget and Finance, Education, Labor and Industrial Relations, Land and Natural Resources, Personnel Services, Regulatory Agencies, Taxation, and Transportation.[44]

But Americans elsewhere may not be as ready as the people in Hawaii to recognize the abilities and qualities of the Japanese American. For example, the recent Watergate hearings have pushed several senators to prominence, including Senator Inouye. Although he is among the most impressive, public discussion of presidential candidates consciously ignores this Japanese American from Hawaii. Of course, it is possible that no one from a state as small as Hawaii would be seriously mentioned as a presidential candidate, but Japanese Americans find it difficult to discount the majority group feeling that the middle positions are considered more appropriate for them. For example, even in Hawaii there has been no Japanese American candidate for the "top" position of governor until today.[45]

The same orientation holds for most other positions in American society. Since very few Japanese expect to obtain positions of prominence and leadership, there develops a self-fulfilling prophecy and a stereotype about the lack of leadership qualities among them. Some hypothesized psychological correlates of groups caught in the middleman position include status anxiety, fear of marginality, and constant questions of identity.[46]

I have detected many of these feelings in my appearances before various Japanese groups, especially on the mainland. The "Who am I" and "How do I fit into this society" themes reflect the questions of people who are unsure and dissatisfied with the relatively fixed positions that are realistically available, and yet are

---

44 Chamber of Commerce of Hawaii, *Who's Who in Government in Hawaii, 1971–1972* (Honolulu, 1972).

45 At this writing, George Ariyoshi has just won election as governor.

46 Kitano, *Japanese Americans,* 96–97.

also proud of having risen from the basement of the social system.

The term middleman minority was used to analyze the position of the Japanese in the United States. In an "ideal model," the middleman would be characterized by visibility, hemmed in by discriminatory barriers, powerless, and limited to certain occupations and status positions. Insofar as the Japanese experience reflects these features, it demonstrates the existence of the middleman position. The familiar phrase, "caught in the middle," is a recognition of this common position in all social systems. In the economic world there is the middleman between producer and consumer; in the family there is often a middle sib; social work and law enforcement are professional middleman positions. My focus has been on a particular ethnic group caught in the middleman position and on the factors which help to explain the development. The process was hypothesized as the interaction among what the immigrants brought with them, the ambience of the host culture, and the visibility and power of the immigrant group.

As noted, the Japanese immigrant came from the lower and lower-middle classes, often the groups most highly conforming to the norms of the culture. Most "knew their place in society," and although there was high motivation to achieve some degree of upward mobility (especially financially), there was also a limit to their expectations; becoming members of a ruling or more powerful elite was not a part of their dreams. They came with a hard-work, high-savings ethic, a strong ingroup orientation, and a high ethnic identification. They maintained their cohesiveness and identity through a strong community and family system. Since they married primarily within the group, they remained structurally pluralistic, partly through their own preferences and partly because of discriminatory practices by the group in power. Horizontal interaction was limited because of the pluralistic structures which emphasized differences. Within the subculture, however, values which emphasized high achievement and education prepared the Japanese to compete in the larger world.

But the America that they encountered was a relatively closed system. The immigrants started at the bottom of the ladder; discriminatory laws forbade citizenship; prejudice and segregation meant that the Japanese were avoided, isolated, and placed at a competitive disadvantage. But in areas where discrimination was not as strong, the group made progress. Education represented the opportunity toward mobility, even though this avenue was used primarily by generations other than the Issei.

It is difficult to appreciate the relative openness of the American system (especially for those of "white" backgrounds) until one spends a period of time in countries where there remain virtually permanent positions based on birth, family, and "acceptable backgrounds." Most Asian and European countries do not automatically grant full citizenship rights to "foreigners," even those born in the country. The granting of American citizenship to the Japanese (Nisei) born in the United States was one important factor in modifying power relationships, especially in an area like Hawaii. But the interaction between the Japanese and the American system fostered the development of a middleman perspective. Very few Japanese expected to achieve leadership positions in the larger society, and most were content merely to rise above the bottom. The dominant community was content to tolerate the ethnic community as long as its members behaved in a less than equal manner.

However, there are many recent changes affecting the Japanese in the United States. One is continued acculturation, so that each generation takes the Japanese further away from the culture of their Issei ancestors of Meiji Japan. Another is the continued upward social mobility of Japanese Americans and the rising rates of intermarriage. As Akemi Kikumura and Harry Kitano have recently reported, the rates of intermarriage in such areas as Honolulu, Fresno, San Francisco, and Los Angeles are at the fifty percent level.[47] This may mean an eventual decrease in the visibility of Japanese Americans; it is an indication of lessening discrimination and a rise in power which should diminish their middleman position.

The dilemma of the Japanese American is also reflected in the position of the Japanese nation. It is interesting to note that a recent best seller in Japan was the book, *The Japanese and the Jews*.[48] The author described the difficulty facing groups and nations caught in the middle. Citing the experiences of the Jews, he warned

---

[47] Akemi Kikumura and Harry H. L. Kitano, "Interracial Marriage: A Picture of the Japanese Americans," *Journal of Social Issues*, XXIX (1973), 67–81.

[48] Ben Dasan, *The Japanese and the Jews* (New York, 1972).

the Japanese that the role of middleman is an especially precarious one. Echoing the same warning was Paul Ehrlich, who, in a 1973 speech in Tokyo, underscored Japan's difficult middle-nation position.[49] Its highly industrialized capacity, coupled with its lack of natural resources, has forced Japan to play the role of economic middleman.

Well-meaning spokesmen for Japanese Americans also talk about a middleman position. They feel that the Japanese American can provide the linkage between whites and blacks, or become the mediator between Japan and the United States. Because so many of them are presently positioned in the middle, the role may be a natural one, but one purpose of this paper is to warn about the consequences of such a choice.

---

[49] Paul Ehrlich, "The Population-Resource-Environment Crisis," manuscript in possession of the author.

Filipinos in the United States

H. Brett Melendy

The author is professor of history in the University of Hawaii.

For most of the twentieth century, Filipinos have been part of the flow of Asian newcomers to Hawaii and to the western shores of the continental United States. The migration has come largely as two distinct movements. The first influx during the 1920s consisted primarily of agricultural workers, while the second, occurring after 1965, was made up of people with a wider range of interests and skills. Since 1968, the Philippines have led all Asian countries in the number of new immigrants, and since 1970 it has led all other nations except Mexico.[1] The purpose of this paper is to review the two major periods of Filipino immigration to Hawaii and to the mainland United States, to discuss the motives of the immigrants, and to describe American attitudes toward the newcomers. Thus far, neither scholars nor the general public have paid much attention to Filipino Americans. Only during the 1930s, when this "third wave" of Asian immigrants who followed upon the heels of the Chinese and Japanese appeared to create problems for West Coast nativists, was any attention given to them or to their problems in becoming part of America's pluralistic society.[2] It is

---

[1] U.S. Commissioner of Immigration and Naturalization, *Annual Report, 1972* (Washington, D.C., 1973), 59.

[2] Filipino immigration and settlement in the United States have not been the subject of intensive study; there is no comprehensive study of those Filipinos migrating since 1965. The major monograph for the first migration period is the work commissioned by the American Council on the Institute of Pacific Relations: Bruno Lasker, *Filipino Immigration to Continental United States and Hawaii* (Chicago, 1931). Other important monographs are John H. Burma, *Spanish-Speaking Groups in the United States* (Durham, N.C., 1954), and Carey McWilliams, *Brothers Under the Skin* (Rev. ed., Boston, 1964). Filipinos have written significant accounts of their immigration and adaptation experiences; see, for example, Manuel Buaken, *I Have Lived with the American People* (Caldwell, Idaho, 1948), and Maximo C. Manzon. *The Strange Case of the Filipinos in the United States* (New York, 1938). The journal,

hoped that this paper will encourage a closer look at these much-neglected people.

For two decades following the annexation in 1898 of the Philippine Islands by the United States, those Filipinos migrating to the mainland came primarily as college and university students. United States citizens welcomed them as trainees in democracy who would eventually return to their islands, carrying the message of democracy to their own people.[3]

Though the students, few in number, pioneered the Pacific crossing, the first major influx experienced by the West Coast occurred during the 1920s. Filipino arrivals increased sharply after 1924 when a new immigration act excluded Japanese immigrants. With the elimination of Japanese labor, California farmers had to find other workers to perform the seasonal tasks in the fields and orchards. Workers were also sought by the salmon cannery industries of the Pacific Northwest and Alaska. Since white Americans were not available in sufficient supply, western employers turned to the Philippines and Mexico for relief. The use of labor from these countries proved temporary, however, for during the depression years of the 1930s the number of available white workers increased. In the face of declining employment opportunities and increasing racial prejudice, the number of Filipinos migrating to the West Coast dropped sharply during this decade.[4]

Filipino immigration to the Hawaiian Islands occurred at the same time as the movement to the West Coast, but it differed in some respects with that to the mainland. Immigration to Hawaii was tied to the fortunes of the islands' sugar companies. Following the 1907–1908 Gentlemen's Agreement, whereby Japan restricted the number of laborers migrating to the islands and to the mainland, the plantations faced a shortage of field and mill hands. From 1907 through 1919, the Hawaiian Sugar Planters' Association experimented with Filipino labor as a replacement for the Japanese. When the experiment proved successful, there followed for a decade after 1919 a heavy influx of workers from the Far East archipelago. During the decade of the 1930s, however, in the face of demand for exclusion and a labor surplus in Hawaii, the number of

---

Sociology and Social Research, has published many analytical articles about these people.

3 Carlos P. Romulo, I Walked with Heroes (New York, 1961), 130–154.

4 Burma, Spanish-Speaking Groups, 138.

migrating Filipinos dropped to a trickle. The one exception occurred in 1946 when, just prior to independence for the new Asian republic, some 7,361 Filipinos migrated to the Territory of Hawaii. Many came at that particular time because they expected easy access to Hawaii to end when the quota system went into effect following Philippine independence. Others came in response to a growing postwar need for labor on Hawaii's sugar plantations. Their arrival was encouraged by the Hawaiian Sugar Planters' Association, which requested the United States Department of Interior, under the terms of the Tydings-McDuffie Act of 1934, to arrange for Filipino immigrants to meet the sugar industry's labor shortage.[5]

The Philippines gained independence on July 4, 1946. Two days earlier, Congress made Filipinos eligible for naturalization in the United States. On July 4, President Harry Truman issued a proclamation fixing the annual quota at 100. This quota remained in effect for two decades.[6] On October 3, 1965, President Lyndon B. Johnson signed a law nullifying prior quotas and abolishing the long-standing national origins system. Under the new legislation, immigration was not based on ethnic considerations, but rather upon the occupational needs of the United States and whether or not a would-be immigrant had relatives in the United States.[7] The latter consideration, in particular, led to increased immigration from Asia, including, of course, the Philippines.

Those Filipinos coming in the wake of the 1965 legislation, as well as those arriving earlier, were representative of at least three different island cultures. Most immigrants, therefore, had to adjust to their own differing cultures as well as to an American culture. For many this intracultural adjustment did not come easily. The Visayan Islands, situated in and around the Visayan Sea, provided one distinct immigrant group with its own language. Those from the Manila area, with easy access to both immigration and transportation agents, formed another group. Their native language, Ta-

[5] Sister Mary Dorita Clifford, "The Hawaiian Sugar Planters' Association and Filipino Exclusion," *The Filipino Exclusion Movement, 1927–1935* (Quezon City, Philippines Institute of Asian Studies, Occasional Papers No. 1, 1967), 14–28; Lasker, *Filipino Immigration*, 350–353; interview with James Misajon, chairman, Hawaii State Commission on Manpower and Full Employment, Dec. 18, 1972.

[6] *U. S. Statutes at Large*, LX, 416, 1353.

[7] *Ibid.*, LXXIX, 911–922; *New York Times*, Oct. 6, 1965, p. 1; U.S. Commissioner of Immigration and Naturalization, *Report, 1970* (Washington, D.C., 1971), 4.

galog, is spoken by more Filipinos than is any of the other eighty or so dialects. The two northern provinces on the island of Luzon, Ilocos Norte and Ilocos Sur, have been and still are the source of most of the immigrants. Their native languge is Ilocano. Two-thirds to three-fourths of all persons of Filipino descent or origin in the United States have come from one of these two Luzon provinces.[8]

Some additional statistics will help put Filipino immigration into sharper relief. By 1920, just prior to the earliest period of heavy immigration, there were more than four times as many Filipinos in Hawaii than on the mainland. They numbered 21,031, most of whom had been brought in on an experimental basis by the sugar growers. Those on the mainland numbered only about 5,600. Most immigrants of the 1920s were single males who were quite young, either in their teens or early twenties. Of those entering California between 1925 and 1929, some 22,767 were males and 1,356 were females. One-third of the males were between 16 and 21 years of age, while another 48 percent were in the 22–29 age range. In Hawaii, the sex imbalance was also present: 42,186 males, 1,468 females, and 750 listed as children.[9]

By 1930, as a result of the growing need for additional labor, the number of Filipinos in Hawaii rose to 63,052, an increase of nearly 66 percent, while the mainland's share during the same decade grew by 88 percent to a total of 45,208.[10] An indication of the rapidity of growth is shown in the figures for the last five years of the 1920s. During these years, 21,123 Filipinos entered through California ports, while some 44,404 entered through Honolulu.[11] With this large influx during the late 1920s, the Filipinos, when compared with other Asian groups, were a rapidly growing minority. In 1920 there were 85,146 Chinese and 220,284 Japanese in the United States and the Territory of Hawaii. Ten years later there were 102,133 Chinese and 278,645 Japanese.[12]

---

8 Horacio Lava, *Levels of Living in the Ilocos Region* (University of the Philippines, College of Business Administration, Study No. 1, 1938); Henry T. Lewis, *Ilocano Rice Farmers* (Honolulu, 1971), 6.

9 Lasker, *Filipino Immigration*, 351; Calif. Dept. of Industrial Relations, *Facts about Filipino Immigration into California* (Sacramento, 1930), 37–38.

10 Andrew W. Lind, *Hawaii's People* (Honolulu, 1967), 28; Trinidad A. Rojo, "Social Maladjustment Among Filipinos in the United States," *Sociology and Social Research*, XXI (1937), 446–457.

11 Burma, *Spanish-Speaking Groups*, 141–145; Lasker, *Filipino Immigration*, 324–325; Manzon, *Strange Case of the Filipinos*, 7.

12 H. Brett Melendy, *The Oriental Americans* (New York, 1972), 183, 187.

During the 1930s, the number of Filipinos on both Hawaii and the mainland remained at about the same level. By World War II, many of the older immigrants had returned home, while the younger Filipinos, who made up the vast majority of the immigrants, had decided to remain in the United States. Since World War II, each decade has seen a substantial increase in the number of immigrating Filipinos. Most of those who came to the mainland continued to settle in California, where, by 1970, 40 percent of the total Filipino population was located. Only 4 percent lived in New York, the mainland state with the second largest population, while Illinois and Washington had but 3.6 percent and 3.4 percent, respectively.[13]

With the diversification of California's industries during and after World War II, Filipinos congregated primarily where many of their fellows had lived during the 1920s and 1930s—in the San Francisco Bay area and Los Angeles. During the 1950s, Filipinos in California continued to shift, as did the general population, from rural to urban areas—from 60 percent in the cities in 1950 to 80 percent in 1960.[14] By comparison, the shift in Hawaii was

TABLE I
Filipinos in the United States

	1920	1930	1940	1950	1960	1970
Mainland	5,603a	45,208b	45,563c	61,636d	107,669e	241,051g
Hawaiif	21,031	63,052	52,659	61,062	68,641	95,680g
TOTAL	26,634	108,260	98,132	122,698	176,310	336,731
Mainland States: Subtotals						
California			31,408c	40,424d	65,459e	135,248g
New York			2,978	3,719	5,403	14,045
Illinois			----	----	3,587	12,355
Washington			2,222	4,224	7,110	11,488

a Lasker, *Filipino Immigration*, 349.

b Rojo, "Social Maladjustment Among Filipinos in the United States," 447.

c U.S. Bureau of the Census, *Nonwhite Population by Race, 1940* (Washington, D.C., 1943), 109.

d *Ibid., 1950* (Washington, D.C., 1953), 65.

e Calif. Dept. of Industrial Relations, *Californians of Japanese, Chinese, Filipino Ancestry*, 16.

f Hawaiian figures for 1920–1960 are from Lind, *Hawaii's People*, 28.

g U.S. Bureau of the Census, *Japanese, Chinese, and Filipinos in the United States, 1970* (Washington, D.C., 1973), 119.

---

13 U.S. Bureau of the Census, *Subject Reports: Japanese, Chinese and Filipinos in the United States, 1970* (Washington, D.C., 1973), 119.

14 Calif. Dept. of Industrial Relations, *Californians of . . . Filipino Ancestry*, 10; Burma, "The Background of the Current Situation of Filipino-Americans," *Social Forces*, XXX (1951), 42–47.

TABLE II
Filipino Immigration to the United States
1948–1971[a]

Year	Immigrants	Year	Immigrants
1948	1,122	1960	2,954
1949	1,068	1961	2,738
1950	595	1962	3,437
1951	760	1963	3,618
1952	1,066	1964	3,006
1953	1,160	1965	3,130
1954	1,633	1966	6,093
1955	1,784	1967	10,865
1956	1,873	1968	16,731
1957	1,996	1969	20,744
1958	2,236	1970	31,203
1959	2,633	1971	28,471
		1972	29,376

[a]U.S. Immigration and Naturalization Service, *Annual Report, 1957* (Washington, D.C., 1958), 37; *Annual Report, 1961* (Washington, D.C., 1962), 43; *Annual Report, 1972* (Washington, D.C., 1973), 59.

slight—only 2 percent.[15] Yet Honolulu possesses the largest Filipino population of any United States city. Other mainland cities, besides those in California, which have developed sizable Filipino populations since the early 1950s are, in order of rank, Seattle, Chicago, New York, and Washington, D.C.[16]

TABLE III
Number of Filipinos Residing in the City of Honolulu
1930–1970

Year	Number
1930	4,776[a]
1940	6,887[b]
1950	17,372[c]
1960	21,807[d]
1970	29,481[e]

[a] U.S. Bureau of the Census, *Population (Second Series), 1940: Characteristics of the Population, Hawaii* (Washington, D.C., 1943), 5.
[b] *Ibid.*
[c] U.S. Bureau of the Census, *Characteristics of the Population, 1950,* II, Part 52, *Hawaii* (Washington, D.C., 1953), 22.
[d] U.S. Bureau of the Census, *Characteristics of the Population, 1960,* I, Part 13, *Hawaii* (Washington, D.C., 1963), 31.
[e] U.S. Bureau of the Census, *General Population Characteristics, 1970: Hawaii* (Washington, D.C., 1971), 27.

[15] Lind, *Hawaii's People*, 28, 50.
[16] Francis J. Brown and Joseph S. Roucek, ed., *One America* (3rd ed., New York, 1952), 361–372.

In 1960, the Filipinos had the following statistical profile: Men in California and Hawaii were older than women. In California, the largest male age group (33 percent) was between the ages of 25 and 34. In Hawaii, 51 percent of the men were in the 45–64 age group, and 29 percent of the women were in the 25–34 age group. The change in the immigration law in 1965 had by 1970 produced a major impact on the age of Filipino immigrants. California's largest male group (62 percent) was under twenty-one years of age. The largest female group (56 percent) was also under twenty-one years of age. The same was true in Hawaii, where 58 percent of the males and 45 percent of the females were under twenty-one.[17]

The motivation for Filipino immigrants during the period of the first influx and after 1965 was the same. They came to the United States in response to economic factors in this country and because of local conditions in the islands. During the 1920s and 1930s, their life plan did not differ greatly from that of other Asians or most Europeans. Many Ilocanos, for example, left their homes for the United States or Hawaii in an effort to assist their families. The lure of comparatively high salaries attracted many who sought to improve their families' economic condition. A common pattern was for the family to mortgage a portion of its land in order to send one son to the United States. In turn he would send money home to pay off the mortgage or to assist a brother to obtain higher education.[18]

The young immigrant's persistent dream was to return home and reestablish his life in familiar surroundings. Any *Hawaiiano* who returned to Norte or Sur Ilocos to buy land became a person of prestige and economic prominence.[19] From 1920 through 1934, as young immigrants arrived at West Coast and Honolulu docks, others returned to their Filipino homes. The number leaving the United States in any one year during these fourteen years ranged from 16 percent to 50 percent of the arrivals for the same year.[20]

As with other immigrant groups, the dreams and hopes that motivated the Filipinos' ambitions frequently did not materialize.

---

17 U.S. Bureau of Census, *Nonwhite Population, 1960* (Washington, D.C., 1963), 88; U.S. Bureau of the Census, *Japanese, Chinese, and Filipinos in the United States, 1970*, 123–124.

18 Lewis, *Ilocano Rice Farmers*, 92.

19 *Ibid.*, 26.

20 Burma, *Spanish-Speaking Groups*, 138.

Wages, which appeared to be extraordinary when viewed from the Philippines, were quickly consumed by a much higher cost of living in the United States. Education often proved more difficult to obtain than had been anticipated by those seeking additional learning experiences. Young men, with a strong sense of pride, did not want to return home as acknowledged failures. While at first not too concerned about adjusting to their new environment, they found that they had to remain a longer time than they had originally planned in order to gain enough money to return home a success. But because they were "birds of passage," they had no inclination to become part of American society. As late as 1944, many Filipinos who had arrived before 1934 still clung to the hope that they would return home. J. C. Dionisio, a member of President Manuel Quezon's World War II exile government, explained the feelings held by those California Filipinos he had interviewed:

The tragedy of our life in America . . . is that it has been predicated on wishful thinking—"I want to go home." We have been sentimental rather than realistic. "Why should I plan, why should I take life seriously here, when this is only an interlude in my life? I am going home. It is there where I am going to take root."
Birds of passage, Mr. President, do not plan. They drift aimlessly.[21]

California agriculture came to rely in large measure upon these men who were caught in a trap, partly of their own making. The state's major farming regions—the Imperial Valley, the San Joaquin Valley, the Delta Region, and the Salinas Valley—relied upon cheap migratory labor to produce a variety of crops. During the 1920s most Filipinos in the Delta area, near Stockton, worked in the asparagus fields. The Salinas Valley, another major Filipino center, has over the years provided seasonal work in the lettuce fields and packing sheds.

Because of the nature of the agricultural work, Filipinos migrated back and forth among farming regions and the larger cities in California and the Pacific Northwest. In his definitive study of the first period of Filpino immigration, Bruno Lasker noted that in 1931 Seattle's summer population of Filipinos consisted of only a few hundred. During the winter, however, some 3,500 of them moved

21 J. C. Dionisio to Manuel Quezon, March 7, 1944, Manuel L. Quezon Papers, National Library of the Philippines, Ermiita, Manila.

into the city's ghettos. Stockton's Filipino summer population during the asparagus season of the same year was 6,000, while its winter population was only a thousand.[22] During the winter Stockton's temporary residents went to Los Angeles or San Francisco to seek other employment and to share with their fellow countrymen the varied experiences of urban living.

This shift from urban to rural to urban was a common way of life for these men, and it has been graphically described by Manuel Buaken, a former field hand. In 1927, after failing to find a city job, he left Los Angeles for Stockton's "Little Manila," the principal Filipino center on the West Coast. He found the city filled with other Filipinos searching for work, but he finally secured employment pulling celery seedlings and transplanting them. He also harvested onions, carrots, and potatoes. His first job paid $2.50 a day plus room and board for a six-day work week. At the end of the season, five months later, he had earned $500.[23] Nationally in 1927, farm workers were earning $2.28 for a ten-hour day, while factory workers made $5.52.[24] The average wage for Filipinos during the 1930 season, three years later, was $600. During the depression, wages sank to $300 a season.[25] It should be noted that "meaningful comparisons" between California farm labor wages and those in other occupations are difficult to make. Even a comparison between various agricultural segments and groups is hard to draw because of piecework payments in many crops.[26]

In general, Filipinos were among the lowest paid agricultural workers during the 1920s and 1930s. This situation is partially explained by racial considerations. Carey McWilliams, in *Factories in the Field*, reported that California farmers in 1937, and in earlier years, paid workers on the basis of race. A study by Harry Schwartz bears out this fact of racial discrimination. His 1928 study showed that farmers employing both white and nonwhite workers paid

[22] Lasker, *Filipino Immigration*, 21.

[23] Buaken, *I Have Lived with the American People*, 59–64.

[24] Harry Schwartz, *Seasonal Farm Labor in the United States* (New York, 1945), 154.

[25] Lillian Galedo, Laurena Cabanero, and Brian Tom, *Roadblocks to Community Building: A Case Study of the Stockton Community Center Project* (Davis, Calif.: University of California Asian American Research Project Working Publication No. 4, 1970, mimeographed), 8.

[26] Lloyd H. Fisher, *The Harvest Labor Market in California* (Cambridge, Mass., 1953), 11.

higher wages to the white. At that time only Mexicans and blacks earned less than Filipinos.[27] Another factor causing the Filipinos to receive lower wages was their own actions. As had the Japanese earlier, they undercut other field labor, such as the Mexicans, by accepting lower wages. In 1935, for example, the Mexicans asked for $5 an acre to thin lettuce, but the Filipinos agreed to do the same work for $3.25 to $4.50. Once ensconced, however, they demanded higher pay.[28]

The Filipinos were used primarily as "stoop labor"—unskilled field hands. Usually the farmer needing labor arranged with a labor contractor to provide for a crew. The contractor arranged for transportation from a nearby town, supervised the work, and kept books. If room and board were furnished the worker, the contractor would deduct the cost from the men's wages. He also collected a service charge from each worker for any service he provided.[29]

Labor was the only commodity that the Filipino had to offer. The one way in which he could change his working conditions was to withhold his work at critical times. American farmers, always on the lookout for cheap labor, stiffly resisted the tactics that their new recruits used to improve wages and working conditions. Many Filipinos responded by adopting techniques—threats of strikes, strikes, and boycotts of hostile farmers—developed earlier by Japanese agricultural workers. The laborers would usually wait until it was time to pick a crop before making their wage demands. The farmer had to accede, obtain other workers, or lose his crop.[30] Not surprisingly, farmers became embittered with the Filipino "troublemakers." "The most unsatisfactory of any unskilled laborers we had ever hired," remembered one farmer. "They were the very essence of independence, taking every advantage to cause the employer trouble. . . ." In 1927, this farmer recalled, "the Filipinos evidently thinking we were in a tight place struck for higher wages. We were already paying a higher price per box than anyone else. . . . We refused to meet their exorbitant demands whereupon general rioting

---

27 Carey McWilliams, *Factories in the Field* (Boston, 1939), 118; Schwartz, *Seasonal Farm Labor*, 83.

28 Fisher, *Harvest Labor Market*, 39–40.

29 *Ibid.*, 38; Benicio Catapusan, "The Filipino Labor Cycle in the United States," *Sociology and Social Research*, XIX (1934), 61–63.

30 Schwartz, *Seasonal Farm Labor*, 92–93; Fisher, *Harvest Labor Market*, 29.

ensued. The Filipinos became enraged and began to destroy everything they could lay their hands on."[31]

Filipinos had become an important part of California agriculture by the 1920s and the early 1930s. But as noted earlier, new immigration declined as a consequence of the depression years. World War II further cut off immigration, and many of those already in the United States moved into industrial occupations. After the war, California farmers began to rely more heavily upon Mexican farm workers than they had in the past. This change to additional Mexican labor gave many farmers an opportunity to rationalize their dislike for the Filipinos. One common complaint was that the quality of work being performed by the Filipinos was below par. At the same time the Mexicans began to supplant the Filipinos in other ways too. In 1955 a study was made of the perceptions of some southern California high school students and farm owners in the Coachella Valley regarding the value of different minorities as agricultural workers. According to those questioned, the Mexican had replaced the Filipino as the least desirable worker.[32] Attitudes of West Coast agriculturalists toward minorities used as field laborers had not changed over the years. Decades earlier, Chinese and Japanese immigrants had experienced a similar contempt.

While Filipinos were readily employed in California agriculture, they also sought, with less success, employment in urban areas. During the 1920s and 1930s, they encountered the same kind of racial discrimination that had been faced by other Asians. While Filipinos could usually find employment as busboys, cooks, dishwashers, domestic help, and gardeners, opportunities in business and professional positions were restricted.[33] During and after World War II, as the industrial base expanded, they found jobs in factories, in some trades, and as wholesale and retail salesmen. They also were able to enter the professions. After 1965 more of them found employment open to them in the cities in unskilled, skilled, and semiprofessional occupations. Nevertheless, union regulations and state licensing provisions have restricted opportunities for qualified Filipinos.

---

[31] Emory S. Bogardus, "American Attitudes Towards Filipinos," *Sociology and Social Research*, XIV (1929), 59–69.

[32] Edward C. McDonagh, "Attitudes Toward Ethnic Farm Workers in Coachella Valley," *Sociology and Social Research*, XL (1955), 10–18.

[33] Burma, *Spanish-Speaking Groups*, 141–145.

Even with the rural to urban move in California, agriculture in 1960 remained the largest employer of Filipinos with 3 percent classified as farmers and farm managers and with another 28 percent classified as farm laborers and foremen. In 1950, these percentages had been about 6 percent and 49 percent, respectively.[34] In Hawaii, Filipinos in 1960 provided the bulk of plantation labor. Forty percent of the gainfully employed males worked in agriculture, a decline of 12.5 percent from 1950. During the 1950s, they began to gain employment as craftsmen and factory workers.[35] According to a socioeconomic study by the California Department of Industrial Relations, Filipinos in California, from 1934 to 1959, had not improved upon their earning power relative to other groups. By the end of the period studied, 1959, the median annual income for male Caucasians in California was $5,109; in Hawaii, it was $3,649. California Japanese males had a median income of $4,388, while Hawaiian Japanese averaged $4,302. Filipino males in California had a median income of $2,925, while in Hawaii their counterparts earned $3,071.[36]

The California Department of Industrial Relations 1965 study of the Japanese, Chinese, and Filipinos graphically showed that as late as 1960 the latter were still largely employed as unskilled laborers. The median annual income in 1959 for the Filipinos was the lowest of the three groups studied. In Hawaii they shared with other Pacific island people the dubious distinction of having the lowest median salary of all ethnic groups. As the "latest arrivals and least fortunately situated" of the immigrant groups, the Filipinos provided most of the unskilled plantation labor which was at the bottom of the wage scale. However, Hawaiian Filipinos have fared better than those in California, largely because the International Longshoremen's and Warehousemen's Union organized Hawaii's agricultural workers and gained wage increases for its members. The union boasts that the sugar industry "pays the highest year-round agricultural wages in the world."[37]

California's agribusiness, on the other hand, successfully resisted unionization of field workers until the 1960s. During most of the

---

34 Calif. Dept. of Industrial Relations, *Californians of . . . Filipino Ancestry*, 12.
35 Lind, *Hawaii's People*, 75, 77.
36 *Ibid.*, 100; Calif. Dept. of Industrial Relations, *Californians of . . . Filipino Ancestry*, 14.
37 Lind, *Hawaii's People*, 76, 78.

1930s, the powerful Associated Farmers of California stayed all efforts to organize migratory farm workers. By the end of the decade, the Filipinos had achieved limited organizing success with their Filipino Agricultural Laborers Association. Created initially in response to a threatened wage cut in asparagus, the union had, by 1941, won several strikes and secured some wage increases and improved working conditions. The union disappeared as an effective force during World War II when most of its members joined the armed forces. The economic motivation for unionism disappeared as farm wages increased during the war years.[38] Following the war, agricultural workers called for improved working conditions and increased wages to meet inflation. California agriculture met this challenge during the 1940s and 1950s by utilizing strikebreakers and court injunctions to hold at bay union activities.[39] But the situation changed dramatically during the 1960s. In 1959, the AFL-CIO formed the Agricultural Workers Organizing Committee (AWOC), and, at about the same time, César Chávez founded the National Farm Workers Association (NFWA). While both unions were racially integrated, the AWOC local, led by Larry Itliong, was predominantly Filipino. These new unions spent several years recruiting members. The climax to these activities came in 1965 over the pay scale of grape pickers in the lower San Joaquin Valley. On September 8, 1965, AWOC launched a strike against thirty-three grape growers near Delano in northern Kern County. Domestic agricultural laborers were being paid about $1.20 an hour, while braceros, under a U.S. Department of Labor ruling, received $1.40 for picking grapes. The domestic workers, including the Filipino Americans and Mexican Americans, demanded $1.40 an hour plus 20 cents a box. Chávez's NFWA joined AWOC's effort eight days later. After a lengthy strike of about seven months, which generated much public sympathy, Schenley Industries, owner of the largest vineyards. recognized NFWA as the sole bargaining agent. NFWA and AWOC continued to organize workers and pressure growers. Chávez's union became the stronger of the two. To end unnecessary conflict, the unions in August 1966 merged as the United Farm Workers Organizing Committee. This new organization became the bargaining agent for the workers of the Di Giorgio Corporation,

[38] Schwartz, *Seasonal Farm Labor*, 100–101.
[39] Mark Day, *Forty Acres, Cesar Chavez and the Farm Workers* (New York, 1971), 36–37; John Dunne, *Delano* (New York, 1971), 77–83.

another large Kern County vineyard owner.[40] The naming of a
bargaining agent for the farm workers marked a turning point in
labor relations in California agriculture.[41] The Filipinos and the
Chicanos, working together in a common effort, were successful in
improving wages and working conditions. They have, through the
UFWOC, continued to struggle together against big agriculture.

Filipino immigrants from both periods of migration, in addition
to the search for economic success, have sought to accommodate
themselves in varying degrees to American society. In 1929, D. F.
Gonzalo, a Filipino student at the University of Southern California, reflected upon the problems of social adjustment faced by recently arrived young Filipinos. For the first few months after arrival, the new immigrant was buoyed by a sense of exuberance and
high anticipation of realizing his dream of success and financial
achievement. The ability to send money home each month further
increased his enthusiasm. He found ready employment as an unskilled worker in those jobs shunned by white labor, and he frequently upbraided his fellow countrymen who had been in the
United States for several years and who appeared to have given up.

The newly arrived immigrant, Gonzalo reported, then moved to
a second phase in his adjustment to the United States. Long hours
of hard work soon dulled his outlook. The young man became lone-
some and began to regret his decision to migrate. He also discovered
that Americans in the United States were different from those he
had met in the Philippines. He became conscious of his color and
language, both different from those of the American majority. He
became aware of acts of discrimination and prejudice aimed at him.
Feeling cut off in an alien world, he sought to draw upon his own
resources which frequently could not cope with those allurements
aimed at capitalizing upon the lonely.[42] Many young men turned to
prostitutes and to dance halls and gambling establishments run by
Caucasians, Chinese, or other Filipinos. Many Filipinos have said
their long hours in the field were really spent working for the "Chinaman"—their name for the gamester. Others noted that they had
been through a comprehensive gaming course at the local "Chinese

---

40 *Ibid.*, 39–43.

41 Walton Bean, *California, An Interpretative History* (2nd ed., New York, 1973),
496–498, 501–505.

42 D. F. Gonzalo, "Social Adjustments of Filipinos in America," *Sociology and Social
Research,* XIV (1929), 167–169.

university."[43] Carey McWilliams, in his *Brothers Under the Skin*, estimated that in Stockton—"the Manila of the United States"— Filipinos spent some two million dollars annually on gambling and prostitution.[44] The *Philippine Free Press* of Manila wrote in 1929 of the ensnarement of the young Filipinos by gambling:

Those Filipinos who send money home are the "blanket boys." These have steady jobs on the farm. . . . The pastime of the "blanket boys" is playing cards. After a day's work they assemble around the improvised table and play cards till late at night. Poker and blackjack are the popular games. Their hard-earned money is easily lost. In the town or city the *Pinoys* may be found in the billiard rooms and pool halls from after breakfast till late at night.

There are many gambling houses, mostly managed and controlled by Chinese. They are popularly known as "sikoy-sikoys". . . . In Stockton there is one gambling house managed and controlled by white men. It is for Filipinos. It is one mile south from the heart of the city. Anyone who wants to go there gets a free ride back and forth. These hired automobiles are owned by Filipinos.

In Walnut Grove there are six "sikoy-sikoys"; in Isleton there are four; in Dinuba one; in Reedley four, and so on. All these gambling houses are patronized by Filipinos and a few Mexicans.

The gambling houses in Walnut Grove and Isleton serve free meals: breakfast at eight o'clock; a dinner at twelve; supper at five; coffee and bread at ten in the evening.[45]

Filipino gambling, although tolerated by native Americans, seemed to be an indication to them that the young immigrants lacked seriousness of purpose. But the sexual relationships of the young Filipino immigrants and white girls led to bitter animosity on the part of adult whites. Throughout California, Filipinos sought female companionship in the dance halls. To cater to the Filipino trade in Los Angeles during the 1930s, six taxi dance halls employed several hundred women. McWilliams opined that the taxi dance provided perhaps the most costly entertainment in the state. Each dance, lasting one minute, cost ten cents.[46]

---

[43] Lillian Galedo and Theresa Q. Mar, "Filipinos in a Farm Labor Camp," in *Asians in America* (Davis, Calif.: University of California Asian American Research Project Working Publication No. 3, 1970, mimeographed), 58; Galedo, Cabanero, and Tom, *Roadblocks to Community Building*, 10.

[44] McWilliams, *Brothers Under the Skin*, 238.

[45] Quoted in Lasker, *Filipino Immigration*, 133–134.

[46] McWilliams, *Brothers Under the Skin*, 238–239.

There were mixed views about Filipinos and prostitution. In Stockton, Charles F. Crook, deputy labor commissioner of San Joaquin County, reflected an unfriendly attitude:

The Filipino never has a dime. . . . His money goes for cars, women, clothes and the like. The Filipino contractor furnishes some of these things. He brings women (white women) into the camp as well as booze and gives each laborer who cares to indulge a ticket. That is, he takes it out of wages.

I know of one taxi company in this city that makes $500 per month running prostitutes into the islands [the San Joaquin River Delta area]. These women must be white, weigh not over one hundred pounds, and be comparatively young—not over 24 or 25 years old. . . . They are worked through the islands and back down the coast toward the city. Then, they are worked back again.[47]

Manuel Buaken, one of the early immigrants, agreed in part with Crook, but he felt that prostitution was based upon the seduction of the Filipinos by white women. "Women professionals," he insisted, "fleeced the innocent Filipino of his money by pretending they loved and so managed to cheat and deceive him."[48]

The 1929 Gonzalo study noted that Filipino immigrants moved through several phases as they attempted to cope with life in the United States. One undesirable aspect, as noted above, was the dependence of many upon gambling and prostitution. Gonzalo concluded that a large number of Filipinos, unable to adapt successfully, had to be classified as bewildered drifters who appeared to have no aim or purpose. The enthusiasm of former days had disappeared, leaving them bitter or resigned. Many who wanted to go home either lacked the money or feared the scorn likely to be meted out to failures. Consequently, they became entrapped in their new environment. From his study of his fellow Filipinos, Gonzalo concluded that they, like many other unskilled immigrants, did not have the background necessary for social adjustment in a country where every wage earner was a specialist of sorts.[49]

The problems noted by Gonzalo persisted for several decades. Aging Filipinos found themselves captive in what was to be their

---

[47] Interview with Charles F. Crook, Feb. 1930, James Earl Wood Papers, Bancroft Library, University of California, Berkeley.

[48] Buaken, *I Have Lived with the American People*, 178.

[49] Gonzalo, "Social Adjustments of Filipinos," 173.

temporary home. Some of those who had migrated in the 1920s were still working in agriculture nearly fifty years later. In 1970, two students of Filipino ancestry, who wanted to understand better their own heritage, interviewed Filipino residents of a Salinas farm labor camp. Those interviewed portray vividly the hopes and frustrations of men who had become a permanent part of California's agricultural labor force. Even though the average age of the men was 65, they still dreamed of returning to the Philippines. Some were semi-retired, working only long enough to pay for their board and room at the camp. Others, too young to retire at the ages of 60-65, worked daily in the fields.[50]

The interviews of these Filipino agricultural workers point up their optimism—the dream of returning to their homeland remained a fond hope. The sadness of it all was that many had come to rely upon an external factor—the big win in gambling—to bring reality to the dream. Brief biographical sketches of three camp residents underscore the difficulties encountered by them and other aging Filipinos who had come to California in the 1920s.

Manong had migrated in 1924 from the Philippines to Hawaii where he had spent three years on sugar and pineapple plantations. Securing financial support from a relative in Stockton, he had then moved to California where he had worked in the potato and asparagus fields of the San Joaquin Delta. In 1938 he had moved to Salinas which became his permanent residence. Like many of his compatriots Manong did not seek citizenship because he always planned to return to his homeland. He claimed that he had an opportunity to return in 1938, but he could not pay for the ticket. Since that time, though he had made no effort to return to the Philippines, he maintained family ties. He sent money home, but that practice had become more difficult as retirement age approached.[51]

Nanding, another of the camp residents, arrived in San Francisco in 1925 with the idea of studying engineering. But his future was more or less determined at dockside when he and others were "greeted . . . by a man from an employment office in Stockton whose job was to pick up a truckload of men and transport them to Stockton." The driver, Nanding reported, made five dollars profit on each passenger by charging more than the normal fare. After his

50 Galedo and Mar, "Filipinos in a Farm Labor Camp," 53–56.
51 *Ibid.*, 56–57.

arrival in Stockton, Nanding worked as an agricultural worker. Once the harvest season had ended, he and several friends enrolled in the seventh grade, but he soon dropped out because he was nineteen and the white students were thirteen; he never went back to school. Nanding subsequently worked as an agricultural field worker, settling finally in the Salinas camp. Like Manong, he never applied for United States citizenship. He viewed that step as unnecessary, "for as soon as he 'makes it in Reno' he plans to return to the Philippines." Although he had never won enough money to cover his transportation costs, he had been able to send money home to support his relatives. Several of these had gained an education because of his financial aid.[52]

Benigno, the third Salinas camp resident, arrived in California in 1924. He began as a field laborer in the Delta regon before moving to Salinas in 1935. There he worked in the lettuce fields until the start of World War II. Drafted into the army, he automatically became an American citizen. He was soon discharged because the Salinas agriculturalists needed his labor—the same reason that caused many other drafted Filipino farm workers to be released from military service. Despite the fact that he was now a citizen, Benigno still wanted to return to the Philippines. Like so many others, he was still "waiting for his big win in Reno" so that he could buy his ticket. Although he had never had much luck, his hopes remained high.[53]

As with other immigrant groups, the Filipinos have responded in many different ways to American life. Some were never able to adapt, while others contributed to the mainstream of American culture. One of the major themes in the history of Filipino immigration has been the difficult and continuing problem of racial prejudice and discrimination. A poignant expression of this was the lamentation uttered in 1937 by Carlos Bulosan, a Filipino immigrant who gained recognition through his writings about his countrymen:

. . . . Western people are brought up to regard Orientals or colored people as inferior, but the mockery of it all is that Filipinos are taught to regard Americans as our equals. Adhering to American ideals, living American life, these are contributory to our feeling of equality. The

52 *Ibid.*, 57.
53 *Ibid.*, 58.

terrible truth in America shatters the Filipino's dream of fraternity.

I was completely disillusioned when I came to know this American attitude. If I had not been born in a lyrical world, grown up with honest people and studied about American institutions and racial equality in the Philippines I should never have minded so much the horrible impact of white chauvinism. I shall never forget what I have suffered in this country because of racial prejudice.[54]

American attitudes toward Filipinos on the mainland and in Hawaii were shaped largely by the white reaction to immigrants of the 1920s. Prejudicial attitudes set at that time persisted for several decades. Emory Bogardus, a University of Southern California sociologist who spent years studying the Filipinos, believed that the general opinions held by white America during the late twenties could be divided into three categories: favorable attitudes, unfavorable attitudes, and the evaluation of an individual on the basis of that person's aims and evident merit. Favorable attitudes, largely paternalistic, developed, he held, from opinions growing out of American colonialism. The White Man's Burden created a sense of benevolent obligation to help Filipinos assimilate into American society. Bogardus believed this view resulted mostly from white contact with Filipinos on a superficial individual basis in hotels and restaurants where the latter held inferior positions.[55]

The more prevalent white view saw the Filipino as a savage, not far removed from the tribal stage. Some American missionaries, self-professed friends of the Filipinos, furthered public apprehension as they recounted the primitive conditions of some of the rural Filipino tribes.[56] The prejudicial attitude held by most Americans paralleled the outlook they had regarding other Asian minorities. Bogardus, in his study, noted that white workers exhibited hatred as Filipinos replaced them in the hotel-restaurant industry and in the maritime trade. White labor unions during the late 1920s and early 1930s were leaders in the opposition to Filipino immigration as they had been earlier against other Asian groups.[57]

In day to day living during the 1920s and 1930s, the Filipinos

54 Carlos Bulosan to Dorothy Babb, Dec. 12, 1937, in Carlos Bulosan, *Sound of Falling Light: Letters in Exile,* Dolores S. Feria, ed. (Quezon City, 1960), 191–192.

55 Bogardus, "American Attitudes," 59–60.

56 *Ibid.,* 63–64.

57 House Committee on Immigration and Naturalization, "Hearings on Exclusion of Immigration from the Philippine Islands," 71 Cong., 2 sess. (1931), 42–46.

also found that their dark skin and their difficulty with the English language set them apart. On the West Coast, they were frequently refused service in restaurants and barbershops, barred from swimming pools, movies, and tennis courts. Californians, in particular, have a long record of discrimination against Asians in real estate and housing. Filipinos, seeking homes in white neighborhoods, were forced into slum areas. Often, because of lack of housing, fifteen or twenty were compelled to live in one room. They accepted these crowded conditions in an effort to save money for those at home, for transportation to the Philippines, or for the purchase of automobiles and American style clothing.[58] Most white Californians were unaware of the contradictions that their attitudes created. One segment of white society welcomed Filipinos to the state because they provided cheap labor. But prejudicial and discriminatory attitudes tended to keep them at a low level of existence. As a consequence, other Californians, critical of the Filipinos' substandard living conditions, attacked them for creating health problems and lowering the American standard of living. Manuel Buaken, another spokesman for his people, cried out about the effect of this denial of adequate housing on the soul of a man:

my personal pride was entirely subdued; I was wounded deeply in heart and soul for on that day I had tasted more pangs of life's bitterness and all the sordidness of this world than I [had] ever known before, and I learned what calamity and what tragic consequences race prejudice can inflict upon a man's life.[59]

The impact of prejudice shook the Filipinos who had had contact with the teachings of Christianity in the Philippines. Many were stunned by the double standards maintained by white Christians during the 1920s and 1930s. One Filipino reported:

During my active membership in church, it always puzzled me to find that many members of the same church would converse with me congenially in the church but when I met them on the streets or in school or later on they acted as if ashamed to talk with me, even more so when they were with their friends. And sometimes when I would talk with

58 Burma, *Spanish-Speaking Groups,* 144; House Committee on Immigration and Naturalization, "Hearings on to Provide for the Return to the Philippine Islands of Unemployed Filipinos Resident in the Continental United States," 72 Cong., 2 sess. (1933), 8–9.

59 Buaken, *I Have Lived with the American People,* 70.

them in spite of their being with their friends, they looked embarrassed and indicated that I should not appear to be knowing them.[60]

While subjected to covert economic and social discrimination, the Filipino was denied fewer civil and property rights than the immigrants from China and Japan. The only direct legislation aimed against the Filipinos involved mixed marriages.

White Californians had long been opposed to Asian males marrying their daughters. In 1901 Californians had enacted a law forbidding whites from marrying blacks, Mongolians, or mulattoes.[61] Although California Attorney General U.S. Webb believed that Filipinos were Mongolians, his opinion did not have the force of a judicial decision. Each county clerk could make his own interpretation as to the racial origin of Filipinos.[62] In 1931, the Los Angeles County clerk, accepting Webb's interpretation, denied a marriage license to Salvador Roldan, who then filed suit against the county. Claiming that the term, Mongolian, did not include Filipinos, Roldan was successful in both superior and appellate courts. In 1933 the county appealed to the California state supreme court which upheld the decisions of the two lower courts on the grounds that the state legislature had not specifically forbidden marriages between whites and Filipinos.[63] The California legislature quickly closed this loophole by amending the state's civil code in 1933 to include persons of the Malay race in the list of people whom whites could not marry. This action nullified the court decision,[64] and it was soon imitated by other state legislatures. By 1937, Nevada, Oregon, and Washington had enacted laws prohibiting marriages between Filipinos and whites.

California's miscegenation law was eventually ruled unconstitutional in 1948 in the case of *Perez* v. *Sharp*. The California supreme court held that legislation limiting the right of members of one race to marry members of another race was a violation of civil rights. Such laws, the court stated, had to be based upon more than "prej-

---

[60] Emory S. Bogardus, "Filipino Immigrant Attitudes," *Sociology and Social Research*, XIV (1930), 469–479.

[61] *California Statutes*, 34th Sess. (1901), 335.

[62] Nellie Foster, "Legal Status of Filipino Intermarriage in California," *Sociology and Social Research*, XVI (1932), 447–452.

[63] *Roldan* v. *Los Angeles County*, 129 Calif. 267 (1933); *San Francisco Chronicle*, March 30, 1933, p. 1.

[64] *California Statutes*, 50th Sess. (1933), 561.

udice and must be free from oppressive discrimination."[65] During the year following the *Perez* decision, some 21,060 marriage license applications were taken out in Los Angeles County. Of these, 100 could be classified as interracial, and Filipinos comprised most of them—40 males and 2 females.[66]

In addition to legal discrimination, there were incidents of violence against Filipinos. Hostility manifested itself in acts of individual violence as well as in riots in Washington and California between 1928 and 1930. The first of these hostilities, which occurred in Washington's Yakima Valley in 1928, grew out of white farm workers' fears that they would be replaced by Filipinos. On September 19, 1928, the white workers forced the Filipinos to leave the valley. A similar incident took place two days later at Wenatchee, Washington, where two hundred whites descended upon a camp of twenty Filipinos and forced them to flee.[67]

California's most violent discrimination came in the form of vigilante action. White motives were based in part upon the fear of economic competition from the Filipino and in part upon concerns about Filipino relationships with white women. The state's first serious riot occurred on October 24, 1929, when a Filipino stabbed a white man at a carnival in Exeter in the San Joaquin Valley. Prior to the stabbing, white farm workers had molested and shoved Filipinos off the town's sidewalks in an effort to intimidate them into leaving the region. At the carnival, whites threw objects at the Filipinos, particularly those who were escorting white women. This provoked the knifing. Following the stabbing, a mob, estimated at 300, rushed to the nearest ranch employing Filipinos and burned the barn. The Filipinos had fled the area before the mob arrived.[68]

The most explosive California vigilante incident occurred in January 1930 near Watsonville. This farm area, with many specialty crops, depended upon large numbers of transient farm workers. By the late 1920s, farmers had come to rely upon Filipino contract labor, which migrated to the region from other parts of the state to harvest the crops. This dependence upon alien labor

---

[65] *Perez* v. *Sharp*, Calif. Reports, 2nd Series, 711 (1948).

[66] Randall Risdon, "A Study of Interracial Marriages Based on Data for Los Angeles County," *Sociology and Social Research*, XXXIX (1954), 92–95.

[67] Buaken, *I Have Lived with the American People*, 94–97; Burma, *Spanish-Speaking Groups*, 152–153.

[68] Calif. Dept. of Industrial Relations, *Facts About Filipino Immigration*, 73–74.

laid the seeds for conflict in Watsonville, a town that was not prepared to accommodate such an influx. Soon the white inhabitants
of the community were voicing a common complaint about the Filipino transients—they spent their money on flashy clothes and new
cars in order to attract the attention of white women. The growing
resentment of the whites was perhaps best expressed by an anti-
Filipino resolution adopted by the northern Monterey County
chamber of commerce.

> Whereas, any foreign people coming to the United States of America
> whose customs, habits and standards of living prohibit them from as-
> similating and adopting our standard of living, are detrimental and
> dangerous to social conditions, and
> Whereas, the unrestricted immigration into the state of California of
> natives of the Philippines is viewed with alarm both from a moral and
> sanitary standpoint while constituting a menace to white labor, there-
> fore be it
> Resolved, That we . . . petition . . . to prevent further immigration.[69]

Judge D. W. Rohrback, a leader of the chamber of commerce and
a respected community leader, added to the growing hostility with
his announcement that Filipinos "possessed unhealthy habits and
were destructive to the living wage scale" of others. He also called
them "little brown men attired like 'Solomon in all his glory,' strut-
ting like peacocks and endeavoring to attract the eyes of young
American and Mexican girls."[70]
At the same time that the Watsonville citizens were becoming
highly agitated about the presence of the farm workers, a small Filipino group leased a dance hall in Palm Beach, a few miles west of
Watsonville on Monterey Bay. About a dozen white women were
engaged as professional dancing partners. The thought of white
women dancing with Filipinos led to demonstrations by self appointed white vigilantes which started on January 19 and lasted
through January 23. On the 20th, about 200 armed men searched
the streets for Filipinos, and, on the next night, they raided the
dance hall. On the 22nd, a mob of 500 went to nearby farms and
fired shots into the camp buildings. One Filipino was killed, several
were beaten, and much property was destroyed. Following this vio-

---

69 Quoted in Buaken, *I Have Lived with the American People*, 169.
70 *Ibid.*, 169–170.

lence, community leaders belatedly formed a law and order group to put down the vigilantes.[71]

Legislation and violence were two weapons often used by exclusionists in the past against Chinese and Japanese. Now fearing a third Oriental wave, the whites set out to eliminate Filipino immigration. Encouraged by such organizations as the American Legion, the California Federation of Labor, the Commonwealth Club of California, and the racist California Joint Immigration Committee, the California legislature in 1929 asked Congress to restrict the immigration of Filipinos because cheap labor "has had a tendency towards destruction of American ideals and American racial unity."[72] However, the exclusionists encountered a unique problem. Since the Philippine Islands were part of the United States overseas territory, the Filipinos had a status different from that of other Asian groups. The Filipinos who migrated to Hawaii and the mainland prior to 1946 were technically American nationals. This status was spelled out rather clearly in the 1924 immigration act, which specified that they were not aliens and were free to enter the United States. The 1924 proviso remained in force until May 1, 1934, when the Philippine legislature accepted the Tydings-McDuffie Independence Act, which limited the number of Filipino immigrants to an annual quota of fifty.[73] Prior to 1946, when the Philippines became independent, Filipinos traveling beyond the territorial limits of the United States or the Philippines carried United States passports, which gave them the apparent status of citizenship. However, in the Philippines the residents had only the fundamental rights of life, liberty, and property as set forth in the Insular Cases.[74]

The different status of the Filipinos did not daunt the exclusionists. At the federal level, Richard Welch, a San Francisco congressman, introduced exclusion and repatriation legislation. Nativist and humanitarian motives were entwined in the proposals. While there was an outright push to eliminate Filipino immigration, there

---

71 *Ibid.*, 75; Buaken, *I Have Lived with the American People*, 97–105; *San Jose Mercury*, Jan. 11–23, 1930.

72 Commonwealth Club of California, *Transactions*, XXIV (1929), 320; Lasker, *Filipino Immigration*, v; California, *Senate Journal*, 48th Sess. (1929), 2690.

73 *U.S. Statutes at Large*, XLIII, 168; Garel A. Grunder and William E. Livezey, *The Philippines and the United States* (Norman, Okla., 1951), 205–233.

74 Manzon, *Strange Case of Filipinos*, 5–6; McWilliams, *Brothers Under the Skin*, 243.

was some concern about the plight of the immigrant farm workers in California. During the depression, Filipinos were among the first workers to be laid off. In 1931, the Philippine Society of California, comprised of recently arrived Filipino immigrants, urged the federal government to use army transports to take unemployed Filipinos home. The society found that thousands of Filipinos wanted to go home but did not have funds to purchase a ticket. Members of the society, who wanted to maintain the option of open access to the mainland for Filipinos, hoped that this voluntary return of the unemployed would reduce the clamor for complete exclusion.[75] But this hope dimmed as white racists continued to push for their goals.

Repatriation, another of the exclusionists' aims, was considered for several years by the House Committee on Immigration and Naturalization. Although cleared for House action by the committee in 1933, final passage of a repatriation bill did not come until 1935. The legislation provided that transportation would be provided at federal expense for those who wanted to return to the Philippines. Those who accepted this aid lost the right of immediate reentry. They could only return as part of the annual quota of fifty immigrants.[76] Repatriation, as an exclusionist tool, did not work. Only 2,190 of the 45,000 Filipinos resident in the United States took advantage of the federal legislation.[77]

Actually, the efforts of the exclusionists were largely unnecessary. With the collapse of the American economy in the early 1930s and the creation of a farm labor surplus, Filipinos stopped coming in any large numbers. The objective of exclusion was at the same time essentially achieved with the establishment of the small quota by the Tydings-McDuffie Independence Act.

While the mainland was concerned about immigration control during the 1930s, the Hawaiian Sugar Planters' Association worried about the lack of enough cheap laborers. Hawaii did not have ready access to the unemployed that California, Oregon, and Washington had. The planters lobbied successfully during the hearings on the

---

75 *San Francisco Chronicle*, Jan. 30, 1931, p. 41.

76 *U.S. Statutes at Large*, XLIX, 478–479; H. Brett Melendy, "California's Discrimination Against Filipinos, 1927–1935," in *The Filipino Exclusion Movement, 1927–1935* (Quezon City, Philippines Institute of Asian Studies, Occasional Paper No. 1, 1967), 10.

77 McWilliams, *Brothers Under the Skin*, 243.

Tydings-McDuffie bill against complete exclusion. Section 8 of the bill permitted unlimited Filipino immigration to the islands if a need could be demonstrated. Determination of a labor shortage and the approval to import additional Filipino laborers were vested with the Department of Interior.[78] Although section 8 represented a major victory for the planters, they found it necessary only once to invoke the provision. This occurred in 1946 when some 7,300 laborers were brought to Hawaii to meet an expected postwar manpower deficit.[79] Nonetheless, from 1946 to the present, Filipino labor has remained important to Hawaii's agriculture.

As noted earlier, Filipino immigration to Hawaii and the mainland increased significantly following the 1965 immigration act. An important study of this recent influx was made in 1971 by the University of Hawaii School of Social Work. Interviews were conducted wth 503 Filipino families on the island of Oahu where most of the new immigrants settled. The study found that 474 (94 percent) of the families came from rural areas in the Philippines. Moving from a rural society to Hawaii's urban setting caused serious problems of adaptation for these new immigrants. Filipinos moving to West Coast cities experienced similar difficulties.[80] As with the earlier waves of Filipino migrants, most of the new arrivals were Ilocanos. Of those families interviewed, 461 (92 percent) came from the northern Luzon provinces, 20 came from the area around Manila, 14 came from the Visayan region, and 6 were from other locations.[81]

The university study also examined the occupational characteristics of the recent Filipino immigrants. Whereas the earlier arrivals were unskilled, those coming after 1965 possessed many different skills. Most of them had been farmers or fishermen (36 percent) in the Philippines; 10 percent had been in service occupations. These newer immigrants were better educated than had been the earlier ones. A significant number had completed high school (23 percent) or had earned a college degree (22 percent).[82]

This post-1965 wave of immigrants has been underemployed in

78 Clifford, "Hawaiian Sugar Planters' Association and Filipino Exclusion," 25–26.
79 Ibid., 26–28.
80 Hawaii, Commission on Manpower and Full Employment, Report of the State Immigration Service Center (Honolulu, Jan. 1972), 46–47; interview with James Misajon, 1972.
81 Hawaii, Report . . . Immigration Service Center, 46.
82 Ibid., 47.

Hawaii and on the mainland.[83] They have not been able to match up their former skills and training with jobs in the United States. Almost a fourth of those interviewed in Hawaii found employment as unskilled labor. Another 25 percent were in the service occupations. Only 15 of the 148 immigrants with technical or collegiate education found positions commensurate with their training.[84] Agricultural employment both in Hawaii and on the mainland still provided jobs for many of the new arrivals.

The white majority has never fully appreciated the contribution made to western agriculture's "factories in the fields" by Filipinos or other migrant workers. That same majority has not understood the dream that motivated the Filipinos to work long hard hours. Instead, the Filipinos have been the object of scorn and prejudice for some Americans. And for others, the Filipinos have been the prey of the unscrupulous and the unethical, who have fleeced them of their earnings. The same white majority during the 1930s, while using these people, also had turned upon them and sought to exclude them from the United States.

With the liberalization of immigration laws and an end to legalized exclusion, Filipinos have again seized the opportunity to migrate to the United States and to make a new life. Unlike the earlier immigrants, most of the recent arrivals wish to establish permanent homes, and this desire has added a new dimension to the history of the Filipinos in the United States.

Much more remains to be learned about the recent immigrants as well as the aging agricultural workers of earlier decades. There is an immediate need for trained oral historians to record more fully the experiences of the immigrants of the 1920s. Especially fruitful would be interviews with those still in the United States and those who have returned to the Philippines so that the experiences of these two groups could be compared. Another important area of investigation would be the involvement of the early Filipino immigrants in the Philippine independence movement and in World War II. The movement of Filipinos since 1965 would provide historians with an opportunity to examine recent adaptation in the United States—economic problems, social adaptation, and the response of the majority and other minorities to this new group. As

83 Interview with James Misajon, Dec. 18, 1972.
84 Hawaii, *Report . . . Immigration Service Center*, 48.

indicated at the beginning of this paper, not much attention has been given to Filipino Americans, yet they have contributed, and continue to contribute, to the American experience. They merit the attention of scholars.

The Korean Experience in America, 1903-1924

Lee Houchins and Chang-su Houchins

Lee Houchins is a member of the history department in Georgetown University and Chang-su Houchins is a member of the anthropology department in the Smithsonian Institution.

THE EXPERIENCE of Korean immigrants in the United States and Hawaii during the years 1903 to 1924 is unique in several respects. Their numbers, when compared with other East Asian immigrant groups, were relatively small.[1] Most, whether students or agricultural laborers, were Christians. More than half emigrated to Hawaii as plantation laborers at a time when the political structure of their home country was on the verge of collapse in the face of steadily increasing pressure from a rapidly modernizing Japan. Like most Asian emigrants, they were motivated by the hope of greatly improving their economic situation. Their emigration was encouraged, however, by a government which innocently hoped that, by doing so, it would somehow acquire a measure of prestige—and support from the United States.

Within less than a decade, the Korean immigrants in America found themselves almost completely cut off from their homeland and in danger of losing their ethnic identity to the Japanese, who had succeeded in annexing Korea. Their identity was preserved, however, by means of their increasingly politicized community organizations and their generally deep involvement in the Korean

---

[1] Between 1889 and 1910, for example, total immigrant entries by group approximated 148,000 Japanese; 22,400 Chinese; and 8,300 Koreans. "Asiatic Immigration to the United States by Race or People, 1899 to 1944," Working File: Immigrants by Race, Immigration and Naturalization Service, U.S. Dept. of Justice Papers, Statistics Branch Offices, Washington, D.C.

independence movement abroad. For these reasons, this paper will emphasize the political history of Koreans in America as well as the basic patterns of the immigration process itself.

The first Koreans to reach the United States were students or political refugees. They arrived in the years after the signing of the Shufeldt treaty that opened Korea to the West in 1882. The United States and the Korean kingdom exchanged ministers in the following year, and, when the Korean mission returned in 1884, one of its members remained behind to pursue his studies in Massachusetts.[2] After the abortive, anticonservative and pro-Japanese coup of December 1884, three political refugees found asylum in the United States. One of these, Sŏ Chae-p'il (Philip Jaisohn), emerged as a leading activist in the Korean independence movement of 1919 and a prominent member of the Korean community in the United States.[3] In an attempt to demonstrate clearly its independence from traditional Chinese domination of its foreign affairs, the Korean government sent resident ministers to Japan, Britain, France, and the United States, where a legation was opened in 1887. This move facilitated the travel of a substantial number of Korean students, sixty-four in all,[4] most of whom were encouraged by Christian missionaries in Korea to study Western life and thought at American colleges and universities. Included in this group were An Ch'ang-ho, Kim Kyu-sik, Pak Yong-man, and Yi Sŭng-man (Syngman Rhee). There followed, until early 1905, small numbers of diplomats and ginseng merchants.

Large-scale Korean emigration to the United States and its territories began in 1903 as the direct result of initiatives on the part of American sugar planters in Hawaii and the very good offices of the American minister at Seoul, Horace D. Allen, and American missionaries. The importation of Koreans for work in Hawaiian sugar plantations was first proposed in November 1896. J. F. Hackfeld, president of a Bremen-based firm heavily involved in underwriting the Hawaiian Sugar Planters' Association (HSPA), made the suggestion to the executive council of the Republic of Hawaii. Hackfeld's

---

[2] This was Yu Kil-chun, whose formal, national dress is on display in the ethnological collections of the Peabody Museum, Salem, Mass.

[3] The other two were Pak Yŏng-hyo and Sŏ Kwang-bŏm, both of whom had visited the United States as members of the first Korean mission, 1883–1884.

[4] Kim Wŏn-Yong, *Chae-Mi Hanin Osimnyŏn Sa* [*Fifty year History of Koreans in America*] (Reedley, Calif., 1959), 29–30.

proposal was rejected, in accordance with the then current anti-Oriental policy of the executive council.[5]

Returning from home leave in March 1902, Horace Allen was intercepted in San Francisco by an HSPA representative. Allen then met with HSPA officials in Honolulu to discuss the feasibility of the importation of Korean plantation workers. In Seoul, Allen sought out David W. Deshler, a fellow Ohioan and junior partner in the American Trading Company operations at Inchon (then Chemulp'o), and asked him to act as the HSPA agent in Korea for the emigration scheme. Allen also introduced Deshler to E. Faxon Bishop, an HSPA representative who had been dispatched to Japan with $25,000 to recruit labor and promote shipping.[6] Deshler had interests in a steamship company operating between Inchon and Kobe and, therefore, stood to profit from transporting emigrants as well as from the fee paid by the HSPA for each Korean laborer to reach its plantations in Hawaii. Horace Allen's motivations are somewhat more difficult to identify. Though he was obviously convinced that Korean laborers would adapt to working conditions on the Hawaiian sugar plantations, and though he may have sincerely felt that such an opportunity would better the lot of individual Koreans,[7] his dominant motivation appears to have been political self-interest.[8] In any case, Allen's well-established role as adviser to the Korean emperor, Kojong, was crucial to his success.

Allen had little trouble persuading the Korean administration of the positive economic value of mass emigration. The social situa-

5 Wayne Patterson, "Koreans to Hawaii: Failure in 1897 and Success in 1902" (Paper presented to the Columbia University Seminar on Korea, May 17, 1974), cited with permission. See also Hilary Conroy, *The Japanese Frontier in Hawaii, 1868–1898* (Berkeley and Los Angeles, 1953), esp. chap. 12.

6 Patterson, "Koreans to Hawaii," 17–18, 21–22; Fred Harvey Harrington, *God, Mammon and the Japanese: Dr. Horace D. Allen and Korean-American Relations, 1884–1905* (Madison, 1944), 186. Ko Sŭng-je identifies Deshler as an HSPA employee and says that HSPA chairman, Charles R. Bishop, met with Deshler at Inchon in 1902, *Han'guk Iminsa Yŏn'gu* [*Studies in the History of Korean Immigration*] (Seoul, 1973), 209.

7 Allen to John Hay and to Sanford B. Dole, Dec. 10, 1902, Diplomatic Dispatches, Korea, 1883–1905, Department of State Papers, Record Group 59, microcopy M-134, reel 13, National Archives.

8 By supporting the emigration scheme enthusiastically, Allen was able to contribute materially to Deshler's personal fortunes. Deshler, in turn, strongly supported Allen's bid for the post of minister in the Seoul legation by organizing the interest and patronage of influential Ohio Republicans, including his stepfather, George K. Nash, a close friend of President-elect William McKinley. Harrington, *God, Mammon and the Japanese*, 186, 294; Patterson, "Koreans to Hawaii," 19–21.

tion in Korea in late 1902 was desperate.[9] A cholera epidemic raged through the summer, exacerbating the effects of a second year of drought, flood, and locust plague. Severe famine prevailed in the three southern provinces and Hwanghae, northwest of Seoul.[10] Large numbers of urban Koreans found themselves in equally distressing circumstances. Yet Allen also appealed to the Korean emperor's sense of prestige: unlike the Chinese, who had been excluded since 1882, Korean laborers would be welcomed in Hawaii or the Philippines.

Allen requested an audience with the emperor in late October,[11] and on November 16, 1902, an edict established the Suminwŏn (Department of Immigration) within the Imperial Household Department.[12] The enlightened Min Yŏng-hwan was appointed director.[13] Early Suminwŏn regulations specified that prospective emigrants be of sound health and good standing in their communities. Destination and intended occupation were to be stated, and, most importantly, it was unlawful to issue passports to Koreans emigrating as contract laborers. Passports, valid only for travel to specific destinations, were to be retained by consular officials abroad and sent to the Department of Immigration when the migrants returned to Korea.[14] The regulations were modified in early December to require close police investigation of departing and returning immigrants as well as punishment for those police who failed to screen passports properly.[15]

---

[9] The Korean situation in the half decade prior to the outbreak of the Russo-Japanese war in February 1904 has been described as follows: ". . . the political, economic, and social conditions of the nation continued to deteriorate under an absolutistic regime dominated by petty, rapacious, and irresponsible court favorites. There were no large scale convulsions; it was a gradual process of system decay." C. I. Eugene Kim and Han-kyo Kim, *Korea and the Politics of Imperialism, 1876–1910* (Berkeley and Los Angeles, 1967), 115.

[10] *Hwangsŏng Sinmun [Imperial City News]* (Seoul), various issues, July 24 to Aug. 29, 1902, facsimile edition in the Korea Section, Orientalia Division, Library of Congress.

[11] *Ibid.*, editorial, Nov. 3, 1902; Allen to Hay, Dec. 10, 1902, Diplomatic Dispatches, Korea, 1883–1905.

[12] *Hwangsŏng Sinum*, Oct. 23, 1902, gives notice of the request without information about its purpose; Allen and Deshler may have attended several audiences at which emigration was discussed. According to Patterson, Allen falsely represented Deshler as an official of the nonexistent Bureau of Immigration of the Territory of Hawaii. Patterson, "Koreans to Hawaii," 24.

[13] *Hwangsŏng Sinum*, Nov. 18, 1902.

[14] *Ibid.*, Nov. 21, 1902.

[15] Allen to Dole, Dec. 10, 1902, Diplomatic Dispatches, Korea, 1889–1905.

The Suminwŏn staff was expanded and branch offices were established in various ports by late November. Official encouragement
of emigration "for the purposes of education, observation, and to
engage in commerce, industry, and agriculture" was publicly announced.[16] Nonetheless, the Suminwŏn's administrative responsibilities were restricted largely to issuing passports, and the bulk of
the recruiting burden fell upon Deshler. With appropriate creden-
tials from the emperor now in hand, Deshler formed the Tonga
Kaebal Hoesa (Korean Development Company) to facilitate his
emigration enterprises for the HSPA. Newspaper advertisements
emphasized several advantages: Hawaii's mild weather; attractive
wages ($16 per month for a sixty-hour work week); free housing,
medical care, wood, and water; and free admission to schools where
the English language would be taught. Unmarried emigrants as
well as those with families would be welcome. Employment opportunities, particularly for farmers, were excellent; furthermore, all
would enjoy the protection of American law. The recruitment message was summed up in the slogan "*Kaeguk chinch'wi*"—The country is open; go forward![17]

The recruiting effort emphasized that those choosing to emigrate
did so as free agents, within the letter and spirit of article six of the
Shufeldt Treaty, and not as contract laborers. Nevertheless, few
Korean emigrants had sufficient funds to achieve the appealing
status of "free agent." Deshler's Tonga Kaebal Hoesa (TKH) paid
passport fees to the Suminwŏn on behalf of prospective emigrants
and loaned each departing individual 100 *wŏn*, in addition to 70
wŏn to be paid as fare for the passage from Kobe to Honolulu. The
loans were made through the newly established Deshler Bank in
Inchon, whose sole depositor was the HSPA,[18] and were to be re-
paid ten months after settling on a Hawaiian plantation. TKH
offices were established in several port cities as well as in the Chŏng-
dong district of Seoul, near the American legation, but the recruiting effort was not immediately successful. Only through the persua-
sion of American missionaries, particularly the Reverend George
Heber Jones, was the first shipload of emigrants collected. Most

---

16 *Hwangsŏng Sinmun,* Nov. 18 and 21, 1902.
17 Kim, *Chae-Mi Hanin Osimnyŏn Sa,* 4.
18 Patterson, "Koreans to Hawaii," 28.

were from the Inchon port area, and nearly half were members of the congregation at Jones's Yongdong church.[19]

The first shipload, carrying 101 emigrants, sailed from Inchon harbor on December 22, 1902, barely five weeks after the establishment of the Suminwŏn, and arrived in Honolulu on January 13.[20] Fifteen additional shiploads in the course of 1903 brought 1,133 more Korean immigrants. In 1904 the flow peaked with thirty-three ship arrivals and 3,434 immigrants. In 1905, the final year of direct Korean immigration to Hawaii, the number of immigrants declined to 2,659. A sense of urgency is suggested by the fact that the average number of emigrants per shipload rose sharply from 73 in 1903 to 104 in 1904 and to 166 in the first half of 1905.[21] The last large group of Korean immigrants to Hawaii arrived in a single shipload on May 18, 1905.[22]

There are, of course, a number of reasons why mass Korean immigration to the United States and its territories was brought to an end in 1905: basic Korean conservatism, particularly regarding absence from ancestors' graves; the opposition of individual Korean politicians and individual American missionaries; and, perhaps, the recall of Horace Allen. The principal reason was, however, the accelerating establishment of Japanese hegemony on the Korean peninsula. "Complete freedom of action in Korea" was one of the major Japanese aims in the 1904–1905 war with Russia. In February 1904, the Korean court was forced to make damaging concessions which allowed the Japanese to interfere in Korean administration and to prevent Korean attempts to seek assistance from other powers. Provisions of the February protocol were expanded in late May, with the effect that the Japanese began to establish a de facto protectorate in Korea.[23] As a means of assuming supervisory

---

[19] Ko, Han'guk Iminsa Yŏn'gu, 208–210.

[20] Only 93 received medical clearance during an intermediate stop at Kobe, according to No Chae-yŏn, Chae-Mi Hanin Sa Ryak [Brief History of Korean Residents in America] (Los Angeles, 1951), 4–5.

[21] Citing Hyŏn Sun, P'owa Yuram Ki [Memoirs of My Hawaiian Sojourn] (Seoul [?], 1909), 5, Ko Sŭng-je gives the size of the first group departing Inchon as 97. Kim Wŏn-yong's figures (121 departing, 101 arriving Honolulu) are somewhat higher.

[22] No, Chae-Mi Hanin Sa Ryak, 29. According to Ko, Han'guk Iminsa Yŏn'gu, 210–211, a small number continued to arrive until November 1905.

[23] Shumpei Okamoto, The Japanese Oligarchy and the Russo-Japanese War (New York and London, 1970), 112–120.

and veto powers over Korean affairs, the Japanese demanded and secured Korean acceptance of foreign advisers on financial and foreign affairs, both of whom would follow the instructions of their respective ministries in the Japanese government. The foreign affairs adviser appointed in August 1904 was Durham White Stevens, an American employee of the Japanese foreign office and a protegé of Theodore Roosevelt. Shortly afterward, the Korean police came under the complete supervision of the Japanese military gendarmerie.[24] The Japanese perceived further Korean immigration as a threat to their newly established political control over Korea.[25] Emigration was effectively suspended and the Suminwŏn dissolved on November 17, 1905, with the signing of the secretly negotiated treaty that formalized the Japanese protectorate in Korea. The Suminwŏn's director, Min Yŏng-hwan, committed suicide, leaving an impassioned plea for independence addressed to the people of Korea.[26]

Of the 7,226 immigrants to Hawaii during the years 1903–1905, 6,048 were male adults, 637 women, and 541 children. Less than sixty percent remained in Hawaii; roughly a thousand immigrants returned to Korea, while two thousand moved on to the continental United States.[27] Unfortunately, we do not have a detailed sociological profile of the immigrants to Hawaii. According to Bernice B. H. Kim, almost all the adult males were between the ages of twenty and thirty. Most were common manual laborers from Korean port cities and towns; the remainder included former soldiers in the Korean army, household servants, policemen, woodcutters, and miners. Few came from rural districts, and less than fourteen percent were farmers.[28] There may have been a few students and

---

[24] Kim and Kim, *Korea and the Politics of Imperialism*, 123–124.

[25] The Japanese anti-emigration policy was further encouraged by the news of the tragic circumstances of Korean contract laborers who had emigrated to Mexico in early 1905. According to Patterson, the Japanese minister to Seoul, Hayashi Gonsuke, successfully demanded an end to emigration in April 1905 ("Koreans to Hawaii," 29), yet 92 emigrants were admitted to Honolulu in July 1905. Ko, *Han'guk Iminsa Yŏn'gu*, 210–211.

[26] Kim and Kim, *Korea and the Politics of Imperialism*, 132.

[27] Kim, *Chae-Mi Hanin Osimnyŏn Sa*, 3, 6. Ko Sŭng-je, whose data are based on Honolulu immigration records and extend into late 1905, has a slightly higher total, 7,296, of whom 715 were women. Both totals are remarkably consistent with data from the *Annual Reports of the Commissioner of Immigration* for 1903–1905.

[28] Bernice Bong Hee Kim, "The Koreans in Hawaii," *Social Science*, IX (1934), 409.

churchmen, but sixty-five percent were illiterate.[29] Clearly, their emigration had almost no impact on the Korean rural economy.

The economic life of most Koreans in America in the early years was not much different from that of other unskilled immigrants. They came as agricultural laborers and so remained until other job opportunities developed. A majority were significantly ill-suited for the rigors of work on the Hawaiian sugar plantations. The daily wage of 69 cents was what recruiters had promised, but little remained after repaying loans. Some immigrants left the plantations for work in railroad construction, fisheries, or the mines. Between 1905 and 1907, some 1,003 Korean laborers fled to the continental United States. Many of them were attracted by the rice farms in California, thinking the work would be more familiar and less strenuous.[30] Railroad construction in the western United States presented another opportunity. A vigorous recruiting effort was conducted in February 1905 by a railroad company agent who established an office in a Korean hotel in Honolulu. Advertisements were placed in local Korean language newspapers with a view toward recruiting 5,000 workers, but the number actually engaged was considerably smaller. Most of the Koreans recruited for railway construction jobs entered at San Francisco; others entered at Seattle, the western terminus of the expanding Great Northern railway system.[31] A relatively large number of railroad workers were established in Salt Lake City by 1906. Some stayed as section hands after construcction was completed, eventually going into truck farming and other agrarian pursuits in Oregon, central California, Colorado, Utah, Kansas, and Montana.[32]

In the face of mounting demands from Californians for Japanese and Korean exclusion legislation, and in the midst of a deepening diplomatic crisis with Japan, the U.S. Congress passed an amendment to the Immigration Act of 1907 which authorized President

[29] Kim, *Chae-Mi Hanin Osimnyŏn Sa*, 7.

[30] Ko, *Han'guk Iminsa Yŏn'gu*, 217–218; Bernice Kim, "Koreans in Hawaii," 411. The 1,003 figure is Ko's; Bernice Kim puts the number at "about a thousand."

[31] *Miju Hanin Ch'ilsimnyŏn Sa* [*Seventy Year History of Koreans in America*] (Seoul, 1973), 59.

[32] No, *Chae-Mi Hanin Sa Ryak*, 26, 57–64. For a brief account of a Korean community established by section hands near Butte, see Dale White, "Koreans in Montana," *Asia and the Americas*, XLV (1945), 156.

Theodore Roosevelt to exclude any immigrant not holding a valid passport to the United States. The President's implementing executive order focused more narrowly on Japanese and Korean trans-migration from Hawaii to the mainland.[33] Once the provisions of Roosevelt's executive order had taken effect, the inflow of Korean immigrants to the United States and its territories slowed rapidly, reaching a low point—eight entries—in fiscal year 1911.[34]

The flow from Hawaii to the mainland was, of course, effectively cut off. But the Korean government continued to issue passports, in the apparent hope that Koreans could continue to immigrate, despite the strong anti-immigration policies of the Japanese protectorate in Korea. In late 1907, the American Secretary of State, Elihu Root, ruled that the United States would not recognize Korean passports, only passports issued by the Japanese Foreign Office.[35]

When the protectorate was formally implemented on November 17, 1905, the incipient decline of American fortunes sharpened in the face of rapidly advancing Japanese commercial operations. The Japanese moved to assure American government and business leaders that Japan intended to adhere to the principles of Open Door Policy in East Asia. Prince Itō Hirobumi, the Japanese resident-general in Korea, sent Durham Stevens to explain Japanese policy and to ameliorate the negative feelings of Americans doing business in Korea.[36]

Stevens arrived in San Francisco on March 20, 1908, and died

[33] Executive Order, March 14, 1907, Theodore Roosevelt Papers, Library of Congress; cf. Charles E. Neu, *An Uncertain Friendship: Theodore Roosevelt and Japan, 1906–1909* (Cambridge, Mass., 1967), chaps. 2 and 3, for domestic and diplomatic background.

[34] U.S. Commissioner of Immigration, *Annual Report, 1911* (Washington, D.C., 1912), 26–27; see also "Asiatic Immigration to the United States by Race or People, 1899–1944."

[35] Oscar Stans to Root, Nov. 6, 1907; Root to Stans, Nov. 12, 1907, Numerical File, 1906–1910, U.S. Dept. of State Papers.

[36] Stevens is a curious and tragic figure. His principal Japanese patron, Hioki Masu, who later served as Japanese minister in Washington, warned him that his position as adviser to the Korean Foreign Ministry would be a difficult one: "When one has to go apparently against the interests of his own countrymen he feels a great burden." Stevens, on the contrary, seemed to delight in the ascription by American businessmen in Korea that he was "more pro-Japanese than the Japanese officials themselves." His assignment in Seoul apparently lasted slightly more than a year. He probably spent the intervening years in Tokyo. Hioki to Allen, Sept. 8, 1905; Stevens to Allen, Oct. 26, 1905; and Townsend to Allen, Nov. 30, 1905, Horace D. Allen Papers, New York Public Library.

there five days later. His public statement in an arrival interview might have convinced Americans that Korea actually benefited under Japanese administration, but it was sufficiently derogatory to infuriate local Koreans. When published in the *San Francisco Chronicle*, Stevens's remarks led to a mass joint meeting of the Taedong Pogukhoe (Restoration Association) and Kongnip Hyŏphoe (Mutual Assistance Association) members and local Koreans in the San Francisco Bay area. A committee of four delegates, selected to confront Stevens at the first opportunity,[37] accosted him at the Fairmont Hotel. When he refused to retract his statements, he was severely assaulted until other hotel guests intervened. Undoubtedly shaken by the incident, Stevens prepared his departure for Washington, D.C., on March 23.

When Stevens arrived at the Ferry Building the following morning to make his railway connection,[38] he was accompanied by the Japanese consul, Koike Chōzō. As they alighted from a limousine, Chŏn Myŏng-un, a member of the Kongnip Hyŏphoe, stepped forward with a revolver. Chŏn failed to shoot Stevens but struck him a vicious blow on the face. In the ensuing scuffle, Chŏn was wounded and Stevens shot by Chang In-whan, a member of the Taedong Pogukhoe. Stevens died on the night of March 25; both Chŏn and Chang were arraigned a week later. Because there was insufficient evidence to show that the assassination was the result of a conspiracy of Korean associations, Chŏn was released in June and Chang tried as the sole plaintiff. In the course of the trial, which lasted seven months, the prosecution naturally received substantial assistance from the Japanese consulate, which sought the maximum penalty. The Korean community in the United States and Hawaii directed its efforts toward defense: hiring lawyers, soliciting defense funds, providing interpreters, and collecting evidence.[39] In view of the circumstances, the defense was rather successful; Chang was convicted of second degree murder, sentenced to twenty-five years in

---

[37] Warren Y. Kim places the mass meeting at the "Korean Mission building." *Koreans in America* (Seoul, 1971), 80. He probably means the Korean Southern Methodist Mission Church at 2350 California St., San Francisco. See No, *Chae-Mi Hanin Sa Ryak*, 62.

[38] Yi Sŏn-gŭn, *Han'guk Sa* [*History of Korea*], VI: *Hyŏndae-p'yŏn* [*Modern Period*] (Seoul, 1963), 965, gives the scene of the shooting as the Oakland railway station.

[39] Overseas Koreans in the U.S., Hawaii, Mexico, China, and Japan contributed $7,390 to the defense. Kim, *Chae-Mi Hanin Osimnyŏn Sa*, 327.

San Quentin penitentiary, and paroled for good behavior after ten years. Chang died in 1930 at age fifty-five; Korean community organizations were heavily represented at his funeral.[40]

The Stevens case involved the first outbreak of nationalism among Koreans in America. It also served to confirm Japanese hostility toward student visa applications. This negative policy was maintained on the grounds that students might become involved in anti-Japanese political agitation; furthermore, any implication that Korean students might prefer an American rather than a Japanese education was highly annoying to the Japanese. By early 1909, however, the Japanese government indicated a willingness to issue passports to Korean students who could show evidence of welcome from the United States government as well as sufficient funds. The American consul-general in Seoul finally agreed to issue student visas to Korean students sponsored by American nationals, provided that the latter would vouch for the students' qualifications and financial ability.[41] During the William Howard Taft administration, the United States government adopted a positive, highly encouraging policy regarding Korean students, and immigration officials were directed to give them "every proper consideration."[42]

During the nine years following the Japanese annexation of Korea in 1910, some 541 students, known to Koreans in America as *sindo haksaeng* (newly arrived students), were admitted for study at American schools and universities.[43] Large numbers made their way to the continental United States via Shanghai on board American flagships without passports or student visas. Most claimed that they were not Japanese subjects, and thus exempt from any requirement to carry a Chōsen Sōtokufu (the Japanese governor-general in Korea) passport, and, furthermore, that they had left Korea before Japan assumed sovereignty over the peninsula. Classifying this group as "working students," the U.S. commissioner of immigration adopted a surprisingly sympathetic policy toward them.[44]

---

40 For a detailed account, including biographical notes on Chŏn and Chang, see *ibid.*, 318–330.

41 Thomas Sammons to T. J. O'Brien, April 14, 1908, Nov. 2, 1908, Jan. 25, 1909, and March 24, 1909, Numerical File, 1906–1910, U.S. Department of State Papers.

42 Charles Nagel to P. C. Knox, March 22, 1909; Knox to O'Brien, March 29, 1909, *ibid.*

43 Kim, *Chae-Mi Hanin Osimnyŏn Sa*, 29.

44 *Miju Hanin Chilshimnyŏn Sa*, 75; U.S. Commissioner of Immigration, *Annual Report, 1914* (Washington, D.C., 1915), 319.

Realizing that most *sindo haksaeng* were essentially political refugees, the leadership of a budding Korean independence movement in America welcomed them as a potentially useful addition to the Korean community. The reaction of Koreans in America to the formal annexation of Korea in the summer of 1910 was directed by the Tae-Han Kungminhoe (Korean National Association). Having anticipated annexation by several months, the Tae-Han Kungminhoe (THK) called on its membership to participate in and contribute financially to a series of patriotic, anti-Japanese programs. Lacking U.S. government interest or support, the THK sent telegrams of protest to both the Korean king and Japanese emperor, a move that produced no apparent result. The THK encouraged the establishment of quasi-military training programs in the hope that military resistance to Japanese rule would become widespread and demanded the participation of young Koreans from the American community. "Military academies" were organized in Hawaii; Claremont and Lompoc, California; Superior, Wyoming; Hastings, Nebraska; and Kansas City. Nearly $60,000 was contributed to the THK in support of the military training program, which continued to function until 1916.[45]

When anti-Japanese activities of Korean immigrants in Hawaii and the United States intensified after the 1910 annexation, the seriously concerned Japanese government decided to grant exit permits to young Korean women who were willing to go abroad under marriage contracts—this as a means to calm political passions among overseas Koreans. Only about ten percent of the 1903–1905 Korean immigrants had been women. The unbalanced sex ratio had brought some immigrants back to Korea in search of wives. Most, however, had lacked sufficient capital to return to the United States or Hawaii, even if they had wished to do so. The Japanese decision to issue exit permits to Korean women resulted in more than a thousand marriages in the period 1910–1924. Most (951) of the brides brought to Hawaii in this fashion were from the southern Korean town of Yongnam and its environs, while most of the 115 brides who came to the U.S. mainland via Shanghai were from the northern provinces,[46] probably Hwanghae and Pyŏng'an. The

45 Kim, *Chae-Mi Hanin Osimnyŏn Sa*, 330–346.

46 *Ibid.*, 27–29. Not all Koreans admitted under these arrangements were young women; the 197 brides who entered at Honolulu in the fiscal years 1918–1921 were accompanied by twenty children and six "parents." The so-called picture bride

preponderance of brides from the southern provinces reflected the continuing socioeconomic effects of overpopulation and low income. The situation of these young women was so distressed that they would willingly risk marrying an unknown person far away.

The picture marriages had a number of important sociological consequences for the Korean immigrant community. They consumed a great deal of accumulated capital because the cost of the marriage arrangements to the typical plantation, farm, or railroad worker was high, usually between $300 and $500; in many cases it was necessary for the prospective groom to borrow from, or simply impose upon, friendly individuals and institutions. The picture groom dealt with marriage brokers in an entrepôt city. His temporary residence in Honolulu or the San Francisco Bay area while waiting for his bride to arrive often involved a change of job, and this, coupled with his reluctance to return with his bride to the plantation worker's life, resulted in a steep increase in the urbanization rate. In Hawaii, increasing numbers of Koreans left the plantations for the Dole pineapple cannery and the Honolulu docks.[47] The picture marriages resulted in rapid growth in the size of the second generation;[48] these immigrants, now largely urbanized, enjoyed vastly improved opportunities for education. The picture marriages contributed to the leveling of values between southern, agrarian brides and northern grooms of urban or near-urban origin. An unfortunate, though temporary, consequence of the common disparity in ages between bride and groom was that second-generation Koreans were often left to spend a considerable number of their formative years with their undereducated, non-English speaking, widowed mothers. The same age difference may account for the relatively high divorce rate among Koreans in Hawaii in the 1914–1926 period.[49]

---

scheme. long used by Chinese and Japanese immigrants, as well as Koreans, should more properly be termed picture marriages; if only one party supplied a photograph it was usually the groom, not the bride, who did so.

[47] Bernice Kim, "The Koreans in Hawaii," 441. The number of Korean sugar plantation workers declined by 50 percent between 1920 and 1924. William Carlson Smith, *Americans in Process: a Study of Our Citizens of Oriental Ancestry* (Ann Arbor, 1937), table IX, 67.

[48] When the picture marriage inflow began in 1910, there were 107 second-generation Koreans in Hawaii; by 1920 there were 345 in the 10-to-17 age group alone, 39 percent of whom lived in Honolulu proper. Smith, *Americans in Process*, table XVI, 212.

[49] At fourteen per thousand, it was the highest of the non-Caucasian ancestral groups. *Ibid.*, table XVII, 215.

In late June 1913, at the height of the anti-Japanese labor movement in California, eleven Koreans were severely beaten as they
attempted to work in an orchard near Riverside. When an official
of the Japanese consulate in Los Angeles visited the victims and
offered assistance, the Tae-Han Kungminhoe (THK) interfered.
Refusing to accept any offer of help from Japanese officials, the
THK's leadership dispatched a telegram to William Jennings
Bryan, U.S. Secretary of State, making the following points: All
Korean residents of the state of California arrived before 1910,
when Korea was annexed by the Japanese; they were Koreans, who
opposed Japanese domination of Korea; Japanese government assistance was refused, particularly because the acceptance of such aid
would imply that Koreans were Japanese subjects; and all matters
regarding Koreans in America should be taken up with the Korean
community organization, the Tae-Han Kungminhoe or Korean National Association of North America. Bryan's prompt response,
favoring the THK position, was widely published, and the THK
gained recognition as a quasi-diplomatic organization representing
the Korean immigrant community.[50]

Along with their deepening involvement in political activities,
increasing numbers of Korean immigrants sought to improve their
economic situations. Especially after 1910, a substantial portion of
Korean males went to the cities where they sought their fortunes
as canning factory workers, or as stevedores, cooks, waiters, jani-
tors, and domestic servants. The general economic stability and
growth of the 1915–1920 period brought some relief to those immigrants, particularly plantation workers, who had been maintaining
themselves at a bare subsistence level.[51] There was a general increase
in wages and the availability of new jobs for both skilled and unskilled immigrants, particularly in industrial and semi-industrial
areas. By this time, Korean immigrants had accumulated sufficient

50 Kim, *Chae-Mi Hanin Osimnyŏn Sa*, 114–117. The Korean National Association
of North America was incorporated as a nonprofit, social service organization under
the laws of the state of California on April 6, 1914. See Ch'oe Hŭi-song, *Ping-Segye
Ch'ilsimnyŏn: Na ŭi chasojon* [*Seventy Years in the Cold World: My Autobiography*]
(Seoul, 1964), 30, for an account of THK representations with Bureau of Immigration
officials at San Francisco on behalf of detained Korean arrivals.

51 The general and sustained poverty among early Korean settlers was partly due
to the demanded, and sometimes forced, financial contributions ("duty money") to
various Korean political organizations. Typical monthly wage scales for the 1903–
1910 period are: plantation workers (Hawaii), $16; farm laborers (California), $36;
railroad construction and mining (Utah and Montana), $60; fishery workers (Wash-
ington and Alaska), $37. Kim, *Chae-Mi Hanin Osimnyŏn Sa*, 283, 298–299.

capital to venture into small business operations: laundry, roominghouse, barber, restaurant, and shoe repair services, as well as retail grocery and used furniture shops. Those who remained in the agricultural sector were now able to operate their own small farms and orchards. The general strike by Japanese plantation workers on Oahu in 1919 gave their Korean counterparts an opportunity to shift from outer-island sugar plantations to stevedoring and cannery work.[52] Despite marked increases in sugar plantation wages, the balance shifted by 1922, and the majority of Korean workers in Hawaii were engaged elsewhere. The trend continued for another decade and only reversed itself slightly due to the employment of small numbers of second-generation plantation workers.[53]

Korean immigrants undertook several ambitious economic enterprises between 1910 and 1925. The grandest schemes were large-scale agricultural ventures sponsored by Korean political organizations. The T'aedong Sirŏp Chusik Hoesa (Great Eastern Industrial Co.) was organized in 1910 by the leadership of the Korean National Association of North America to finance its political activities. One thousand $50 stock certificates were issued to capitalize the purchase of 2,430 acres of farmland in Manchuria. The THK intended to build a model farm village accommodating two hundred families, but the selection of the farm site was unfortunate, and the venture was a complete loss.[54] A similar venture in California was less disastrous. The Hŭngsadan (Corps for the Advancement of Individuals) formed the Puk-Mi Sorŏp Hoesa (North American Farming Industry Company) in 1917. Capitalized at $95,000, the company began rice farming with the hope that a model village for Hŭngsadan members would eventually be constructed.[55] This dream was never realized, and after a decade the company was dissolved.[56]

Smaller scale, nonpolitical business ventures were notably more

52 Bernice Kim, "Koreans in Hawaii," 441.
53 Ko, *Han'guk Ilminsa Yŏn'gu*, 218–219; Smith, *Americans in Process*, 67–69.
54 Kim, *Chae-Mi Hanin Osimnyŏn Sa*, 286. For a reproduction of one of the stock certificates, dated August 10, 1910, see *ibid.*, 287.
55 *Miju Hanin Ch'ilsimnyŏn Sa*, 103.
56 According to Kim, *Chae-Mi Hanin Osimnyŏn Sa*, 289, the rice farming business began to decline in 1920. No, *Chae-Mi Hanin Sa Ryak*, 103, gives the organization and dissolution dates as 1912 and 1929, and states that the company was most successful during World War I.

successful. Early immigrants in Hawaii had little opportunity to free themselves from the sugar plantations, but some few did manage to open small businesses. By 1922, there were twenty-two Korean entrepreneurs operating in Hawaiian cities with capital investments between $1,000 and $20,000. In addition to the traditional Asian immigrant hotel, restaurant, and grocery enterprises, Koreans engaged in thirteen different commercial operations, including variety goods and furniture retailing, ready-to-wear clothing manufacturing, and construction contracting.[57] On the Pacific Coast, economic opportunities were limited by more intense and effective racial prejudice. Entrepreneurial activity within the Los Angeles Korean community was extremely modest and conventional. The largest enterprise by 1939 was the Oriental Food Products Co., which specialized in the wholesale distribution of canned and other processed Oriental foods. But it was in agriculture that the greatest scale and level of success of Korean entrepreneurial skill was achieved.

Korean settlers in California, Oregon, Colorado, Montana, Kansas, and Nebraska began vegetable farming as early as 1911. They followed with successful ventures in orchards, nurseries, and vineyards. In 1916, a group of sixty Koreans in the Manteca, California, area pooled their resources to lease 1,300 acres for experimental sugar beet production. Business thrived, and a small cooperative village was organized nearby. A smaller group of Koreans in Logan, Utah, succeeded with a 292-acre melon farm. By far the most successful of all Korean enterprises before 1924 were the rice and fruit farming operations in the San Joaquin Valley. One California Korean, Kim Chong-nim, celebrated as the "Rice King" in 1917, was able to expand his operations to 2,085 acres in rice. Near Reedley, two brothers, Kim Ho and Kim Hyŏng-sun, began a truckfarming business in 1921, eventually working 500 acres. Their business grew to $100,000 annually, as they expanded into nectarine and other fruit production and wholesaling along with canning and large-scale nurseries.[58]

Korean immigrants began building churches and church-related

<hr>

57 *Hawai-zai Chōsenjin Ippan Jōtai* [*General Situation of the Koreans in Hawaii*], cited by Ko, *Han'guk Iminsa Yŏn'gu*, 218–219.

58 Kim, *Chae-Mi Hanin Osimnyŏn Sa*, 299, 302–305. No Chae-yŏn gives slightly different totals for participants and acreage involved in cooperative ventures. No, *Chae-Mi Hanin Sa Ryak*, 119–128.

schools in their first years of settlement in Hawaii and the United States and continued to do so in ensuing years. The churches and schools served as community life centers and provided a source of hope for an uncertain future. Korean immigrants viewed the establishment of the Japanese protectorate in 1905 as a clear danger signal, and, when their worst fears were confirmed with outright annexation in 1910, large numbers of them became virtually obsessed with maintaining their identity as Christians and as Koreans. More than half of the early settlers had been active members of missionary church groups when they left Korea;[59] the remainder willingly participated in church activities as the only organized social activity available.

The first Korean church service was held at Mokolia plantation on July 4, 1903, barely six months after the arrival of the first group of immigrants. The Korean Methodist Church of Hawaii was established in November of the same year; the Korean Episcopal Church in January 1905, and the Korean Christian Church of Hawaii in 1918. The Korean Methodist Church of San Francisco held its first service in October 1905, and in 1906 the Korean Presbyterian Church was established in Los Angeles. By the end of the first decade, there were in the Hawaiian territory alone over thirty-one churches and church-schools, with congregations of 2,800, while on the mainland there were seven church missions with approximately 450 constant members.[60] Churches of various other denominations were organized in the next two decades. By the mid-1920s, Korean churches were established in Chicago and New York City, as well as in several California cities. The Methodist and Presbyterian congregations were the largest and most active; while there were modest congregations of Episcopalians and Baptists, the number of Buddhists and Catholics remained negligible.[61] Over the years, in a definite manifestation of the growing sense of Korean nationalism, the Korean Christian movement became increasingly independent of American church leaders and their organizations.

Nearly every Christian mission in Hawaii provided Sunday school and Korean language classes for children and English language classes on various plantations designed to reduce the illit-

---

[59] Kim, *Chae-Mi Hanin Osimnyŏn Sa*, 40.

[60] *Ibid.*, 41.

[61] Warren Y. Kim, *Koreans in America* (Seoul, 1971), 31–40.

eracy rate among Korean workers. Korean language books and
periodicals were imported for this purpose. The first institution
devoted primarily to education was the Hanin Kisuk Hakkyo (Korean Boarding School or "Korean compound"), which was established in Honolulu in 1906 by the Korean Methodist mission.[62]
Various courses were offered for boys aged seven to twelve as preparation for admission to American secondary schools; the Korean
language was included in the curriculum. For a brief period, the
school was known as the Girls' Seminary, but in 1918 it was expanded as a coeducational institution and its name changed to
Hanin Kidok Hagwŏn (Korean Christian Institute). It was eventually converted to an orphanage in 1928.[63] Both Pak Yong-man
and Syngman Rhee were closely connected with the Korean boarding school in Honolulu, and, it is said, their celebrated political
rivalry began with a dispute over school administration.[64]

Six Korean language schools were in operation on the mainland
between 1906 and 1940. All these were located in California—San
Francisco, Los Angeles, Sacramento, Dinuba, Reedley, and Delano.
After 1931, the number of mission and church-related language
schools in rural areas declined as increasing numbers of Korean
immigrants and their families moved into the cities. The organization of language schools in large California cities in 1906 demonstrated the resistance of the Korean community to the San Francisco Board of Education's decision to segregate all Chinese, Japanese, and Korean school children in a separate Oriental school.[65]

But it was the politically oriented organizations, rather than the
churches or language schools, which came to dominate the structure of the Korean community in America. The first attempt to
organize Korean immigrants occurred in 1903, when An Ch'ang-ho
formed a small fraternal group of San Francisco area students called
the Ch'inmokhoe (Friends' Association). With the burst of anti-Japanese feelings among Korean immigrants attending the estab-

62 Kim, *Chae-Mi Hanin Osimnyŏn Sa*, 243. Cf. Arthur L. Gardner, *The Koreans in Hawaii: An Annotated Bibliography* (Honolulu, 1970), entry 30.

63 Kim, *Chae-Mi Hanin Osimnyŏn Sa*, 246, gives 1928 as the closing date of the institute; in his severely abridged English-language version, *Koreans in America*, 44, the date is given as 1933.

64 For a partisan account of Rhee's involvement, see Robert T. Oliver, *Syngman Rhee, The Man Behind the Myth* (New York, 1954), 122–123.

65 The board's earlier resolution to pursue a segregation policy inspired the formation of the Japanese-Korean Exclusion League in May 1905. Neu, *An Uncertain Friendship*, 23–25.

lishment of the Japanese protectorate in Korea in 1905, the Ch'in-mokhoe was reorganized as the Kongnip Hyŏphoe (Mutual Assistance Association), giving a definite political cast to an otherwise traditional immigrant community mutual benefit society. By 1908, the membership had grown to 130, distributed among six California local branches.[66] Under similar political motivation, Korean community leaders in Honolulu saw a need to mobilize the more than twenty Korean clubs and societies in various localities. In 1907 they organized the Hanin Hapsŏng Hyŏphoe (United Korean Society), with headquarters in Honolulu.

The efforts to mobilize proliferating community organizations and, more importantly, to bring the Hawaiian and mainland Korean communities into closer cooperation were greatly accelerated by the Stevens case of 1908. The Tae-Hanin Kungminhoe (Korean National Association of North America) was formed in 1909 for the express purpose of uniting all Korean organizations in the United States and its territories in a concerted effort to protect Koreans and, at the same time, to channel their political energies and sustain their commitment to Korean culture. The THK central headquarters was established in San Francisco, with chapter headquarters in Hawaii, Siberia, and Manchuria. Of the 116 local branches, 78 were in Hawaii, where their role has been described as a "government within a government."[67] All Koreans in America were required to join the THK and were subject to its membership dues.

The THK movement in Hawaii reached its peak in 1915, by which time the association had invited Syngman Rhee to Hawaii. There ensued protracted factional controversy between Rhee and An Ch'ang-ho and Pak Yong-man, the most prominent Korean political activists in America, which greatly weakened the organization. The central issue of the bitter controversy was the means to be used to achieve the goal of Korean independence; Pak Yong-man favored an activist, militant approach, while Rhee favored a

---

66 In Oakland, Los Angeles, Redlands, Riverside, Boyd, and Rockspring; an unknown number of chapters were also established in the Far East. Kim, *Chae-Mi Hanin Osimnyŏn Sa*, 88.

67 Gardner, *Koreans in Hawaii*, 3. The central headquarters was moved to Los Angeles in 1913. Kim, *Chae-Mi Hanin Osimnyŏn Sa*, 111.

slower course, emphasizing education and diplomacy.[68] With his designation as premier and later as chief executive of the Korean Provisional Government (KPG), established in 1919 at Shanghai, Rhee's prestige greatly increased. For the next two years, as "president" of the provisional government, he devoted himself to a vain attempt to secure support at international conferences. Rhee organized the Tongjihoe (Society for the Like-Minded) in Honolulu in 1921 to reinforce his position vis-à-vis the KPG. But the KPG was already on the verge of collapse because of divergent political strategies and the style of Rhee's leadership.[69] Rhee returned to Honolulu to demand that Tongjihoe members remain exclusively loyal to him; in 1924 he was elected to a life term as the society's executive-general. Tongjihoe branch organizations were formed in Chicago, Detroit, Butte, New York, and Los Angeles, where a chapter was established in 1929.[70]

The Hŭngsadan (Corps for the Advancement of Individuals)[71] was formally organized in San Francisco on May 13, 1913, when An Ch'ang-ho mobilized a small group of young Korean students in the San Francisco Bay area. With the motto "virtue, intellect, and health," the Hŭngsadan's immediate purpose was to improve the lives of individual overseas Koreans, particularly youths, and its long-range goal was to provide elitist leadership which would eventually manage the restoration of Korean sovereignty and subsequent reconstruction.[72] As means to these ends, the Hŭngsadan rejected radical revolutionary methods, choosing instead a patient program of individual improvement involving both formal education and self-study.

---

[68] Gardner, *Koreans in Hawaii*, 3–4. Rhee essentially relied on propaganda directed to the United States. Chong-sik Lee, *Politics of Korean Nationalism* (Berkeley and Los Angeles, 1963), 135.

[69] Lee, *Politics of Korean Nationalism*, chap. 8, *passim;* cf. Frank Baldwin, "The March First Movement: Korean Challenge and Japanese Response" (Ph.D. dissertation, Columbia University, 1969), 105–107, for external reasons for the KPG's "predetermined failure."

[70] Tongjihoe membership ranged from 150 to 400; monthly dues were $1.25. For a full historical account, including organizational structure, operational rules and regulations, and biographical notes, usually critical, on Rhee, see Kim, *Chae-Mi Hanin Osimnyŏn Sa*, 198–209.

[71] Translation from Lee, *Politics of Korean Nationalism*, 239.

[72] Kim, *Chae-Mi Hanin Osimnyŏn Sa*, 176–177.

In its early years, the Hŭngsadan concentrated on recruitment. An Ch'ang-ho made it a point to interview every student immigrant on arrival at San Francisco, with a view toward selecting the most impressive as candidates for Hŭngsadan membership. One such student recalled his 1916 meeting with An:

An came to visit me one day when I was picking oranges on a farm. He told me that, though each individual is free to pursue his studies and other activities, we Koreans should unite to do "anything" for our fallen mother country. If not, we would be like wandering Jews [without a country] . . . . I became a member, but first had to go through a rather intensive "question-and-answer" process of selection. I passed the examination and took an oath of allegiance at a ceremony conducted by An and previously selected student members.[73]

When An went to Shanghai in 1919 to join the Korean Provisional Government he continued Hŭngsadan recruitment. One of his most illustrious recruits was Yi Kwang-su, now considered to be the father of modern Korean literature.[74] Of his encounter with An, Yi wrote:

An Ch'ang-ho impressed me very deeply. After hearing about the [Hŭngsadan's] principles . . . I was convinced that the independence of our nation could not be attained through a [radical] movement, but only through cultivating the strength of the nation . . . through strengthening individuals and organizing them.[75]

Thus began Yi Kwang-su's transformation from a student radical idealist to a gradualist committed to feasible intermediate goals in the Hŭngsadan style.[76] Actually, the Hŭngsadan never functioned as an active political organization. Most members were, in fact, members of the Korean National Association of North America.

The public dynamics of Korean immigrant politics are recorded in Korean community publications. More than thirty Korean language periodicals appeared in Hawaii and the continental United States between 1903 and 1924.[77] Most were conspicuously short-

---

73 Ch'oe, *Ping-segye Ch'ilsimnyŏn*, 37.
74 Cf. Peter H. Lee, *Korean Literature: Topics and Themes* (Tucson, 1965), 102, 112.
75 Yi Kwang-su, *Nae Kobaek* [*My Confessions*] (Seoul, 1948), 138–139, as cited and translated in Lee, *Politics of Korean Nationalism*, 239–240.
76 *Ibid.*, 239.
77 Taehan Min'guk Kukhoe Tosŏgwan [National Assembly Library, Republic of Korea], *Han'guk Sinmun Chapchi Ch'ong Mongnok, 1883–1945* [*Catalogue of Korean*

lived, suggesting that many ambitious publishers were richer in good intentions than in financial resources. A large number of weeklies and monthlies lasted for less than a year; others survived for several years. Periodicals associated with political associations reflect the turbulent histories of such organizations: frequent reorganization, and title changes, widely fluctuating availability of funds, and abrupt shifts of editorial policy. Still, precisely this type of publication enjoyed the greatest longevity.

Three well-known periodicals served the Korean community for periods ranging from a decade to more than seventy years. The oldest Korean publication is the *Sin-Han Minbo* [*New Korea*], the organ of the Korean National Association of North America, currently published in Los Angeles as a weekly. The first issue appeared in San Francisco in 1905 as the *Kongnip Sinmun* [*Korean News*], a publication of An Ch'ang-ho's Kongnip Hyŏphoe. The *Kongnip Sinmun* was absorbed in 1910 by the THK's *Sin-Han Minbo*. The second oldest publication is the *T'aep'yŏngyang Chubo* [*Korean Pacific Weekly*], which was first published in 1913 as a monthly magazine in Honolulu under Syngman Rhee's editorship. Another publication worthy of notice was the *Sin Han'guk po* [*United Korean News*], published by the Hawaiian committee of the THK under Pak Yong-man's leadership between 1909 and 1913. Previously published as a daily beginning in 1907, it continued weekly publication under various titles and changing format until December 1968.[78]

Nearly all of the Korean community publications were political. Both news content and editorial policy were designed to instill in the immigrant reader a sense of Korean nationalism. The most frequently reported topics and editorial themes centered on the Korean independence movement in Korea proper and overseas, the spirit of *aeguk chŏngsin* (patriotism), and the dream of *kwangbok* (restoration of Korean independence). In addition to the publications of various Korean student associations, there were several distinctive, special-purpose Korean language periodicals. The *Tansan Sibo* [*Korean Report*], for example, was published in 1925

Periodicals, 1883–1945] (Seoul, 1966), 133–176. See also Kim, *Chae-Mi Hanin Osimnyŏn Sa*, 259–279, which contains a comprehensive list of overseas Korean publications, including monographs.

78 Cf. Gardner, *Koreans in Hawaii*, entries 47, 101, 178, 181, and 187–189.

by a Korean communist group in Honolulu;[79] while the Korean
Socialist-Labor party organization in Los Angeles published
Tongmu [*Comrades*] in 1921.[80] The overseas Korean periodicals
that survived probably did so because the subsidizing political organizations required subscriptions as a condition of membership.

Korean political activists in both America and China were struck
by the relevance to their situation of President Woodrow Wilson's
Fourteen Points speech of January 8, 1918. As is well known, article
five of Wilson's address stressed the principle of self-determination,
especially the more specific idea that colonial claims should be
adjusted to reflect the interests of the colonized population, not just
those of the colonial governments. Charles R. Crane, traveling as
Wilson's unofficial emissary, arrived in Shanghai in late November
and was regarded by local Koreans as a possible means of communication with the President. Encouraged by a preliminary individual encounter with Crane, the Korean Shanghai group hurriedly
formed the Sin-Han Ch'ŏngnyŏn Tan (New Korea Youth Party)
as an organizational base for their petition. The petition was de-
livered to one of Crane's entourage, and an additional copy was
placed in the hands of Thomas Millard, the editor of the influential
Millard's Review. Encouraged by these events, the leadership of
the Sin-Han Ch'ŏngyŏn Tan (SHCT) summoned Kim Kyu-sik,
American educated and fluent in English, from Tientsin to send
him to the Paris Peace Conference. Difficulties in booking passage
were overcome when Kim was allowed to travel in company with
the Chinese delegation, which left Shanghai in late January 1919.[81]

The response of the Korean community in America was not well
coordinated. Nonetheless, it had important consequences. The New
Korean Association, recently organized by the University of Nebraska student, Chŏng Han-gyŏng (Henry Chung), met in New York
in late November 1918 to write a lengthy petition for American
assistance in the achievement of Korean self-determination. The
petition was circulated to President Wilson, the House and Senate
foreign relations committees, and the U.S. delegation to the Paris
Peace Conference. This appeal by Koreans in America was reported a fortnight later by the *Japan Advertiser* in Tokyo, where

79 Taehan Min'guk Kukhoe Tosŏgwan, *Han'guk Sinmun Chapchi Ch'ong Mongnok,* 169.

80 Kim, *Chae-Mi Hanin Osimnyŏn Sa,* 262.

81 Baldwin, "The March 1st Movement," 39–44.

the newspaper was seen by a Korean student. As Frank Baldwin has argued, awareness that Koreans in America had taken positive action, coupled with news of the Shanghai group's plans to send Kim Kyu-sik to Paris, led directly to a flurry of demonstrations by Korean students in Tokyo, culminating in their proclamation of a Korean declaration of independence on February 8, 1919. This, in turn, stimulated the political consciousness of key sectors of Korean society, with the result that the March First Independence Movement was launched.[82]

The immediate opportunity for the mobilization of mass demonstrations by Koreans for independence came with the death of the Korean emperor, Kojong, a death popularly attributed to the Japanese. The emperor's funeral was originally scheduled for March 1, but Korean nationalist leaders, working in close collaboration with Korean Presbyterian and Methodist clergy, moved with alacrity in organizing nationwide demonstrations centering on a mass meeting for independence in Seoul.

Meanwhile, there was a concerted effort on the part of An Ch'ang-ho's Korean National Association (the THK) to mobilize Koreans in America in an effective independence movement. By December 1918, the THK plan involved sending Chŏng Han-gyŏng (Henry Chung) to Paris to present Korea's case; Syngman Rhee, head of the THK's Hawaiian branch, along with Min Ch'an-ho, would attend the League of Small Nations activities in New York; and Kim Hŏn-sik, who signed the New Korea Association's appeal the previous December, would direct Korean propaganda activity throughout the United States. The more exciting aspects of this program, as reported in Tokyo and Korea by the Japanese press services, served to inspire Koreans in Tokyo and Korea; the Shanghai group was equally well informed.[83]

Responding to THK notification, Syngman Rhee arrived at the San Francisco THK headquarters in mid-January 1919. Rhee announced to a large gathering at a Korean church that he would cooperate with his old rival, An Ch'ang-ho; that the Honolulu branch of the THK approved of the THK central committee's plans; that he and the THK Honolulu branch would cooperate with the THK central committee; that he had brought $1,000 to

[82] Ibid., 45–46.

[83] Ibid., 125 and 291n. There is no mention of these episodes in Oliver's partisan, and often unreliable, Syngman Rhee.

cover his expenses for attendance at the Conference of Small Nations in New York; and that he wished the question of his representation at the Paris Peace Conference left open. When Rhee met with An in Los Angeles, they disagreed over fund raising for the independence movement; An argued that the THK had already raised $10,000 in the United States and that he should go to Hawaii to raise an equal amount and, failing that, Rhee should help redress the imbalance. Rhee refused on both counts.[84]

In the meanwhile, Sŏ Chae-p'il (Philip Jaisohn), the George Washington University graduate now permanently settled in medical practice in Philadelphia, proposed that additional funds be raised from the Korean community to subsidize an English language magazine which would publicize the Korean effort at the Paris conference. It was agreed that such a magazine would provide a basis for cooperation among contending Korean groups in America.[85] This was the genesis of *Korea Review*, the first issue of which appeared in May 1919.

Rhee, however, went off on an increasingly independent path. Exploiting the apparent lack of political unity among Koreans in the United States, especially in the East, Rhee wrote to his followers in Hawaii, urging them not to cooperate with the THK. His subsequent request to the State Department for a travel permit was forwarded to Paris, where Secretary of State Robert Lansing rejected it with the prediction that the conference would not entertain Korean claims against Japan, largely because the Korean issue was not related to the resolution of the World War I conflict. The State Department publicly announced the substance of this decision, adding that the two Koreans (Rhee and Chŏng) who had applied for travel permits were Japanese subjects.[86]

The efforts of Kim Kyu-sik, who had reached Paris in mid-March, were largely in vain. He did manage to engage the interest of a personal aide to Colonel Edward House, as well as Stanley Hornbeck, the chief of the Bureau of Far Eastern Affairs, but the Lansing position on the irrelevance of the Korean question had taken a firm hold among the senior American delegates. Acting on a request from Rhee, Kim tried without success to reopen the question of passport issuance to Korean delegates from the United

84 *Ibid.*, 127.
85 *Ibid.*, 127–218; *New York Times*, March 9, 1919.
86 Baldwin, "The March 1st Movement," 128–129, 170.

States.[87] By now it was clear that Korean independence movement leaders in the United States would have no opportunity for direct participation at the Paris conference. And by now, also, news of the March 1st independence demonstration in Korea—and their brutal suppression by the Japanese military and police—had reached Korean organizations in America. Rhee and Chŏng abandoned their attempts to reach Paris and turned to collaboration with Sŏ Chae-p'il in the organization of a public meeting and other efforts to attract the attention and support of the American public.

The Korean independence movement's propaganda offensive in the United States began with a series of communications to President Wilson and Acting Secretary of State Frank Lyon Polk.[88] The first of these was a letter of April 17, 1919, to Wilson from Earl K. Paek (Paek Il-gyu), acting president of the Korean National Association, which forwarded a translation of the March 1st Korean declaration of independence. Paek's covering letter stressed that "thousands of Koreans have been educated abroad in recent years . . . [and] these men are trained in the best thought of the western world."

In mid-June, Rhee addressed similar letters to Polk and Wilson, informing them that, on April 23, "Korea became a completely organized, self-governed democratic state." The new state had adopted a "Constitution or Manifesto," and, he added, he was honored by being elected as the president of the Republic of Korea. Rhee simultaneously announced the establishment of a Washington "headquarters" for the Republic of Korea. Though Rhee made no mention of Japan or the notion of self-determination, he referred to the Shufeldt Treaty of 1882 and the commitment of "protection" given by the United States and implied in article one.[89] Polk ignored this entire flurry of correspondence. The cautious Polk, in fact, marked one of Rhee's letters with a bold "File, Do *not* acknowledge. FLP."

One of the most articulate political statements of the Korean community propaganda campaign to reach the State Department in this period was an undated, three-and-a-half page manifesto submitted by Young L. Park, representative of the United Asiatic So-

---

[87] Rhee to Polk, Rhee to Wilson, April 23, 1919, U.S. Dept. of State Papers, Decimal File, 1910–1929, Korea (Chosen) Internal Affairs, microcopy M-426, reel 2.

[88] These letters are in *ibid.*

[89] Rhee to Wilson, June 16, 1919, *ibid.*

ciety of Detroit. Park's statement emphasized the notion of self-determination, presented a comprehensive historical review of the Japan-Korea relationship, and announced the convening of the "first Korean Congress on foreign soil" to be held at Liberty Hall, Philadelphia.[90]

Rhee's agents in Washington persisted in forwarding his numerous and varied requests to Wilson and the State Department, none of which appears to have elicited a written response. Late in June, Rhee cabled Wilson to protest Japanese authority over Korea at the conference.[91] On the same day, he sent a lengthy letter protesting Japanese oppression, asserting that the Korean emperor was poisoned by the Japanese, and arguing that the Japanese prohibition of Korean education abroad was a violation of article eleven of the Shufeldt Treaty. As something of an afterthought, Rhee appended a copy of his mid-June letter to the emperor of Japan which proposed that Japan and Korea enter a "new era of perpetual peace and good will."

By now, the THK leadership realized that there was little hope for an opportunity to participate actively in the postwar settlement, nor to establish effective KPG representation in Washington. Sŏ Chae-p'il's propaganda approach to the American public and the U.S. Congress was successful enough for him to continue the effort for several years. The Korean Commission, which had represented the KPG in Washington since late 1919, was supported by Sŏ Chae-p'il's Korean Information Bureau, whose resources included the influential *Korea Review*.[92] Despite considerable discussion, congressional support for de facto recognition of the KPG died on the floor of the Senate and in the House Foreign Relations Committee.

Abandoning his attempt to gain a voice for Korea at the Paris Peace Conference, Rhee shifted to an effort to assume direct control over the KPG. The KPG was already weakening when he arrived at the organization's headquarters in Shanghai late in 1920. He failed to rally his provisional government and soon came under personal attack for, among other things, his handling of finances. As Chong-sik Lee has pointed out, Rhee's personality was simply not suited to the kind of compromise necessary to overcome the

---

[90] Rhee to Wilson, June 14, 1919, *ibid.*
[91] Rhee to Wilson, June 27, 1919, *ibid.*
[92] Lee, *Politics of Korean Nationalism*, 142–146.

intense factionalism of the KPG's leadership, and the provisional government collapsed within three years.[93]

Koreans in America made a last effort to present their aspirations when they appeared at the Washington Disarmament Conference, which convened on November 12, 1921, to discuss naval arms limitation and Pacific and Far East problems.[94] This move also failed.

Like the March First Movement in Korea, the Korean independence movement in America was initially inspired by Wilsonian idealism. Yet it was the residual realism of Wilson and his advisers that frustrated the movement. Confused by this inconsistency, the Korean political leadership in America sought to identify scapegoats within its own ranks. Factional conflict within the Korean community was intensified by the collapse of the KPG at Shanghai in 1923. As politically oriented as it was, the Korean community, and particularly the leadership of its community organizations, fell into disarray, and it was not until the eve of Pearl Harbor that the THK of North America was able to undertake the painful process of reunification.[95]

The modestly successful effort to gain American congressional and popular support faded in the face of mounting pressures from interest groups promoting an Oriental exclusion policy. With the implementation of the Immigration Act of 1924, Korean immigration dwindled rapidly to an entry rate of twenty per year. The deepening of the Great Depression and simultaneous heightening of Japanese military activity in northeast Asia further reduced the Korean entry rate to a mere trickle. A net outflow of returnees over Korean immigrants was established as early as 1926, a trend which would not reverse itself until 1948.[96] The Korean immigrant community in America was no longer capable of substantial population expansion. Without the unifying force of the Korean independence movement, it devoted itself to economic growth, problems of cultural identity, and, particularly, education.

---

[93] *Ibid.*, 152–154.

[94] For the text of the Korean Commission's statement to the conference, see *Cong. Rec.*, 66 Cong., 2 sess. (Dec. 14, 1921), 344–345. See Lee, *Politics of Korean Nationalism*, 171–173, for an extensive treatment of this episode.

[95] Rhee eventually emerged as the principal beneficiary of reunification when he was installed as president of the Republic of Korea.

[96] "Asiatic Immigration to the United States by Race or People, 1899 to 1944"; miscellaneous undated records in the U.S. Dept. of Justice files, Immigration and Naturalization Service, Statistics Branch Offices, Washington, D.C.

The Forgotten Asian Americans: The East Indian Community in the United States

Gary R. Hess

The author is professor of history in Bowling Green State University.

Between 1820 and 1972, some 70,140 immigrants from India entered the United States. This immigration has been concentrated in two distinct phases. Between 1907 and 1920, approximately 6,400 Indians, mostly agricultural workers, were admitted and settled predominantly in California. Their modest numbers, by contrast with the Chinese and Japanese immigrants, did not protect the "Hindus," as immigrants from India were generally called, from the anti-Asian sentiment especially prevalent in California. Their Asian origin alone engendered fear of a "Hindu invasion" and demands for their exclusion and for reduction of their political and economic rights. Poorly educated, untrained in any skills, and ignorant of American society, the preponderance of these early East Indian immigrants were ill-equipped to cope with the situation they encountered in the United States. They quickly became and generally remained an alienated minority near the bottom of the socioeconomic scale.

During the period since World War II, and especially after the

The author wishes to thank Joan M. Jensen for her suggestions and for permitting him to read her manuscript, "Outcasts in a Savage Land: The East Indian in North America," a detailed and thoughtful study of the East Indian experience.

1965 immigration law, a much larger wave of East Indians, nearly all easily assimilated professionals and their families, have migrated to the United States. Between 1946, when the American government modestly relaxed restrictions on Indian immigration, and 1965, nearly 6,000 immigrants settled in the United States. From 1966 to 1972, immigrants from India totaled 50,990, a number equivalent to more than seventy percent of all the East Indian immigrants over the last one hundred and fifty years.[1]

The East Indian community has not been fully studied. It is, of course, too early to examine very thoroughly the more recent arrivals, but even the earlier East Indian immigrants have been virtually ignored by both American and Indian scholars.[2] During the early twentieth century, the "Hindus" never approached the size of the Japanese and Chinese communities, and after 1920 they were outnumbered by the Filipinos as well. In California, the "Hindus" constituted a very small minority—both numerically and in terms of political influence—in a state of many minorities. Thus, studies of Asian Americans and of California's racial history have given scant, if any, attention to the East Indians. Scholars interested in Indian emigration have concentrated on the experiences of the more numerous overseas groups, especially those in Africa, Southeast Asia, the Pacific, and the Caribbean.[3]

By drawing on the available documents and the few studies of East Indians, it is possible to trace the history of this community

---

[1] U.S. Dept. of Justice, Immigration and Naturalization Service, *Annual Report, 1955* (Washington, D.C., 1955), 43–45; *Annual Report, 1960* (Washington, D.C., 1960), 43; *Annual Report, 1971* (Washington, D.C., 1971), 53; *Annual Report, 1972* (Washington, D.C., 1972), 34–36. Reference to the number of immigrants per year are to fiscal years ending June 30; this is the practice followed in the annual reports of the Immigration and Naturalization Service.

[2] The principal studies of East Indians are Rajani Kanta Das, *Hindustani Workers on the Pacific Coast* (Berlin, 1923); Yusuf Dadabhay, "Circuitous Assimilation among Rural Hindustanis in California," *Social Forces*, XXXIII (1954), 138–141; Harold S. Jacoby, *A Half-Century Appraisal of East Indians in the United States* (Stockton, 1956); Lawrence A. Wenzel, "The Rural Punjabis of California: A Religio-Ethnic Group," *Phylon*, XXIX (1968), 245–256. Das based his book, a comprehensive examination of the early immigrants, on an investigation of East Indians which he made in 1921–1922 while working for the Labor Department. The works of Jacoby and Wenzel are based on thorough investigations and observations of the East Indians in California. Both Jacoby and Wenzel question the conclusions reached by Dadabhay.

[3] C. Kondapi, *Indians Overseas, 1838–1949* (Bombay, 1951), 201–211, deals only with the legal status of East Indians in the U.S.; Barton M. Schwartz, ed., *Caste in Overseas Indian Communities* (San Francisco, 1967), draws some generalizations from the experience of other East Indian overseas communities which can be useful in understanding the East Indians in the United States.

in the United States. This paper will endeavor to examine not only the patterns of Indian emigration to the U.S., but also the East Indian political, social, and economic experiences, most of which proved similar to those of the other principal Asian American groups.

The early East Indian community was comprised mainly of unskilled agriculturists who arrived on the West Coast during the first decade of the twentieth century. From the beginning, however, a number of intellectuals, mostly students, also came to the United States and would later provide the leadership of the community. This migration to North America represented a very small fraction of the number of Indians who migrated overseas during the nineteenth and early twentieth centuries. Indian emigrants consisted principally of two groups: small entrepreneurs and unskilled laborers; the latter group included nearly all the emigrants to the United States and Canada. These emigrants came from the rural districts of the Punjab and, to a lesser extent, from Bengal, Gujarat, and the United Provinces (the present state of Uttar Pradesh). They were attracted by the propaganda of Canadian employers, notably railroad interests aided by steamship companies. These Canadian agents had their greatest success in northern India, especially among Sikhs. Some of the Indian immigrants had already worked overseas, usually for the British government in police and army stations in Singapore, Shanghai, and Hong Kong. Contacts with Westerners had acquainted these men, again almost all Sikhs, with the prospects for employment in America; those who had returned to India frequently experienced difficulties in adjusting to their homeland. Originating in these diverse areas, Indian emigration to Canada increased sharply; from forty-five arrivals in 1905 and 387 in 1906, the Indian immigrants in 1907 totaled 2,124 and, in the following year, they reached 2,623. In response to public pressures, the Canadian government in 1909 effectively ended Indian immigration through various means, including: (1) utilization of the "continuous voyage" provision of the Canadian immigration law, which permitted excluding immigrants who had failed to travel in a single, direct voyage from their native country; (2) a reprimand of the steamship companies for their misleading propaganda on economic opportunities available in Canada; (3) an increase in the amount of money required for immigrants to remain in the country. This Canadian policy caused much concern in the British colonial office in London, since Indians, as citizens of the British empire, had the right of migration. The effect of the exclusion policy of the Canadian government was to channel more East Indian immigrants to the United States.

Even before their exclusion from Canada, some Indians had migrated to the United States after either brief stays in British Columbia or denial of entry at Vancouver. The first relatively sizable influx of East Indian immigrants into the United States occurred in 1907 when 1,072 entered; this represented more than the total number of arrivals from India (885) between 1899 and 1906. In 1908, an additional 1,710 Indians were admitted.[4]

Many of these immigrants sought work in the lumber industry of Washington, but they quickly encountered the resentment of white workers who feared the competition of cheap Asian laborers. On September 5, 1907, several hundred whites raided the living quarters of the "Hindu" workers in Bellingham. The mob forced about seven hundred East Indians to flee across the Canadian border. In early November, five hundred wokers in Everett rounded up the "Hindus" and drove them from the city.[5] The East Indians who remained in Washington faced a worsening economic situation. When employers increased their wages in order to avoid charges of relying on cheap labor, the public regarded the East Indians as overpaid in terms of their physical and intellectual capabilities. Such pressures, and the relative attractiveness of the California climate, prompted many Indians to move south and settle in California. The few hundred East Indians in Washington after 1910, although not posing any serious economic threat to the white workers, were still the victims of racial prejudice, which was especially manifest in residential segregation. For instance, when an Indian endeavored to purchase property in Port Angeles in 1913, real estate brokers entered into a covenant not to sell to "Hindoos

---

4 Das, *Hindustani Workers*, 3–6; H. A. Millis, "East Indian Immigration to British Columbia and the Pacific Coast States," *American Economic Review*, I (1911), 72–76; S. Chandrasekhar, "Indian Immigration in America," *Far Eastern Survey*, XIII (1944), 138–141; Chandra Jayawardena, "Migration and Social Change: A Survey of East Indian Communities Overseas," *Geographical Review*, LVIII (1968), 426–428.

5 *Outlook*, LXXXVII (Sept. 14, 1907), 51–52; Werter D. Dodd, "Hindu in the Northwest," *World To-Day*, XIII (Nov., 1907), 1157–1160; Robert E. Wynne, "American Labor Leaders and the Vancouver Anti-Oriental Riot," *Pacific Northwest Quarterly*, LVII (1966), 174–177.

or Negroes." The agreement, published in a local newspaper, rested on the premise that when "Hindoos and Negroes" settled in an area, they "have depreciated value of adjacent property and injured the reputation of the neighborhood, and are generally considered as undesirable."[6]

The incidents at Bellingham and Everett focused public attention for the first time on the latest group of Asian immigrants. Opponents of Asiatic immigration, most prominently the San Francisco-based Asiatic Exclusion League, took the initiative in warning of the East Indian "menace." In his first reports on the "Hindoo question," A. E. Yoell, secretary of the League, presented a stereotype of the East Indian as untrustworthy, immodest, unsanitary, insolent, and lustful. Responding to pressure from the Exclusion League, immigration officials, beginning in late 1908, denied admission to many East Indians. Between 1908 and 1910, some 1,130 Indian arrivals were rejected, forty-one percent on the grounds that they would likely become public charges. Thus in 1909 only 377 East Indians entered the United States.

But in 1910, a demand for construction workers on the Western Pacific Railroad led to a relaxation of immigration restrictions. In that year, 1,782 East Indians were admitted, mostly at San Francisco. The 1910 census reported a total of 5,424 East Indian immigrants residing in the United States, with about half (2,742) in California.[7]

This influx of a few thousand East Indians into the California labor force made the "Hindus," for a brief period, the focus of anti-Oriental sentiment. On behalf of the Exclusion League, Yoell protested in December 1909 to officials in Washington against the "wholesale landings of large numbers of Hindoos," many of whom, he charged, suffered from diseases and all of whom competed against white labor. When Daniel J. Keefe, commissioner general of immigration, replied that the immigrants were not numerous and did not threaten the jobs of native Americans, Yoell recalled that Japanese immigration had started modestly only to increase by 2,000 percent in a decade. The League endorsed bills introduced in Con-

---

6 Joan M. Jensen, "Apartheid: Pacific Coast Style," *Pacific Historical Review,* XXXVIII (1969), 335–340.

7 *Proceedings of the Asiatic Exclusion League,* Feb., 1908, pp. 8–10; *ibid.,* Sept., 1908, pp. 11–12; *ibid.,* Jan., 1910, pp. 5–11; *ibid.,* March, 1910, pp. 7–10; Das, *Hindustani Workers,* 17–20; H. A. Millis, "East Indian Immigration to the Pacific Coast," *Survey,* XXVIII (June 1, 1912), 380–381.

gress to exclude immigrants ineligible for citizenship, but some believed that such legislation, designed to keep out all nonwhites as well as East Indians, might not be enough. They feared that the federal courts might accept "Hindus" as "white persons" eligible for citizenship. In a report of April 1910, the League reflected concern over any suggestion of racial affinity between "whites" and "Hindus":

Students of ethnological subjects all agree that the Hindus are members of the same family that we are, and consequently all legislation based upon racial distinction might fail so far as keeping them out of the United States is concerned. As a matter of fact, we, the people of the United States, are cousins, far removed, of the Hindus of the northwest provinces, but our forefathers pressed to the west, in the everlasting march of conquest, progress, and civilization. The forefathers of the Hindus went east and became enslaved, effeminate, caste-ridden and degraded, until today we have the spectacle of the Western Aryan, the "Lords of Creation," if we may use the simile, while on the other hand the East Aryans have become the "slaves of Creation" to carry the comparison to its logical conclusion.

And now we the people of the United States are asked to receive these members of a degraded race on terms of equality. Or if they came under the law they may become citizens, and what would be the condition in California if this horde of fanatics should be received in our midst.[8]

The popular press augmented this campaign, frequently relying on the exaggerated reports of the Exclusion League. For instance, *Collier's* carried an article on the "Hindu invasion" based on the League's estimate of 10,000 East Indians in California. In October 1910, *Survey* told its readers that 5,000 "Hindus" had entered at San Francisco within the past year. In "The Tide of Turbans" published in *Forum*, Herman Scheffauer depicted the new immigrants as a "dark, mystic race," and warned that the "Hindoo invasion is yet in its infancy; only the head of the long procession has entered the Golden Gate."[9]

The primary thrust of the anti-Indian campaign was directed against the San Francisco commissioner of immigration, Hart H. North. In meetings with officials of the Exclusion League, North

---

[8] *Proceedings of the Asiatic Exclusion League*, April, 1910, p. 8.

[9] "Hindu Invasion," *Collier's*, XLV (March 26, 1910), 15; "The Hindu, the Newest Immigration Problem," *Survey*, XXV (Oct 1, 1910), 2–3; Herman Scheffauer, "The Tide of Turbans," *Forum*, XLIII (June 1910), 616–618.

defended his relaxation of restrictions on the grounds that the East Indians could easily find employment in the San Francisco area. The League petitioned President William Howard Taft to remove North, accusing him of incompetence and personal gain from the employment of the cheap Indian labor. In 1910, the League's agitation encouraged a thorough examination of the East Indian community by H. A. Millis, superintendent of immigration commission investigations on the Pacific Coast. Millis's findings tended to support the League's position. While the East Indians were employed in railroad construction and in agricultural work, they were paid considerably less than other Asian laborers and were frequently employed for only brief periods. Employers, especially the railroad companies, regarded them as the least efficient workers. On the basis of his observations and interviews, Millis concluded that no other group was so strongly opposed, and the demand for its exclusion was nearly unanimous.[10]

By 1911, the campaign to end Indian immigration had been effectively won. Washington officials encouraged North's resignation and immigration authorities at San Francisco began rejecting a majority of the East Indian arrivals. In 1911, some 517 were admitted and 861 were debarred. That trend continued during the next decade; less than 600 were admitted during the next five years before Congress virtually ended Indian immigration in 1917. Altogether, between 1911 and 1920, some 1,462 East Indians were admitted, while 1,782 were denied entry, most on the grounds that they would probably become public charges. The admissions did not equal East Indian departures; approximately 1,400 Indians voluntarily left the United States between 1911 and 1920 while an additional 235 were deported.[11]

Despite this trend toward a leveling of the East Indian population, pressures continued to formalize the exclusion policy. In Congress, Democratic Representative Denver S. Church of Fresno, California, waged a determined campaign for exclusionist legislation, but found little support. Nonetheless, his goal was accom-

---

10 *Proceedings of the Asiatic Exclusion League,* Sept., 1910, pp. 45–52; *ibid.,* Oct., 1910, pp. 59–60; H. A. Millis, "East Indian Immigration to the Pacific Coast," *Survey,* XXVIII (June 1, 1912), 379–386.

11 *Cong. Rec.,* 64 Cong., 1 sess. (1916), 4810; Gurdial Singh, "East Indians in the United States," *Sociology and Social Research,* XXX (1946), 210–211; Das, *Hindustani Workers,* 12–16.

plished as part of the 1917 immigration law which was intended to restrict immigration from southern and eastern Europe, but also provided for a "barred zone" by which laborers from nearly all of Asia, including India, were prohibited from entering the United States.[12]

The continual concern with the "Hindus," despite their numerical insignificance, underscored the pervasiveness of the anti-Oriental sentiment in California. As evidenced in the reports of the Exclusion League and the popular press, East Indians were commonly seen as but part of an Asiatic horde moving across the Pacific; they were not distinguished from the more numerous groups. Labor organizations accepted without question that Asians had to be excluded; as noted by one historian, anti-Orientalism had become an inherited and irrational act of faith. In this context, anti-Orientalism made for sound politics; thus California Progressives could couple legislation reflecting concern for the living conditions of European immigrants with other laws, for example, the 1913 Alien Land Law, showing enmity for Asians. And as recent studies have observed, California's racism reflected a national racist society. Except for its anti-Oriental emphasis, California was not unique; and its outlook toward Asians eventually gained national endorsement in the 1920s.[13]

In this atmosphere of marked hostility toward Asians, the few thousand East Indians gradually established themselves primarily in California and relied chiefly on agriculture as a means of livelihood. Typically the Indians sought work in groups with a leader serving as their agent in negotiating with employers. Owing in part to the desire of many farmers to break the Japanese monopoly on the labor supply in those areas, they had little difficulty finding employment in the Sacramento and San Joaquin valleys. Also, Indians moved into the Imperial Valley, another rapidly growing

12 *Cong. Rec.*, 63 Cong., 2 sess. (1914), Appendix, pp. 842–845; 64 Cong., 1 sess. (1916), 724; 64 Cong., 2 sess. (1917), 2452–2457, 2616–2629; *Biographical Directory of the American Congress, 1774–1961* (Washington, D.C., 1961), 691.

13 Roger Daniels and Spencer C. Olin, Jr., eds., *Racism in California: A Reader in the History of Oppression* (New York, 1972), v-viii; Roger Daniels, *The Politics of Prejudice: The Anti-Japanese Movement in California and the Struggle for Japanese Exclusion* (Berkeley, 1962), 65–91; Robert F. Heizer and Alan J. Almquist, *The Other Californians: Prejudice and Discrimination under Spain, Mexico, and the United States to 1920* (Berkeley, 1971), 178–200; Spencer C. Olin, Jr., "European Immigrant and Oriental Alien: Acceptance and Rejection by the California Legislature of 1913," *Pacific Historical Review*, XXX (1966), 303–315.

agricultural area. By 1920, many had become farm operators, leasing ranches on a share or cash basis for periods ranging from one to three years. In the vineyards and fruit orchards of the San Joaquin and Sacramento valleys, they operated farms averaging about forty acres; in 1920, Indians were operating some 85,000 acres in each of the valleys. In the Imperial Valley, they leased farms in the cotton and rice districts, and altogether were operating about 30,000 acres. Indebtedness was common, as the operators had to borrow heavily in order to meet preharvest rent payments. In addition, many other Indians worked, usually in groups, as itinerant farm laborers, who were often the victims of considerable seasonal unemployment.[14]

The social adjustment proved very difficult and accounted for most of the voluntary returnees to India. The 1909 Immigration Commission investigation of the East Indians suggested that they appeared the least assimilative of any immigrant group. Most of the Indians were illiterate and learned little English. They remained isolated, generally living in small groups on farms or on the fringes of towns. For all but a few, family life was unknown, at least during their first several years in America. Only a handful had managed to bring their wives from India. The possibilities for marriage in America were very restricted. The Indians regarded themselves as superior to Negroes, while whites were prejudiced against any dark-skinned people. The most acceptable and accessible mates were the Mexican women living in southern California, and, by 1920, a few East Indians had married Mexican women.[15]

The East Indians' isolation was enhanced by their retention of native customs and dress (especially the turban which was of religious significance to Sikhs). Modest Sikh temples were established, with one of the workers serving as part-time priest. At Stockton, a Sikh temple was constructed and became the headquarters of the Pacific Coast Khalsa Diwan Society. The Moslem Association of America, established at Sacramento, and the Hindustani Welfare and Reform Society of America, with its office at El Centro, sought

---

14 Das, *Hindustani Workers,* 22–26, 31–32, 49–50, 93–95; S. Chandrasekhar, "Indian Community in the United States," *Far Eastern Survey,* XIV (June 6, 1945), 147–149; Subhindra Bose, "Asian Immigration in the United States," *Modern Review* (Calcutta), XXV (May 1919), 524–526.

15 Das, *Hindustani Workers,* 77–80, 109–110; Millis, "East Indian Immigration to the Pacific Coast," 385–386.

to serve the needs of the non-Sikh population. Efforts of Christian groups to proselytize among the East Indians had negligible effect.[16]

On the political level, East Indians sought both immediate and distant objectives. Led by East Indian political refugees, they were active on behalf of their rights in America and for their native country's independence. During World War I, some nationalist leaders endeavored to mobilize the Indian immigrants for revolutionary activity against the British raj; this activity became popularly known by the British-inspired term, "Hindu conspiracy."

Political activity among the West Coast "Hindus" began as early as 1908 when Taraknath Das, a student at the University of Washington who had fled India to avoid imprisonment for his political agitation, began publishing *Free Hindustan*. In the next few years, several Indian revolutionaries sought asylum in America. Determined in their political goals, they frequently utilized the Sikh organizations as a vehicle for propagating among their fellow countrymen. In 1911 Har Dayal, who had resigned a scholarship at Oxford University as a protest against the British educational system in India, arrived in San Francisco and provided effective leadership for the West Coast political movement. He taught briefly at Stanford, but was dismissed for overplaying his university affiliation on behalf of political causes. Aided by Ram Chandra, Das, and others, Dayal organized the Ghadr (meaning "revolution" or "mutiny") party and published a weekly newspaper, *Ghadr,* and various revolutionary materials in English, Urdu, and other Indian languages. In his writings and speeches, Dayal urged his countrymen to return home for revolutionary work. In a speaking tour that brought him before gatherings of East Indians in California in 1913, he was greeted enthusiastically and secured considerable financial support. Following a speech before an anarchist rally in San Francisco, he was arrested as an undesirable alien and ordered deported, but he fled to Switzerland and then to Germany where he secured backing for Ghadr activities.[17] An immigration official in 1914 assessed the effectiveness of the revolutionary propaganda: "most of the Indian

---

16 Das, *Hindustani Workers,* 88–92; Lee M'Crae, "Self-Exiled in America: Something about the Hindus in California," *Missionary Review,* XXXIX (July 1916), 525–526.

17 Kalyan Kumar Banerjee, *Indian Freedom Movement Revolutionaries in America* (Calcutta, 1969), 7–13; L. P. Mathur, *Indian Revolutionary Movement in the United States of America* (Delhi, 1970), 18–25.

students . . . are infected with seditious ideas. Even Sikhs of the laboring class have not escaped their influence."[18]

After the outbreak of the First World War, Ghadr leaders believed that the time was now opportune to launch revolutionary projects in India. At meetings in Fresno, Sacramento, and Stockton, several hundred East Indian immigrants pledged to take part in revolutionary expeditions to India. In the fall of 1914, some four hundred East Indians left the United States in several Ghadr-organized revolutionary missions. The Ghadr party's projects to disrupt the British imperial system aborted, however, and they did so primarily because of poor planning, the effectiveness of British surveillance, and the lack of popular support in India.[19]

By 1917 the Ghadr movement in America had virtually collapsed. The British government pressured officials in Washington to curtail Ghadr activities. In early 1917, British agents helped the New York City police uncover the work of C. K. Chakravarty, who had been sent by the German government a year earlier to head the revolutionary work in the United States. Shortly afterward, the federal government indicted 105 persons on charges of conspiracy to violate the neutrality laws; only thirty-five, including seventeen East Indians, were brought to trial. At the conclusion of the well-publicized five month trial, Ram Chandra was assassinated by another Indian defendant who was immediately shot and killed by a U.S. marshal. The fourteen convicted "Hindu conspirators" received sentences ranging from four to twenty-two months.[20]

With the United States at war by the time of the trial, the "Hindus" were thus cast as traitors. It appears, however, that by the time of American intervention most East Indian workers had lost interest in the Ghadr party. The failure of the Ghadr leadership to sustain

---

[18] Mathur, *Indian Revolutionary Movement*, 30.

[19] *Ibid.*, 26–29, 72–73; Banerjee, *Indian Freedom Movement*, 13–17; Jacoby, *Half-Century Appraisal of East Indians*, 25; Mark Naidis, "Propaganda of the Gadar Party," *Pacific Historical Review*, XX (1951), 252–253; Giles T. Brown, "The Hindu Conspiracy, 1914–1917," *ibid.*, XVII (1948), 299–300.

[20] Banerjee, *Indian Freedom Movement*, 73; Don K. Dignan, "The Hindu Conspiracy in Anglo-American Relations during World War I," *Pacific Historical Review*, XL (1971), 57–76. The British government maintained an extensive surveillance of Indian nationalists, including the use of private detective and military intelligence agents. Joan M. Jensen, "Outcasts in a Savage Land: The East Indian in North America" (Unpublished manuscript), 488–572, details the British activities and their relation to the conspiracy trial.

its following resulted from several factors. First, the party had virtually ignored the economic and social problems of the East Indian
workers. Second, the majority of the East Indians were committed
to remaining in the United States and found little appeal in the
Ghadr's schemes. Once the United States had become a belligerent,
the preponderance of the East Indians were loyal to the Allied
cause. In this sense, the East Indian immigrants reflected the sentiment of the Indian people at home; the Indian National Congress,
the Muslim League, and other political groups supported the British war effort. Finally, communalism and personal rivalries hin-
dered efforts at cooperation in the Ghadr movement. By 1916, suspicions among the Sikhs, Muslims, and Hindus substantially weakened the Ghadr party. The "Hindu conspiracy" trial was marked by
incessant bickering and disagreement among the East Indian de-
fendants, culminating in the murder of Chandra.[21]

The moderate, but less-publicized, activities of Lala Lajpat Rai
reflected more accurately the aspirations and plans of the majority
of Indian nationalists at home and in America. Rai, who had long
been active in the Indian National Congress, visited the United
States in 1906 and returned in 1914, convinced that he could mobilize American opinion behind the nationalist cause. From his
base in New York, he devoted the next five years to propagandizing
the Congress party's commitment to self-government through constitutional means. He founded the India Home Rule League, lec-
tured, and wrote extensively; his writings included the periodical,
Young India, and a book, *England's Debt to India.* He cultivated
the support of American politicians, especially those representing traditional anti-British constituencies, and liberal spokesmen,
including Oswald Garrison Villard, George Kirchwey, Norman
Thomas, J. G. Phelps Stokes, Roger Baldwin, Robert Morss Lovett,
and John Hayes Holmes. J. T. Sunderland, a Unitarian minister
who had twice visited India, lent enthusiastic backing to the Indian
cause, including his book, *India in Bondage.* Yet Rai's intensive
efforts were far removed from the majority of East Indians in the
United States. The Home Rule League collapsed after Rai's departure in 1919, but most subsequent nationalist activities in the

---

21 Brown, "The Hindu Conspiracy," 307–309; Naidis, "Propaganda of the Gadar
Party," 254–258; Mathur, *Indian Revolutionary Movement,* 155.

United States followed the pattern set by Rai of relying for support on educated Indians and American liberals.[22]

After World War I, a resurgent anti-Orientalism adversely affected the status of East Indians and encouraged many to leave the United States. This agitation was not directed specifically at "Hindus"; rather it represented principally a renewal of the longstanding drive to exclude formally the Japanese. East Indians, however, suffered serious deprivations. With California Senator Hiram Johnson and V. S. McClatchy, retired editor of the *Sacramento Bee*, providing much of the leadership, a movement to legislate Japanese exclusion gained wide support. The Supreme Court, in the *Ozawa* decision of 1922, declared that Japanese were ineligible for citizenship; this facilitated the exclusionist campaign by enabling Congress to base the barring of the Japanese on the criterion that they were ineligible for citizenship.[23]

East Indian leaders initially welcomed the *Ozawa* decision, for it seemed to confirm their claim that persons of Indian origin were entitled to American citizenship. Since 1907 about seventy Indians had been granted citizenship, although the Justice Department had consistently contested the cases. The lower federal courts had adhered, however, to the precedent established in the 1910 *U.S.* v. *Balsara* and the 1913 *re Akhoy Jumar Mazumdar* decisions which held that Indians were Caucasians and thus entitled under the naturalization legislation of 1790 and 1875 to be considered "white persons" eligible for citizenship. The Supreme Court's position in the *Ozawa* case—that "white person" was synonymous with Caucasian—appeared to affirm the East Indians' right to citizenship. Although it was possible for East Indians to find support in the *Ozawa* decision, the Supreme Court justices were not concerned with the implications of their definition of "white persons" with respect to East Indians—a fact which became evident a year later.

In 1923 the Supreme Court, in the case of *U.S.* v. *Bhaghat Singh Thind*, relied on the "understanding of the common man" to rule that Indians were ineligible for naturalization. Thind, who had

22 Haridas T. Muzumdar, *America's Contribution to India's Freedom* (Allahabad, 1962), 9–12; Naeen Gul Rathore, "Indian Nationalist Agitation in the United States: A Study of Lala Lajpat Rai and the Indian Home Rule League of America, 1914–1920" (Ph.D. dissertation, Columbia University, 1965), 284–293, *passim*; Diwaker Prasad Singh, "American Official Attitudes toward the Indian Nationalist Movement, 1905–1929" (Ph.D. dissertation, University of Hawaii, 1964), 235–264.

23 Daniels, *Politics of Prejudice*, 92–102.

been granted citizenship by a federal court in Oregon, was a somewhat controversial figure owing to his friendship with some of the "Hindu conspirators" and his advocacy of Indian independence. In a unanimous decision, the Supreme Court held that the term "white person" in the naturalization statutes was not to be defined simply on the basis of race (as the *Ozawa* case suggested), but rather in accord with popular definition. Thus, it was argued that the Congress of 1790 associated "white persons" with immigrants from northern and western Europe, while the 1870 legislators assumed that "white persons" included immigrants from all parts of Europe. Moreover, the "barred zone" provision of the 1917 immigration law provided additional evidence that East Indians were not regarded as fit for naturalization; in denying immigration privileges to East Indians, Congress was also expressing opposition to their naturalization. Through this reasoning, the Court concluded that the public and Congress never intended that East Indians be given naturalization privileges; "Hindus" and their children "would retain indefinitely the clear evidence of ancestry."[24]

Critics of the case frequently noted that Justice George Sutherland, who wrote the court's decision, had been born in England; perhaps, the *Modern Review* of Calcutta observed, Sutherland had been unable to overcome his prejudice against Indians.[25] It would be inaccurate, however, to hold one man responsible; the *Thind* decision represented but one phase of a widespread effort, backed by a popular consensus, to reduce non-Anglo-Saxon influences in America.

The ramifications of the *Thind* case extended beyond the establishment of a precedent for denying citizenship requests of East Indians. It provided as well a basis for annulling previous grants of citizenship. During the first three years following the *Thind* decision, federal authorities secured cancelations of the naturalizations of some fifty Indians; the courts consistently upheld the government's contention that the naturalization certificates had been illegally procured. Finally, in November 1926, the Ninth Circuit Court of Appeals, in the case of *U.S.* v. *Sakharam Ganesh Pandit*, denied a government request by upholding the argument of Pandit,

24 *U.S.* v. *Bhagat Singh Thind*, 261 U.S. 204–215 (1923); *New York Times*, Feb. 20, 1923; Taraknath Das, "Stateless Persons in U.S.A.," *Calcutta Review*, XVI (July 1925), 40–43.

25 *Modern Review*, XXXIII (June 1923), 770.

a lawyer in California, that his naturalization in 1914 had been granted by a court fully empowered to act and hence had been procured legally. The *Pandit* decision slowed but did not end the government's efforts to disallow Indian citizenship; as late as the mid-1930s, the government was still contesting the naturalization certificates of East Indians.[26]

In addition to its effect on the Indians' claim to citizenship, the *Thind* decision also subjected East Indians to the more restrictive provisions of the California Alien Land Law, which prohibited leasing or sale of land to aliens ineligible for citizenship. For several years prior to the *Thind* case, the Exclusion League and others had been calling attention to the rapid increase of agricultural land being leased or purchased by the "Hindus." It was especially for this reason that California newspapers, including the *Sacramento Bee,* the *San Francisco Chronicle,* and the *Fresno Morning Republican,* and various political leaders praised the *Thind* decision.[27]

In the face of these pressures, many East Indians left the United States. Between 1920 and 1940, some 3,000 returned to India; most left voluntarily, although a few hundred were deported. By 1930, the "Hindu" population had dropped to 3,130 and, in 1940, to 2,405. But during this same period, 3,000 East Indians, by conservative estimate, entered the United States illegally; they were mostly farm laborers who came via Mexico. Many of these men were apprehended and deported, but others, certainly at least several hundred, managed to remain and became absorbed in the East Indian community.[28] Although the preponderance (sixty percent) of the East Indians in 1940 still lived in California, their numbers in California had declined by forty-six percent since 1910 (from 2,742 to 1,476).

The status of the small community had not improved over the

---

[26] Das, "Stateless Persons in U.S.A.," 43–44; Singh, "East Indians in the United States," 211; *New York Times,* Jan. 26, 1933; James W. Garner, "Denationalization of American Citizens," *American Journal of International Law,* XXI (Jan. 1927), 106–107.

[27] *Literary Digest,* CXVII (March 10, 1923), 366–367.

[28] U.S. Department of Commerce, Bureau of Census, *Fifteenth Census of the United States 1930,* Vol. II: *General Report, Statistics by Subjects* (Washington, D.C., 1933), 64; Jacoby, *Half-Century Appraisal of East Indians,* 7–9; Theodore Fieldbrave, "East Indians in the U.S.," *Missionary Review,* LVII (June 1934), 291–293; D. P. Pandia and Mme. Kamaldevi, "Justice for Hindus in America," *Christian Century,* LVII (March 13, 1940), 357.

years. By 1940 only a handful (four percent) were professionals; nearly half were farm laborers, fifteen percent were farmers or farm managers, and an additional twenty percent were engaged in non-farm labor. Of the 1,600 East Indians over age twenty-five, more than a third had not completed even a year of schooling. The median school years completed among East Indians were 3.7. This was lower than the educational accomplishment of any other racial and ethnic group reported in the 1940 census. (The Chinese were next at 5.5 median school years completed.) Moreover, the East Indians now constituted an aging community; fifty-six percent were over age forty, thirty-two percent over fifty, and nine percent over sixty.[29]

Indeed, it seemed to some observers that the East Indians were losing much of their cultural identity. Due to their small numbers and pattern of living in isolation, they had difficulty in forming a strong community. The strongest unifying force was religion, with East Indians from throughout California visiting the mosques and temples on holy days; the Sikh Temple at Stockton still served as the principal center of religious and social contacts. Occasionally, the rural East Indians found a sense of community among the Mexican Americans with whom they worked. Owing to similarities in physical appearance and socioeconomic status, the East Indians were frequently identified with the Mexicans. Generally, the Mexicans accepted the East Indians. Thus, some of the East Indians were assimilated within the Mexican-American culture, a process typically completed with marriage to Mexican women.[30]

During World War II, East Indian political activity in the United States intensified. The principal effort was to enlist American support for the Indian National Congress in its struggle to secure a British commitment to independence. The India League of America, led by the enterprising J. J. Singh and other Indian businessmen and intellectuals living in the eastern United States, attracted the support of the spokesmen of American liberalism, including those who had backed the India Home Rule League during World War I, as well as many labor groups and politicians. The writings, speeches, and other work of Anup Singh, Krishnalal Shridharani, Kumar Goshal, Taraknath Das, B. Shiva Rao, Syud Hossain, and

---

29 U.S. Department of Commerce, Bureau of Census, *Sixteenth Census of the United States, 1940—Population: Characteristics of the Nonwhite Population by Race* (Washington, D.C., 1943), 2–7, 17, 34, 37.

30 Dadabhay, "Circuitous Assimilation Among Rural Hindustanis," 138–141.

Haridas Muzumdar helped to reinforce the American public's sympathy for the Indian cause. The India League, however, had difficulty sustaining public interest after the failure of the National Congress's "Quit India" movement in August 1952. Further, intensive British imperialist propaganda helped to reduce the pro-Indian sentiment in the United States. Generally, the India League made no effort to utilize the East Indian farmers and laborers in its political campaigns. The most notable exception occurred in early 1945 when Mrs. Vijayalakshmi Pandit, the sister of Jawaharlal Nehru, visited the United States and campaigned on behalf of the nationalist cause among East Indian audiences in California.[31]

This nationalist activity during the war sought a secondary objective which held important ramifications for the East Indian community. The India League of America and the India Welfare League, led by Mubarak Ali Khan and the American voice of the All-India Muslim League, won considerable sympathy, predominantly from American liberals, for granting Indians an immigration quota and extending naturalization privileges to East Indians. Overcoming the opposition of some congressional leaders and the problems caused by disagreements on strategy between the India Welfare League and the India League of America, champions of the Indian immigration-naturalization measure finally maneuvered a bill through Congress in early 1946 which President Harry S. Truman signed on July 2. It gave natives of India an annual quota of a hundred, thus ending nearly thirty years of virtual exclusion, and made Indians eligible for American citizenship, thus reversing the *Thind* decision of twenty-three years earlier.[32]

This liberalization of American immigration and naturalization policy facilitated an increase in the East Indian community and changes in its character. Between 1947 and 1965, nearly 6,000 immigrants from India were admitted to the United States. During the first few years after India's independence, the number of Indians returning to their homeland almost equaled the new immigrants, but by the early 1950s few Indians were leaving the United States. Moreover, the number of persons born in India and entering through other countries also increased. During this period, non-

---

31 Gary R. Hess, *America Encounters India, 1941–1947* (Baltimore, 1971), 16, 19, 85–90, 113–129, 151–155.

32 Gary R. Hess, "The 'Hindu' in America: Immigration and Naturalization Policies and India, 1917–1946," *Pacific Historical Review*, XXXVIII (1969), 71–77.

quota immigrants generally equaled or surpassed those admitted under the annual quota: most nonquota immigrants were husbands, wives, and children of American citizens. The largest number of the post-World War II immigrants were professional men and their families. The East Indians took advantage of the opportunity for American citizenship. Between 1948, when twenty-six East Indians were naturalized, and 1965, a total of 1,772 persons of former Indian allegiance acquired United States citizenship.[33]

The recent arrivals reinvigorated the older East Indian community. A 1954 study suggested that the agricultural workers in California were experiencing a "circuitous assimilation" into American culture through the Mexican-American subculture.[34] But that finding has been questioned by other more thorough investigations of the East Indians—a 1956 report based on extensive interviews and a 1968 survey of nine hundred East Indians residing in the Sutter County area of north central California.[35] Taken together, these studies provide a comprehensive account of the development of the rural East Indians into a stronger and more unified community.

Several factors helped in this process. To begin with, the older East Indian men never lost their preference for East Indian wives. Although many intermarried, perhaps half the men chose to remain single. After it became possible to bring Indian women to America, some brought wives from India. The younger male immigrants from the Punjab married, almost without exception, East Indian women. Even the children of East Indian-Mexican marriages were not absorbed within the Mexican-American group; one sample of twenty-one marriage-age sons of such families showed that, while eight married Mexican-American girls, six found wives of mixed East Indian-Mexican parentage.

Economically and culturally, the rural East Indians have been notably strengthened. Aided by the virtual disappearance of overt anti-Orientalism and their characteristic thrift and hard work, the East Indians have increased their agricultural holdings and are, as

---

33 U.S. Department of Justice, Immigration and Naturalization Service, *Annual Report, 1949* (Washington, D.C., 1949), table 13; *Annual Report, 1950* (Washington, D.C., 1950), tables 6, 7, 13A; *Annual Report, 1955* (Washington, D.C., 1955), 45, 48, 50, 53, 55, 114–115; *Annual Report, 1960* (Washington, D.C., 1960), 23, 41, 78–80; *Annual Report, 1965* (Washington, 1965), 97.

34 Dadabhay, "Circuitous Assimilation Among Rural Hindustanis," 138–141.

35 Jacoby, *Half-Century Appraisal of East Indians*, 27–32; Wenzel, "The Rural Punjabis of California," 245–256.

a group, much more prosperous than thirty years ago. The Sikh heritage still provides the strongest cultural focus, with Sikhism represented in nearly all institutionalized activities. The political efforts of the early immigrants are not forgotten. Among the holidays celebrated by the East Indians is "Martyrdom Day," in recognition of the martyrs for Indian independence, and given special emphasis is the involvement of the East Indians in the Ghadr party. Other traditions and practices have been preserved, notably a continued preference for Indian food and the speaking of Indian languages at gatherings of East Indians.

As has generally occurred in overseas Indian communities, the caste system has had negligible influence. This has been especially true among Indian immigrants engaged in farm labor, which undermined traditional occupations, and where there was a shortage of Indian women, which served to weaken the demographic basis of caste by necessitating marriage between castes. An additional factor in the American scene was the predominance of Sikh immigrants, whose religion disavowed caste. There is, however, some evidence that among rural East Indians, caste affiliation has not been entirely forgotten, but serves more as an indication of status and prestige than of exclusiveness and privileges.

Although the members of the older East Indian community have adopted American material comforts, dress, and other features of American life, they have experienced only slight social integration and, as noted, retain important aspects of their own culture. The acculturation of the rural East Indians thus remains limited.[36]

While the East Indians as a group never exerted much political influence, one immigrant, Dalip Singh Saund, did achieve political prominence. Saund, who in 1919 migrated from the Punjab to study at the University of California, became a prosperous farmer in the Imperial Valley. During the 1920s and 1930s, he was active politically, working on behalf of the rights of Indian immigrants and writing a book in response to Katherine Mayo's *Mother India*, a widely-read criticism of Indian culture. After being naturalized in 1949, he joined the Democratic party and was elected a county judge. In 1956 he won election to the United States Congress as

---

[36] Jacoby, *Half-Century Appraisal of East Indians*, 10–21, 26–32; Jayawardena, "Migration and Social Change," 441; Wenzel, "The Rural Punjabis of California," 245–256.

representative of the district covering Imperial and Riverside coun-
ties. Saund served three terms in the House of Representatives. A
massive stroke incapacitated him during his unsuccessful 1962 re-
election campaign; he remained an invalid from then until his
death in April 1973.[37]

Since the passage of the 1965 immigration law eliminating the
quota system, East Indian immigration has increased dramatically.
Between 1965 and 1970, immigrants born in India showed a higher
percentage increase than newcomers from any other country. The
overwhelming majority of the immigrants are professional men
and their families; for instance, of the 10,114 persons born in India
and admitted in 1970, some 5,171 were classified as holding professional occupations and 4,284 were housewives and children. These
newer immigrants are predominantly young; of the 1970 arrivals,
one out of seven was under ten years of age and more than three of
five were under thirty years. Also there has been a sharp increase
in naturalization; between 1966 and 1972, some 2,972 persons of
former Indian allegiance were granted United States citizenship.
Many more are anticipating naturalization; from 1970 to 1972,
over 16,000 Indians were granted permanent resident status. It is,
of course, too early to write definitively about this urban-centered,
well-educated, affluent East Indian community, which already out-
numbers the older, predominantly rural group. Certainly the newer
arrivals can be more easily assimilated, but the evidence that they,
like the older immigrants, prefer marriage to East Indians also
suggests that a sense of Indian cultural identity will prevail.[38]

37 *New York Times*, April 25, 1973; *Biographical Directory of the American Congress, 1774–1961*, 1563.

38 U.S. Department of Justice, Immigration and Naturalization Service, *Annual
Report, 1970* (Washington, D.C., 1970), 4–5, 49, 63–64, 110; *Annual Report, 1971*
(Washington, D.C., 1971), 34, 38, 41, 47–50, 99–101; *Annual Report, 1972* (Washington,
D.C., 1972), 32, 103.

The above comments on recent East Indian immigration deal only with immigrants
from India and do not include those from Pakistan. Until the last few years, the
number of Pakistani immigrants was very small. After the partition of India in 1947,
the United States gave Pakistan an annual quota of a hundred immigrants. The
immigrants from Pakistan actually averaged about 150 per year, however, because
some were admitted as nonquota immigrants. Between 1958 and 1965 the total
Pakistani immigration was 1,224. Since 1966, the number of Pakistani immigrants has
increased sharply; the total from 1966 to 1972 was 7,911. U.S. Department of Justice,
Immigration and Naturalization Service, *Annual Report, 1967* (Washington, D.C.,
1967), 62; *Annual Report, 1969* (Washington, D.C., 1969), 47; *Annual Report, 1972*
(Washington, D.C., 1972), 34.

The East Indian experience in the United States has thus been largely shaped by the changes in American attitudes and policies toward Orientals. The older Indian community in California may still have little social and political integration with white Americans; nonetheless its relative prosperity and growth are not the target of any significant resentment. The "Hindu invasion" feared sixty years ago is occurring in the 1970s without any perceptible public concern. It is this group of new arrivals which will, in the next generation, contribute a fascinating new dimension to the history of Asian Americans.

Index

Index

A

Agricultural Workers Organizing Committee (AWOC), 113
The Alien and the Asiatic in American Law (Milton R. Konvitz), 14
alien land acts (1913, 1920), 13, 90, 164, 171
Allen, Horace D., 130, 131–132, 134
All-India Muslim League, 173
Ambassadors in Arms (Thomas W. Murphy), 19
American Federation of Labor (AFL), 72
The American Japanese Problem (Sidney Lewis Gulick), 13
Americans Betrayed (Morton Grodzins), 17
An Ch'ang-ho, 130, 146, 147, 148, 149, 150, 152–153
Angell, James B., 63
An Anti-American Literary Collection on the Exclusion of Chinese Laborers [*Fang-Mei hua-kung chin-yueh wen-hsueh chi*] (A Yin, pseud.), 55–56 n.9
anti-Chinese movement, 8–9, 34–35, 47, 55, 61–62, 89; Communist Chinese historians on, 61, 64–65
The Anti-Chinese Movement in California (Elmer C. Sandmeyer), 8
anti-Orientalism, 1, 2, 7–8, 13–14, 164, 169, 174–175. *See also* immigration laws; specific immigrant groups
Asian American study centers, 23, 24 n.73
Asiatic Exclusion League, 161–163, 164, 171
Associated Farmers of California, 113
A Yin [pseud.]. *See* Chien Hsing-ts'ung

B

Bailey, Thomas A., *Theodore Roosevelt and the Japanese-American Crisis*, 14
Bancroft, Hubert Howe, 1, 4–5
Barth, Gunther, 64 n.36; *Bitter Strength*, 11
Bayard, Thomas, 62
Beauty Behind Barbed Wire (Allen H. Eaton), 19

Bendetsen, Karl R., 15–16, 18
Bishop, E. Faxon, 131
Bitter Strength (Gunther Barth), 10–11
Blalock, Hubert, Jr., 81–83
Bloom, Leonard, and Ruth Reimer, *Removal and Return*, 18–19
Broom, Leonard, and John I. Kitsuse, *The Managed Casualty*, 18–19
Buaken, Manuel, 116, 120; *I Have Lived with the American People*, 109
Buell, Raymond Leslie, 13–14
Bulosan, Carlos, *Sound of Falling Light*, 118–119
Burlingame Treaty (1868), 60, 63
Burns, John, 96

C

Chakravarty, C. K., 167
Chandra, Ram, 166, 167, 168
Chang In-whan, 138–139
Chang Jen-yu, *A History of Imperialistic American Exclusion against the Chinese* [*Mei-ti p'ai-hua shih*], 60–62
Chang Yin-huan, *Diary of the Three Continents* [*San-chou jih-chi*], 62
Chávez, César, 113
Cheng Kuan-yin, 54
Chien Hsing-ts'ung [pseud. A Yin], 64, 66; *An Anti-American Literary Collection on the Exclusion of Chinese Laborers* [*Fang-Mei hua-kung chin-yueh wen-hsueh chi*], 55–56 n.9
Chih-kung T'ang, 39, 43. *See also* Sun Yat-sen; Triad Society
Chinatown (San Francisco): conflict in, 48–52; development of, 27–28, 47–48; *hui kuan* in, 33–37; political organization of, 28–30; prominent clans in, 31
Chinese: and racial discrimination, 3, 4–5, 6, 9, 26–27, 33–34, 47–48, 55, 61–62; in California, 4 n.6, 27, 89; in Hawaii, 4 n.6; study of, in U.S., 9–10
Chinese communities (Chinatowns), 21, 24, 26–27, 28–29, 31–32
Chinese Consolidated Benevolent Association (San Francisco), 33–35, 48
Chinese Exclusion Act (1882), 2, 6

Chinese immigration, 2, 3, 54 n.6, 55 n.7;
Communist Chinese historians on, 54,
60–61, 66
Chinese Immigration (Mary Roberts
Coolidge), 7–8
*The Chinese in the United States of
America* (Rose Hum Lee), 10
Chinese laborers, 6–7, 36, 60–61, 64–65.
See also labor movement
Chinese mutual aid societies, 26–27, 30
Chinese Peace Society, 27, 41
Chinese Six Companies. *See* Chinese
Consolidated Benevolent Association
(San Francisco)
Chinese Society of Free Masons. *See*
Triad Society
Ching Ju-chi, 59, 60, 65, 66; *A History of
American Aggression against China
[Mei-kuo chin-hua shih]*, 57 n.12–58
Ch'inmokhoe (Korean Friends' Associa-
tion), 146–147
Ch'i-ying, 57
Chŏn Myŏng-un, 138
Chung, Henry (Chŏng Han-gyŏng), 151,
152, 154
Chun Ti Chu, 34 n.35
Church, Denver S., 163–164
Chu Shih-chia, 60, 63, 64, 66; *Historical
Materials Concerning America's Perse-
cution of Chinese Laborers [Mei-kuo
p'o-hai hua-kung shih-liao]*, 58 n.15–59,
63
clans (Chinese), 26, 27, 30–32, 43–44,
47–49, 51. See also *hui kuan;* secret so-
cieties (Chinese)
The College Nisei (Robert W. O'Brien),
19
Communist Chinese historiography, 53–
55, 60–61, 63–66
Comrades [Tongmu], 151
Concentration Camps USA (Roger Daniels), 20
Conn, Stetson, "The Decision to Evacuate the Japanese from the Pacific
Coast," 18
Conroy, Hilary, *The Japanese Frontier
in Hawaii, 1868–1898*, 14
Coolidge, Mary Roberts, 1; *Chinese Immigration*, 7
coolie trade, 56, 57 n.11–60
Crane, Charles R., 151
Cushing, Caleb, 57

D

Daniels, Roger: *Concentration Camps
USA*, 20; *The Politics of Prejudice*, 15
Das, Taraknath, 166, 172
Dayal, Har, 166
"The Decision to Evacuate the Japanese
from the Pacific Coast" (Stetson Conn),
18
Deshler, David W., 131, 132 n.12, 133
De Silva, Joseph, 72, 77–78, 79
De Witt, General John L., 18
*Diary of the Three Continents [San-chou
jih-chi]* (Chang Yin-huan), 62
Doi, Masato, 96

E

East Indian community, 172–174
East Indian immigration, 157, 158, 160,
173, 176
East Indian laborers, 160, 161, 164–165.
See also labor movement
East Indians, 22 n.69, 157–158, 159; and
American racism, 157, 160–162, 171,
177; and naturalization, 169–171, 172,
174; demographic profile of, 165, 172,
174–176; exclusion of, 163, 164, 169–
171; in California, 164–165, 171, 174;
in Canada, 159–160; political organizations of, 165–166; violence against, 160
Eaton, Allen H., *Beauty Behind Barbed
Wire*, 19
Eaves, Lucille, *A History of Labor Legislation in California*, 8

F

Filipino Agricultural Laborers Association, 113
Filipino immigration, 3, 101, 102, 104,
107, 124–125
Filipino laborers, 110–111, 113–114, 125–
126. *See also* labor movement
Filipinos, 22 n.69, 101–103, 124; and
American racism, 109–111, 114–116,
119–122, 123; and citizenship, 3, 103;
demographic profile of, 107, 126–127;
in California, 4 n.6, 102, 104–108, 109–
114, 117, 118; in Hawaii, 4 n.6, 102–107,
112; social adjustments of, 114–117;
violence against, 122–124

Fong Ching ("Little Pete"), 42, 44
Fong Yue Ting v. *U.S.*, 34 n.35
Free Hindustan, 166
Fruit & Vegetable Store Employees' (Japanese) Union Local 1510, 79, 80 n.34

G

Geary Act (1892), 34 n.35, 63
Gentlemen's Agreement (1907–1908), 3, 88, 102
Ghadr, 166
Ghadr party, 166–168, 175
Gibson, Reverend Otis, 6
Girdner, Audrie, and Anne Loftis, *The Great Betrayal*, 19–20
Gonzalo, D. F., "Social Adjustments of Filipinos in America," 114–116
The Great Betrayal (Audrie Girdner and Anne Loftis), 19–20
Great Eastern Industrial Co. (T'aedong Sirŏp Chusik Hoesa), 143
Grodzins, Morton, *Americans Betrayed*, 17
Gulick, Sidney Lewis, 12–13; *The American Japanese Problem*, 13
Gullion, Provost Marshal General Allen W., 18

H

Hackfeld, J. F., 130–131
Hakka-Punti War (1855–1868), 44, 45. *See also* Weaverville War (1854)
Hamilton, Gary, 82, 83–84
Hasuike, Susumu, 75
Hawaiian plantations, labor requirements of, 86–88, 134, 135
Hawaiian Sugar Planters' Association (HSPA), 102, 103, 125–126, 130, 131, 133
"Hindu conspiracy" trial, 167–168
Hindustani Welfare and Reform Society of America, 165–166
Hip Sing Tong, 40
Historical Materials Concerning America's Persecution of Chinese Laborers [*Mei-kuo p'o-hai hua-kung shih-liao*] (Chu Shih-chia), 58–59, 63
A History of American Aggression against China [*Mei-kuo chin-hua shih*] (Ch'ing Ju-chi), 57–58
A History of Imperialistic American Exclusion against the Chinese [*Mei-ti p'ai-hua shih*] (Chang Jen-yu), 60–62
A History of Labor Legislation in California (Lucille Eaves), 8
Hong Ah Kay, 40
Hop Sing Tong, 40
Hsieh Fu-ch'eng, 54
hui kuan, 32–37, 43–44, 49, 51. *See also* secret societies (Chinese)

I

I Have Lived with the American People (Manuel Buaken), 109
immigration laws, 3, 102, 103, 136–137, 156, 264
India Home Rule League, 168–169, 172
India League of America, 172, 173
India Welfare League, 173
The Indispensable Enemy (Alexander Saxton), 9
Inouye, Senator Daniel, 1, 96, 97
Insular Cases, 124
International Longshoremen's and Warehousemen's Union, 112
Issei, 85–86, 88, 95
Itliong, Larry, 113

J

Jackson, Helen Hunt, 5–6
Jaisohn, Philip. *See* Sŏ Chae-p'il
Japanese, 5, 71, 98–99; and agricultural economy, 68, 70, 80, 89–90; and American racism, 5, 12, 13–14, 15, 20, 67–68, 94, 95–96; as middleman minority, 86, 87–88, 90, 91, 94, 96, 98–99, 100; in California, 4 n.6, 21, 67, 69–70, 84, 85, 89–90, 91, 94, 95; in Hawaii, 4 n.6, 14, 84–89, 94, 95; and relocation centers, 1, 15–21; legal discrimination against, 3, 13, 90–91; success of, 20 n.61, 96–97
Japanese Americans, 1, 20–23, 92–93. *See also* Nisei
Japanese Americans (Harry H. L. Kitano), 20–21
The Japanese Frontier in Hawaii, 1868–1898 (Hilary Conroy), 14
Japanese immigration, 3, 12–13, 14, 85, 88
Japanese-Korean Exclusion League, 146 n.65

Jones, Reverend George Heber, 133–134

K

Kapitan China, 29 n.8
Kawakami, K. K., 12, 13
Kikuchi, Charles, 22
Kim Chong-nim (the "Rice King"), 144
Kim Kyu-sik, 130, 151, 152, 153–154
Kitano, Harry H. L., *Japanese Americans,* 20–21
Koike, Chōzō, 138
Konvitz, Milton R., *The Alien and the Asiatic in American Law,* 14
Korea, Japanese annexation of, 134–135, 137, 139, 145, 147
Korean Christian Institute (Hanin Kidok Hagwŏn), 146
Korean Christian movement, 145
Korean community, 146–156
Korean Corps for the Advancement of Individuals (Hungsadan), 148–149
Korean Development Company (Tonga Kaebal Hoesa), 133
Korean immigration, 129, 130, 134
Korean laborers, in Hawaii, 131–134, 136
Korean Mutual Assistance Association (Kongnip Hyŏphoe), 138, 147, 150
Korean North American Farming Industry Company (Puk-Mi Sorŏp Hoesa), 143
Korean Pacific Weekly [*T'aep'yŏngyang Chubo*], 150
Korean Provisional Government (KPG), 148, 149, 155–156
Korean Report [*Tansan Sibo*], 150–151
Korean Restoration Association (Taedong Pugukhoe), 138
Koreans, 23 n.69, 129, 135–136, 138–140, 145–146; and American racism, 144; economic enterprises of, 142–144; exclusionary legislation against, 136–137; in California, 4 n.6; in Hawaii, 4 n.6, 129, 130–131, 134–135, 141, 143
Korean students, 139–140
Korea Review, 153, 155
Kwong Duck Tong, 40

L

labor movement, 5, 7–8, 9, 71, 72, 79, 102, 112–114, 117; anti-Orientalism of, 9,

15, 64–65, 160–163; and immigrants' organizations, 36, 71–75, 76–77, 79–80, 113, 143
Larson, T. A., *Wyoming's War Years,* 19
Lee, Rose Hum, *The Chinese in the United States of America,* 10
Liang Ch'i-ch'ao, 54
Liu Ta-nien, 56 n.10, 65
Loewen, James W., *The Mississippi Chinese,* 11

M

McCarran Act (1952), 3
McCloy, John J., 18
McCreary Amendment, 35 n.35
McWilliams, Carey, 16, 115
The Managed Casualty (Leonard Broom and John T. Kitsuse), 18–19
March First Independence Movement (Korea), 151–152, 154, 156
Matsunaga, Spark, 96
middleman minority, definition of, 81–84, 86, 94, 95, 96, 97, 98
Miller, Stuart Creighton, *The Unwelcome Immigrant,* 9
Millis, H. A., 163
Mink, Patsy, 96
Min Yŏng-hwan, 132, 135
The Mississippi Chinese (James W. Loewen), 11
Mock Wah, 40
Moslem Association of America, 165
Mountain of Gold (Betty Lee Sung), 10 n.23
Mubarak Ali Khan, 173
Murphy, Thomas W., *Ambassadors in Arms,* 19

N

National Farm Workers Association (NFWA), 113
Neutral Thousands, The, 73 n.14, 76, 78 n.29
New Korean Association, 151
New Korea [*Sin-Han Minbo*], 150
New Korea Youth Party (Sin-Han Ch'ŏngnyŏn Tan, SHCT), 151
Nisei, 67, 68–69, 71, 73, 95–99
North, Hart H., 162–163
Num, Sing Bark, 40

O

O'Brien, Robert W., *The College Nisei*, 19
On Yick Tong, 44, 45, 46
Ozawa decision, 169, 170

P

Pacific Coast Khalsa Diwan Society, 165
Pakistani immigration, 176 n.38
Pak Yong-man, 130, 146, 147, 150
Pandit, Mrs. Vijayalakshmi, 173
Perez v. Sharp, 121–122
Philippine Independence Act (1934), 3
Philippine Society of California, 125
picture marriages, 140 n.46, 141
The Politics of Prejudice (Roger Daniels), 15

R

Rai, Lala Lajpat, 168–169
re Akhoy Jumar Mazumdar, 169
relocation centers, 1, 15, 18, 19 n.57, 20, 92
Removal and Return (Leonard Bloom and Ruth Reimer), 18–19
Retail Clerks International Protective Association, AFL, 72, 79
Retail Food Clerks Local 770 (Los Angeles), 71–75, 79–80
Roldan v. Los Angeles County, 121
Root, Elihu, 137
Royce, Josiah, 5

S

The Salvage (Dorothy S. Thomas), 17
Sandmeyer, Elmer C., *The Anti-Chinese Movement in California*, 8
Sata, Robert K., 79
Saund, Dalip Singh, 175–176
Saxton, Alexander, *The Indispensable Enemy*, 9
Scott Act (1888), 62, 63
secret societies (Chinese), 26–28, 30, 37–43, 44–45, 48–49, 51
Shufeldt Treaty (1882), 130, 133, 154
Singh, J. J., 172
Sino-American treaty (1880), 62, 63
Sŏ Chae-p'il, 130, 153, 154, 155

"Social Adjustments of Filipinos in America" (D. F. Gonzalo), 114–116
Sound of Falling Light (Carlos Bulosan), 118–119
Southern California Retail Produce Workers Union (SCRPWU), 73, 75, 76–77
The Spoilage (Dorothy S. Thomas), 17
Stevens, Durham, 137–139, 147
Stimson, Henry L., 18
Sue Hing Association (San Francisco), 27
Suey Sing Tong, 45
Suminwŏn (Korean Department of Immigration), 132, 133, 135
Sung, Betty Lee, *Mountain of Gold*, 10 n.23
Sun Yat-sen, 38–39, 46
Swift, John F., 63
Syngman Rhee (Yi Sŭng-man), 130, 146, 147–148, 150, 152, 156

T

Tae-Han Kungminhoe (Korean National Association of North America, THK), 140, 142, 143, 147–149, 150, 152, 155
Theodore Roosevelt and the Japanese-American Crisis (Thomas A. Bailey), 14
Thind decision. See *U.S. v. Bhaghat Singh Thind*
Thomas, Dorothy S., 15; *The Salvage*, 17; *The Spoilage*, 17
Three Star Produce Company (Los Angeles), 74, 76–77
Tongjihoe (Society for the Like-Minded), 148
tongs. See secret societies (Chinese)
tong wars, 27, 43–44, 48–49
Topaz (relocation camp), study of, 19
Trescot, William H., 63
Triad Society, 37–38, 42–43
Tydings-McDuffie Act (1934), 103, 124, 125, 126

U

U.S. v. Balsara, 169
U.S. v. Bhaghat Singh Thind, 169–170, 173
U.S. v. Sakharam Ganesh Pandit, 170–171
United Farm Workers Organizing Committee (UFWOC), 113–114.

United Korean News [*Sin Han'guk po*], 150
United Korean Society (Hanin Hapsŏng Hyŏphoe), 147
University of California Japanese American Evacuation and Resettlement Study, 15–16, 17–18, 22
Unwelcome Immigrant, The (Stuart Creighton Miller), 9

W

Wai, Elmer Wok, 40

Wanghia, Treaty of (1844), 57–58, 59
War Relocation Authority, 15, 16
Weaverville War (1854), 44, 45, 48
Wilson, Woodrow, 6–7, 151, 154–155, 156
Wyoming's War Years (T. A. Larson), 19

Y

Yamate, Thomas Hiromu, 73, 74–76, 77
Yan Hoi group (San Francisco), 27
Yi Kwang-su, 149
Yoell, A. E., 161

The Asian American was composed in linotype Baskerville
  with Bulmer display
by Kimberly Press, Inc., Goleta, California
Jacket and cover art were executed by Raymond Glass;
copy editing and proof reading were done by John R. "Jack" Raup;
  indexing was by Barbara Phillips.
The entire job was prepared for the offset printing process
  by Graphics 2, Los Angeles, California.
The book was printed on a 26-inch offset press by
  R. R. Donnelley and Sons Co., Crawfordsville, Indiana.
The text stock is a Dontique cream white offset,
  bulking at 352 pages per inch;
  basis weight is 60 pounds.